A New Europe?

Foreign Affairs Readers

A New Europe? (1999)
The Rise of China (1998)
Is Global Capitalism Working? (1999)
Asia: Rising or Falling? (1999)
Democracy (1998)
War in the Balkans (1999)

Foreign Affairs Agenda: The New Shape of World Politics (1997)
The Marshall Plan and Its Legacy (1997)
Clash of Civilizations: The Debate (1996)
Competiveness: An International Economics Reader (1994)

For information, or to order Foreign Affairs Readers, visit www.foreignaffairs.org.

A New Europe?

Noel Malcolm
John Newhouse
George Soros
Tony Judt
Timothy Garton Ash
Ralf Dahrendorf
Richard Medley
C. Fred Bergsten
Martin Feldstein
William Wallace *and* Jan Zielonka
Jacob Heilbrunn
Josef Joffe
Fritz Stern
Dominique Moïsi

A FOREIGN AFFAIRS READER

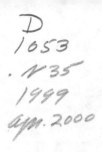

D
1053
. N35
1999
afr. 2000

A FOREIGN AFFAIRS READER

ISBN: 0-87609-266-0

CONTENTS

INTRODUCTION   **1**

POLITICS
The Case Against 'Europe'   **2**
Noel Malcolm
March/April 1995

Europe's Rising Regionalism   **19**
John Newhouse
January/February 1997

Can Europe Work?   **37**
George Soros
September/October 1996

The Social Question Redivivus   **44**
Tony Judt
September/October 1997

Europe's Endangered Liberal Order   **67**
Timothy Garton Ash
March/April 1998

The Third Way and Liberty   **82**
Ralf Dahrendorf
September/October 1999

Europe's Next Big Idea   **87**
Richard Medley
September/October 1999

EURO-NOMICS
The Dollar and the Euro 92
C. Fred Bergsten
July/August 1997

EMU and International Conflict 105
Martin Feldstein
November/December 1997

America and Europe: Clash of the Titans? 119
C. Fred Bergsten
March/April 1999

Misunderstanding Europe 134
William Wallace and Jan Zielonka
November/December 1998

GERMANY
Germany's New Right 149
Jacob Heilbrunn
November/December 1996

Mr. Heilbrunn's Planet 168
Josef Joffe et al.
March/April 1997

Germany's Choice 178
Timothy Garton Ash
July/August 1994

Freedom and Its Discontents 195
Fritz Stern
September/October 1993

FRANCE
The Trouble With France   213
Dominique Moïsi
May/June 1998

Introduction

Foreign Affairs *Readers bring together important essays first published in* Foreign Affairs. *We include a variety of articles, serving different purposes. Some may be pieces of reportage, others may strongly argue a specific point of view, still others may be statesmen's memoirs.*

Each volume presents a structured, focused set of our best essays on a specific topic. Both the topic and the essays have been chosen with a particular purpose in mind — classroom use. Most of the essays advance a thesis or provide important information that is likely to stimulate students to think and discuss the broader subject. Some are current, others were written a while ago. The latter are included because the arguments they advance are still crucial to understanding the issues. We exclude many articles, which, while excellent in other respects, might not contribute as much to discussion in the classroom.

For over 75 years, Foreign Affairs *has prided itself on publishing only the very best analytic writing on political, economic, and social trends around the globe. We hope that this collection succeeds in linking scholarship and the reality of today's world.*

A complete listing of Foreign Affairs Readers *appears at the front of this volume.*

The Case Against 'Europe'

Noel Malcolm

A FLAWED IDEAL

THE CASE against "Europe" is not the same as a case against Europe.
Quite the contrary. "Europe" is a project, a concept, a cause: the final
goal that the European Community (EC) has been moving toward
ever since its hesitant beginnings in the 1950s. It involves the creation
of a united European state with its own constitution, government,
parliament, currency, foreign policy, and army. Some of the machinery for this is already in place, and enough of the blueprints are in circulation for there to be little doubt about the overall design. Those
who are in favor of Europe—that is, those who favor increasing the
freedom and prosperity of all who live on the European continent—
should view the creation of this hugely artificial political entity with
a mixture of alarm and dismay.

The synthetic project of "Europe" has almost completely taken
over the natural meaning of the word. In most European countries
today, people talk simply about being "pro-Europe" or "anti-Europe";
anyone who questions more political integration can be dismissed as
motivated by mere xenophobic hostility toward the rest of the continent. Other elements of the "European" political language reinforce
this attitude. During the 1991-93 debate over the Maastricht treaty,
for example, there was an almost hypnotic emphasis on clichés about
transport. We were warned that we must not miss the boat or the bus,
that we would be left standing on the platform when the European

NOEL MALCOLM is a political columnist for London's *The Daily
Telegraph*. His latest book is *Bosnia: A Short History*, published by New
York University Press.

[52]

train went out, or that insufficient enthusiasm would cause us to suffer a bumpy ride in the rear wagon. All these images assumed a fixed itinerary and a preordained destination. Either you were for that destination, or you were against "Europe." The possibility that people might argue in favor of rival positive goals for Europe was thus eliminated from the consciousness of European politicians.

The concept of "Europe" is accompanied, in other words, by a doctrine of historical inevitability. This can take several different forms: a utopian belief in inevitable progress, a quasi-Marxist faith in the iron laws of history (again involving the withering away of the nation-state), or a kind of cartographic mysticism that intuits that certain large areas on the map are crying out to emerge as single geopolitical units. These beliefs have received some hard knocks from twentieth-century history. Inevitability is, indeed, a word most often heard on the lips of those who have to turn the world upside down to achieve the changes they desire.

ON LITTLE CAT FEET

THE ORIGINS of the "European" political project can be traced back to a number of politicians, writers, and visionaries of the interwar period: people such as the half-Austrian, half-Japanese theorist Richard Coudenhove-Kalergi, former Italian Foreign Minister Carlo Sforza, and Jean Monnet, a French brandy salesman turned international bureaucrat. When their idea of a rationalized and unified Europe was first floated in the 1920s and 1930s, it sounded quite similar in spirit to the contemporaneous campaign to make Esperanto the world language. Who, at that stage, could confidently have declared that one of these schemes had the force of historical inevitability behind it and the other did not? Both had theoretical benefits to offer, although they were almost certainly outweighed by the practical difficulties of attaining them. It is not hard, surely, to imagine an alternative history of Europe after World War II in which the EC never came into existence and in which, therefore, the project of a united Europe would occupy a footnote almost as tiny as that devoted to the work of the International Esperanto League. Things seem inevitable only because people made them happen.

The impetus behind the "European" idea came from a handful of politicians in France and Germany who decided that a supranational enterprise might solve the problem of Franco-German rivalry, which they saw as the root cause of three great European wars since 1870. For this purpose alone, an arrangement involving just those two countries might have sufficed. But other factors coincidentally were at work, in particular the Cold War, which made the strengthening of Western Europe as a political bloc desirable, and the barely concealed resent-

ment of French President Charles de Gaulle toward "les Anglo-Saxons," which made him look more favorably on the EC as an Anglo-Saxon-free area that could be politically dominated by France.

Even with these large-scale factors at work, however, it is doubtful whether the "European" project would have got off the ground without the ingenuity of a few individuals, notably Monnet and former French Foreign Minister Robert Schuman. The method they invented was what political theorists now call "functionalism." By meshing together the economies of participating countries bit by bit, they believed a point would eventually be reached where political unification would seem a natural expression of the way in which those countries were already interacting. As Schuman put it in 1950, "Europe will not be built all at once, or as a single whole: it will be built by concrete achievements which first create de facto solidarity."

And so the method has proceeded, from coal and steel (European Coal and Steel Community Treaty), through agriculture and commerce (Treaty of Rome), environmental regulation and research and development (Single European Act), to transport policy, training, immigration policy, and a whole battery of measures designed to bring about full economic and monetary union (the Maastricht treaty). Step by step with these developments has been the march toward political unification, with the growth of a European Court, the development of the European Parliament from a talking-shop of national appointees into a directly elected assembly with real legislative powers, the extension of majority voting at the Council of Ministers, and even the announcement, in the Maastricht treaty, of something called European citizenship, the rights and duties of which have yet to be defined. Almost every one of these political changes was justified at the time on practical grounds: just a slight adjustment to make things easier, or more effective, or to reflect new realities. The economic changes and the transfers of new areas of competence to EC institutions are likewise usually presented as mere practical adjustments. At the same time, many continental European politicians (such as German Chancellor Helmut Kohl and French President François Mitterrand) talk openly of the ultimate grand political goal: the creation of a federal European state.

There is a strange disjunction between these two types of "European" discourse, the practical and the ideal. But this is just a sign of functionalism successfully at work. The argument for "Europe" switches to and fro, from claims about practical benefits to expressions of political idealism and back again. If one disagrees with advocates of "Europe" about the practical advantages, they say, "Well, you may be right about this or that disadvantage, but surely it's a price worth paying for such a wonderful political ideal." And if one casts doubt on the political desirability of the ideal, they reply, "Never mind about that, just think of the economic advantages." The truth is that both arguments for "Europe" are fundamentally flawed.

DUNCE CAP

THE ECONOMIC project embodied in the European Economic Community (EEC) was a true reflection of its origins in a piece of Franco-German bargaining. German industry was given the opportunity to flood other member states with its exports, thanks to a set of rules designed to eliminate artificial barriers to competition and trade within the "common market." France, on the other hand, was given an elaborate system of protection for its agriculture, the so-called Common Agricultural Policy.

The general aims of the CAP, as set out in Article 39 of the Treaty of Rome, included stable markets and "a fair standard of living for the agricultural community." On that slender basis, France established one of the most complex and expensive systems of agricultural protectionism in human history. It is based on high external tariffs, high export subsidies, and internal price support by means of intervention buying (the most costly system of price support yet invented, since it involves collecting and storing tens of millions of tons of excess produce). By the time this system was fully established in 1967, EEC farm prices had been driven up to 175 percent of world prices for beef, 185 percent for wheat, 400 percent for butter, and 440 percent for sugar. The annual cost of the CAP is now $45 billion and rising; more than ten percent of this is believed to be paid to a myriad of scams. Thanks to this policy, a European family of four now pays more than $1,600 a year in additional food costs—a hidden tax greater than the poll tax that brought rioters out onto the streets of London.

Even the most hardened advocates of "Europe" are always a little embarrassed by the CAP. The massive corruption that flows from it— phantom exports picking up export subsidies, smuggled imports relabeled as EC products, nonexistent Italian olive groves receiving huge subsidies, and so on—is embarrassing enough, but it is the system itself that requires defense. Ten or twenty years ago, one used to hear its proponents arguing that at least there would be stocks of food available if Western Europe came under siege. That argument seemed thin then and sounds positively fatuous today. If pressed, they will insist that the CAP is gradually being reformed, pointing out that the beef mountains and wine lakes are getting smaller. These reforms, however, are achieved only by spending more money in such schemes as the infamous set-aside payments given to farmers as a reward for not growing anything. More commonly, though, the defenders of "Europe" will say that the CAP is just an unfortunate detail, that they are aware of its problems, and that one really should not use it to blacken "Europe's" name.

But the CAP is not just a detail. It is, by a huge margin, the largest single item of EC spending, taking up roughly 60 percent of the budget every year. It dominates the EC's external trade policy, distorting the world market and seriously undermining the ability of poorer countries elsewhere to export their own agricultural produce. It almost broke the Uruguay round of the General Agreement on Tariffs and Trade (GATT), thanks to the French government's irrational obsession with agricultural protectionism—irrational, that is, because agriculture accounts for only four percent of French GDP, and much of the other 96 percent would have benefited from lower world tariffs.

No account of the economic functioning of "Europe" can fail to begin with the CAP, and no study that examines it can fail to conclude that it is a colossal waste of money. Even the European Commission, which administers the scheme, has admitted that "farmers do not seem to have benefited from the increasing support which they have received." Enthusiasts for "Europe" often wax lyrical about European achievements such as the German highway system or the French railways—things that were built by national governments. Almost the only major achievement of the EC—the only thing it has constructed and operated itself—is the CAP. It is not an encouraging precedent.

LEVELING THE PLAYING FIELD

THE CAP sets the tone for other areas of the EC's trading policy. Although it would be unfair to describe the EC as behaving like a "Fortress Europe" (so far), it is nevertheless true that "Europe" has evolved an elaborate system of tariffs and discriminatory trading agreements to protect its sensitive industries. Agriculture has the highest tariffs; ranging below it are such products as steel, textiles, clothing, and footwear (as Poland, Hungary, and the Czech Republic have discovered to their dismay—food, steel, textiles, clothing, and footwear being their own most important products). The EC has been at the forefront in developing so-called voluntary export restraints with countries such as Japan. In addition, "Europe" has shown extraordinary ingenuity in adapting the GATT's "antidumping" measures to block the flow of innumerable imports: electronic typewriters, hydraulic excavators, dot-matrix printers, audiocassettes, and halogen lights from Japan; compact disc players from Japan and Korea; small-screen color televisions from Korea, China, and Hong Kong, and so on.

A recent study of EC trade policy by L. A. Winters uses the phrase "managed liberalization" to describe the EC's foot-dragging progress toward freer trade. "Managed liberalization," notes Winters, "is a substitute for genuine liberalization, but a poor one, because it typically attenuates competition in precisely those sectors which are most in need of improved efficiency." Nor is this surprising, since the trade policy emerges from a system of political bargaining in which the governments

8

of EC member states compete to protect their favorite industries. Massive state subsidies to flagship enterprises (French car manufacturers, Spanish steel mills, Belgian and Greek national airlines) are common practice. In addition, the officials at the European Commission in Brussels are strongly influenced by the French *dirigiste* tradition, which sees it as the role of the state to select and nurture special "champion" industries. This was the driving force behind the new powers granted to the EC in 1986 to "strengthen the scientific and technological basis of European industry." In practice, this means spending millions of taxpayers' dollars developing French microchips that will never compete with East Asian ones on the open market.

Inside the tariff wall, a kind of free trade area has indeed been created. Many obstacles to trade have been removed (though important barriers remain in the realm of services, as British insurance firms are still discovering when they try to break into the German market), and industry as a whole has benefited from this process of internal liberalization.

> Brussels forces labor costs up to German standards, penalizing small enterprises.

However, the long-term effects may be more harmful than beneficial. In their attempt to create a level playing field for competition on equal terms within the EC, the administrators of "Europe" have leveled up, not down. They have tried to raise both the standards and the costs of industry throughout the community to the high levels practiced in Europe's foremost industrial country, Germany. When this process is complete, industrialists inside the EC may indeed sell goods to one another on equal terms, but their goods will all be uncompetitive on the world market.

This leveling up occurs in two areas. The first is the harmonization of standards. Brussels has issued a mass of regulations laying down the most minute specifications for industrial products and processes; the dominant influence on these has been the German Institute for Norms, which has the strictest standards in Europe. Harmonization is meant to simplify matters for producers, who now have only one standard within the EC instead of various national ones. But in many cases, as the task of matching product to standard becomes relatively simpler, it is also made absolutely more expensive. In addition, the EC has powers relating to environmental protection and health and safety at work, which are increasingly used to impose German-style costs on industries and services. The costs fall especially heavily on small enterprises, which have to pay disproportionately for monitoring equipment, inspection, and certification.

> "Europe" will stumble under the weight of its costs like a woolly mammoth sinking into a melting tundra.

This distorts the market in favor of large corporations, penalizing the small enterprises that are the seed corn of any growing economy.

The second way in which the playing field is leveled up to German standards is in the social costs of labor. German employers pay heavily for the privilege of giving people jobs: there are generous pension schemes to pay for health insurance, long holidays, maternity and paternity leave, and other forms of social insurance. As a consequence, labor costs are $25 per hour in the former West Germany (the highest in the world), as opposed to $17 in Japan, $16 in the United States, and $12 in the United Kingdom. German work practices mean that a machine in a German factory operates an average of only 53 hours a week, as opposed to 69 hours in France and 76 in Britain. And the average worker in Germany spends only 1,506 hours each year actually at work, as opposed to 1,635 hours in Britain, 1,847 in the United States, and 2,165 in Japan.

Over the last five years, the European Commission has proposed a whole range of measures to increase the rights of workers and limit their working hours. When measures in this so-called social action program could not gain the required unanimous support from member states (notably Britain), they were dressed up as health and safety matters, for which only a majority vote is required. Further costs on employers were imposed by a "social protocol" added to the Maastricht treaty. Although Britain was able to gain a special exemption from this agreement, it is likely that many of the new measures adopted under the protocol eventually will filter back to Britain through other parts of the "European" administrative machine.

Some of these measures are inspired, no doubt, by concern for the plight of the poorest workers in the community's southern member states. But the general aim of the policy is clearly to protect the high-labor-cost economies (above all, Germany) from competitors employing cheaper labor. In the short or medium term, this policy will damage the economies of the poorer countries, which will have artificially high labor costs imposed on them. In the long term, it will harm Germany, too, by reducing its incentive to adapt to worldwide competition. "Europe," whose share of world trade and relative rate of economic growth are already in decline, will enter the next century stumbling under the weight of its own costs like a woolly mammoth sinking into a melting tundra.

The final expression of this leveling-up syndrome is the plan for monetary union. As outlined in the Maastricht treaty, the idea is to create a Euro-deutsche mark, operated by a body closely modeled on the Bundesbank and situated in Frankfurt. Earlier moves in this direction were not encouraging: the European Exchange Rate Mechanism, which linked the currencies of member states to the deutsche mark, fell apart spectacularly in October 1992. In the process, the British government spent nearly $6 billion in a doomed attempt to prop up the pound, and Germany is thought to have spent roughly $14 billion in an equally futile effort to support the Italian lira. The artificially high interest rates that countries such as Britain had imposed to maintain their currency's parity with the deutsche mark severely intensified the 1989-93 recession; the human costs of the unnecessary indebtedness, bankruptcies, and unemployment cannot be calculated.

The Exchange Rate Mechanism was, as Professor Sir Alan Walters, an adviser to former British Prime Minister Margaret Thatcher, famously put it, "half-baked." Currencies were neither fully fixed nor freely floating but pegged to so-called fixed rates that could be changed. This provided the world markets, at times of pressure on any particular currency, with an irresistible one-way bet. That problem, of course, will not arise once the currencies of "Europe" are merged into a single Euro-mark—though the activities of the world currency markets in the days just before the conversion terms are announced will be a wonder to behold.

Once the Euro-mark is in place, a different set of problems will arise. Whatever the "economic convergence programs" dutifully embarked on by the governments of member states, this single currency will be covering a number of national economies with widely varying characteristics. Hitherto, changes in the values of their national currencies have been one of the essential ways in which the relative strengths and weaknesses of those countries were both expressed and adjusted. With that mechanism gone, other forms of expression will operate, such as the collapse of industries or the mass migration of labor.

The European Commission understands this problem and has a ready solution: massive transfers of money to the weaker economies of "Europe." The machinery to administer this huge program of subsidies is already in place, in the form of regional funds, "structural" funds, and "cohesion payments." All that is lacking so far is the actual money, for which purpose the outgoing president of the European Commission, Jacques Delors, recently proposed increasing the European budget by more than $150 billion over the next five years.

A model for the future of an economically unified Europe can be found in modern Italy, which united the prosperous, advanced provinces of the north with the Third World poverty of the south. After more than a century of political and economic union, huge disparities still remain between the two halves of Italy—despite (or indeed partly because of) all the subsidies that are poured into the south via institutions such as the Cassa del Mezzogiorno, the independent society established by the Italian government to help develop the south. As southern Italians have had the opportunity to discover, an economy based on subsidies unites the inefficiencies of state planning with almost limitless opportunities for graft and corruption. It is a sad irony that today, just as the leaders of "Europe" are preparing for unification, the politicians of Italy are seriously considering dismantling their country into two or three separate states.

DECAFFEINATED POLITICS

So much for the economic benefits of European unity. At this point the advocates of "Europe" usually shift to their other line of defense. This is not just a money-grubbing enterprise, they say, to be totted up in terms of profit and loss: "Europe" is a political ideal, a spiritual adventure, a new experiment in brotherhood and cooperation. Has it not made war in Europe unthinkable? Is it not the natural next step for mankind, at a time when the old idea of national sovereignty is evidently obsolete? Does it not show the way to the abolition of old-fashioned national feeling, with all its hostilities, prejudices, and resentments?

The answer to all these questions, unfortunately, is no. The argument that the EC is responsible for the lack of war in post-1945 Europe is hard to substantiate. A far more obvious reason is the Cold War, which obliged Western Europe to adopt a common defensive posture and a system of deterrence so effective that war between Western and Eastern Europe never happened. The fact that a group of West European countries were able to cooperate in the EC was more a symptom of the lack of belligerent tensions in postwar Western Europe than a cause. Liberal democracies had been established in most West European countries after 1945; even if the EEC had not existed, it is hard to imagine a scenario in which Germany would have wanted to invade France, or France drop nuclear bombs on Germany. Even if one concedes for the sake of argument that the EEC did ensure peace for the last generation or two, this cannot be used as a reason for closer integration, since the EEC had this supposed effect at a time when it was not a unified supranational entity but a group of cooperating nation-states.

The idea of "Europe" is founded, however, on the belief that the nation-state is obsolete. This is an article of faith against which rational arguments cannot prevail. It is no use pointing out that the most successful countries in the modern world—Japan, the United States, and indeed Germany itself—are nation-states. It matters little if one says that some of the most dynamic economies today belong to small states—South Korea, Taiwan, Singapore—that feel no need to submerge themselves in large multinational entities. And it is regarded as bad taste to point out that the multinational federations most recently in the news were the U.S.S.R. and the Federal Republic of Yugoslavia. They are merely the latest in a long list of multinational states that have collapsed in modern times, from the Austro-Hungarian Empire to the various postcolonial federations set up by the British in central Africa, east Africa, and the West Indies. Nigeria, for example, kept Biafra only by warfare and starvation; India needs armed force to retain Nagaland and Kashmir. "But Europe will not be like that," say the federalists. "We have traditions of mutual tolerance and civilized behavior." Yes, we have some such traditions; they are the traditions that have evolved within fairly stable nation-states. Whether they last indefinitely under the new conditions of multinational politics remains to be seen.

What will political life be like in the sort of European federation currently proposed in Brussels and Bonn? Some of the powers of national governments will be transferred upward to the European level, while others will move down to a "Europe of the regions" (Catalonia, Bavaria, Wales, etc.). The official vision of political life at the uppermost level is essentially that of Jean Monnet, the original inventor of the community: a technocrat's ideal, a world in which large-scale solutions are devised to large-scale problems by far-sighted expert administrators. (The most common argument for abolishing nation-states is that problems nowadays are just too big for individual states to handle. In fact, there have always been issues that cross international borders, from postal services to drug enforcement to global trade. It cannot be the size of the problem that dictates that it must be dealt with by supranational authority rather than international cooperation, but some other reason that the advocates of European federation have yet to explain.)

> A federal Europe would revive the politics of nationalist hostility and resentment.

This technocratic vision is of a decaffeinated political world, from which real politics has been carefully extracted. Things will surely turn out differently. Real politics will still operate at the European level. The one form it will not take, however, is that of federation-wide democratic politics. For that, we would need "Europe"-wide parties, operating across the whole federation in the way that the Republican and Democratic parties operate across the United States.

There are already some ghostly transnational groupings in the European Parliament: the Socialist Group, the European People's Party (the Christian Democrats), and so on. But these are just alliances formed at Strasbourg by members of the European Parliament elected on the tickets of their own national parties. No one can really envisage ordinary voters in, say, Denmark being inspired by the leader of their preferred Euro-party, who might make his or her speeches in Portuguese. The basic facts of linguistic, cultural, and geographic difference make it impossible to imagine federation-wide mass politics ever becoming the dominant form of political life in Europe. Instead, the pursuit of national interests by national politicians will continue at the highest "European" levels. Yet it will do so in a way subtly different from the way in which local representatives within a national political system press for the interests of their localities. Although a member of parliament for Yorkshire may push hard on Yorkshire's behalf, on all major issues the member votes according to what he or she thinks is in Britain's interest; the MP belongs to a national party that addresses those issues with national policies.

The art of "European" politics, on the other hand, will be to do nothing more than dress up national interests as if they were Europe-wide ones. With any particular nation paying only a small proportion of the European budget, each set of national politicians will seek to maximize those European spending projects that benefit their own country. The modus operandi of European politics, therefore (already visible in the Council of Ministers today), will be logrolling and back-scratching: you support my pet proposal, even though you think it is a bad one, and in return I shall back yours. This is a recipe not only for nonstop increases in spending, but also for radical incoherence in policymaking. And with politics at the highest level operating as a scramble for funds, it is hard to see how politicians at the lower level of Europe's "regions" can fail to replicate it: they will have fewer real governmental powers but more populist opportunities to woo their voters with spending.

This type of political life is accompanied by two grave dangers. In any system where democratic accountability is attenuated and the powers of politicians to make deals behind closed doors is strengthened, the likely consequence is a growth in political corruption. Corrupt practices are already common in the political life of several European countries: their exposure has led recently to the prosecution, flight into exile, or suicide of former prime ministers in Italy, Greece, and France. A federal Europe, far from correcting these vices, will offer them a wider field of action.

A more serious danger, however, lies in store for the political life of a federal "Europe": the revival of the politics of nationalist hostility and resentment. Aggressive nationalism is typically a syndrome of the dispossessed, of those who feel power has been taken from them. Foreigners are often the most convenient focus of such resentment, whatever the true causes of the powerlessness may be. But in a system where power really has been taken from national governments and transferred to European bodies in which, by definition, the majority vote will always lie in the hands of foreigners, such nationalist thinking will acquire an undeniable logic. Of course, if "Europe" moves ever onward and upward in an unprecedented increase in prosperity for all its citizens, the grounds for resentment may be slight; that is not, however, a scenario that anyone can take for granted.

In this respect, the whole "European" project furnishes a classic example of the fallacious belief that the way to remove hostility between groups, peoples, or states is to build new structures over their heads. Too often that method yields exactly the opposite result. The most commonly repeated version of this argument is that Germany needs to be "tied in" or "tied down" by a structure of European integration to prevent it from wandering off dangerously into the empty spaces of Mitteleuropa. If Germany really has different interests from the rest of "Europe," the way to deal with it, surely, is not to force it into an institutional straitjacket (which can only build up German resentment in the long run), but to devise ways of pursuing those interests that are compatible with the interests of its allies and partners. So far, Germany's involvement in "Europe" looks rather like the action of a jovial uncle at a children's party who, to show goodwill, allows his hands to be tied behind his back. It is not a posture that he will want to stay in for long, and his mood may change when he becomes aware of innumerable little fingers rifling through his pockets.

FIRST AS FARCE . . .

THE FINAL question is whether "Europe" has a valuable role to play on the world stage. The "Europe" we have at present is a product of the Cold War era. Now that the whole situation in Eastern Europe has changed, one might expect the engineers of the EC to go back to the geopolitical drawing board. Instead, they are pressing ahead with the same old set of plans at a faster pace. Some enthusiasts for "Europe," such as former EC Commissioner Ralf Dahrendorf or British Foreign Minister Douglas Hurd, have even claimed that the internal development of the EC in the 1980s played a decisive part in bringing about the fall of communism in the east. One rather doubts many East European dissidents ever said: "Have you heard about the new Brussels Directive on Permitted Levels of Lawnmower Noise? This means we really must bring down the communist regime!" The Hurd/Dahrendorf thesis bears a curious resemblance to the recent Michael Jackson music video entitled "Redeeming Eastern Europe," in which the pop star defeats the Red Army singlehandedly while adoring children chant messages of goodwill in (coincidentally) Esperanto.

Since the removal of the Iron Curtain, the new democracies of Eastern Europe have found their ostensible savior strangely reluctant to help it in the one way that matters—namely, by buying their goods. They all want to join "Europe," of course, for two simple reasons: because it is a rich man's club in which fellow members possess huge funds for investment, and because they want to be part of some kind of security grouping. The first requirement could be met by any economic club of nations, of the sort that the EC was for its first couple of decades; it does not call for European political integration. Indeed, any such development would be a strange reward for those East European countries that have only just freed themselves from the embrace of another multinational empire.

The question of European security raises a similar point. The long-term effect of the end of the Cold War will be a gradual reduction in the American defense commitment to Europe. This prospect even causes some pleasure in those parts of Europe—above all, France and Germany—where anti-Americanism has long flourished. Clearly, the Europeans will have to take more care of their own defense. But the question is whether this requires political integration, a Euro-army, a Euro–foreign policy, and a Euro-government. For more than 50 years, NATO has managed to defend Western Europe without any such political integration, and NATO is clearly the most successful international organization in modern history.

"Of course," comes the reply, "NATO was able to function as a loose intergovernmental body because its members were facing a clear common threat. The threats and challenges will be more various now, so intergovernmental agreement will be harder to obtain." But that is precisely why such matters should not be funneled into a "European" government operating by majority vote. "Europe" is indeed a collection of countries with different national interests and foreign commitments. On each separate security issue, individual states may have concerns of their own that are not shared by their fellow members (Britain over the Falklands, France over North Africa, Germany and Italy over Yugoslavia, and so on). To try to form a single "European" policy on such issues, whether by unanimity, consensus, or majority voting, is to guarantee at best ineffective compromise and at worst total self-paralysis.

This simple truth has been demonstrated twice in the last four years—the first time as farce, the second as tragedy. The farce was "Europe's" reaction to Iraq's 1990 invasion of Kuwait, when Germany agonized over sending a few trainer jets to Turkey, France sent an aircraft carrier to the Persian Gulf bearing helicopters instead of planes, and Belgium refused to sell ammunition to the British army. The tragedy is Yugoslavia. "This is the hour of Europe!" cried the egregious Jacques Poos, foreign minister of Luxembourg, when Yugoslavian President Slobodan Milošević's army first opened fire in Slovenia and Croatia in the summer of 1991. "We do not interfere in American affairs; we trust that America will not interfere in European affairs," said Jacques Delors, voicing the only consistent and distinctive theme of "European" foreign policy: graceless anti-Americanism. The desire to produce a foreign policy by consensus was just strong enough to ensure that those countries who did understand what was happening in Yugoslavia (above all, Germany) were kept in check by those who did not (above all, Britain). As a result, the recognition of Croatia and Slovenia was delayed by six months, and when it finally came it did so unaccompanied by any measures to protect Milošević's other prospective victims from attack.

The mentality behind the drive for a "European" foreign policy displays a childlike logic. "Think how strong and effective our foreign policies will be if we add them all together!" it says. Similarly, one might say: think what a beautiful color we can make if we mix all the colors of the paint box! The result, inevitably, is a muddy shade of brown. ✿

Europe's Rising Regionalism

John Newhouse

DEVOLUTION OF AUTHORITY

THE NATION-STATE is too big to run everyday life, and too small to manage international affairs. So say many of Europe's regional and big-city leaders, who are themselves gaining influence and authority. European cities and regional governments are acquiring bigger budgets and developing more professional bureaucracies. National cultures are being squeezed between a broader popular culture and briskly reviving regional cultures.

Europeans are finding national interests hard to see, let alone define. The role of European governments is just as ambiguous. National leaders had an easier time during the Cold War, when, thanks to NATO, they could satisfy the essential need, military security. But in this transitional time, economic security is far more pressing, and far more elusive. A second industrial revolution is causing serious social dislocations. The nation-state's inability to keep unemployment at a tolerable level while maintaining the social safety net has accelerated Europe's growing devolution of authority.

With European governments losing or ceding control of national economies, their constituencies are turning to the market for help. Two parallel and related processes have emerged. One is regionalism, the other globalization; instead of working through national capitals, European regions are linking themselves directly to the global economy.

JOHN NEWHOUSE is a Guest Scholar at the Brookings Institution and consultant to the State Department. This article is drawn from his forthcoming book on Europe in the post–Cold War era, which Pantheon will publish this fall.

[67]

As the role of central governments shrinks, democratic societies are being fragmented and factionalized politically, culturally, and linguistically. Mainstream political parties, especially in Europe, are losing their credibility and support. The institutions of government are under even heavier pressure. At varying speeds and to varying degrees, authority is drifting down from national capitals to provinces and cities. Regionalism, whether within or across national borders, is Europe's current and future dynamic. Its sources vary, but it is judged on many sides to be partly a protest against the authority of national capitals by people who see themselves as belonging, historically and otherwise, more to "Europe" than to a nation-state of clouded origins and dubious boundaries.

> ocal entities feel better suited to manage their affairs than distant bureaucracies.

The nation-state is in most cases a relatively recent formation, and in many places the process of cobbling it together left a deposit of sour memories. With the Cold War over, people are indifferent to whether Germany acquires a seat on the U.N. Security Council or Poland is admitted to NATO. Foreign policy has to be concerned with crime, drug trafficking, and immigration. Local authorities feel that they, not national governments, are best suited to deal with such matters, even though they must compete with their capitals for adequate funding.

Officials in some provincial cities see growing regional sentiment as a reaction to burdensome regulations descending from European Union headquarters in Brussels. But many regional leaders and officials are self-professed Europeans; they talk about bypassing national capitals and dealing directly with Brussels. The deeply controversial Treaty on European Union concluded at Maastricht in December 1991 took account of the trend by creating a Committee of the Regions, although that body's mandate is still not clear.

What is clear is that in this age of global trade and capital flows, not to mention information highways and high-speed travel, local entities feel better placed to manage their affairs than distant bureaucracies, whether in national capitals or in Brussels. The German state of Baden-Württemberg, for example, is making its own foreign and trade policies; it has signed several hundred agreements with other regions and entities. In this more freewheeling environment, bankers and industrial planners have begun to view Europe at least as much as a group of distinct economic regions as an assortment of nation-states.

Creating the climate for faster growth is a top priority for any government, and one that European cities and regions believe themselves better equipped to achieve than their national capitals. Regionalism is also partly about infrastructure. Raising taxes to finance infrastructure projects is probably not an option for most EU governments; their revenues already average nearly half of GDP, compared with less than a third in the United States. Much of the investment in large projects is thus being done at the regional or local level, often in cooperation with neighboring regions with which the region or locality has strong economic ties.

Regionalism is much more than a return to cultural roots or a distancing from national capitals. It has as much to do with wealth creation as anything else. Many and probably most of the wealthiest provinces of Western Europe are interacting with one another (and in some cases with parts of Central Europe) and together creating super-regions— large economic zones that transcend national boundaries.

RIPE BANANAS

VARIOUS BANKING and business circles believe that Europe's industrial and financial heartland is dividing into banana-shaped configurations. Jordi Pujol, the president of Catalonia, Spain's dominant political figure and Europe's most conspicuous prophet of regionalism, will sketch the two most highly developed "bananas" for visitors to his Barcelona office. The first zone, which he considers more important, stretches from southeastern England through northern France and the Benelux countries and down the Rhine Valley into Switzerland. The second forms an arc from the Veneto in Italy, west through Lombardy and the Piedmont into the Rhône-Alpes, across France's Mediterranean coast and hinterland, and into Catalonia. Pujol calls this second "banana" Europe's Sunbelt, noting that it is undergoing the kind of economic growth that transfigured America's Sunbelt a few decades ago.

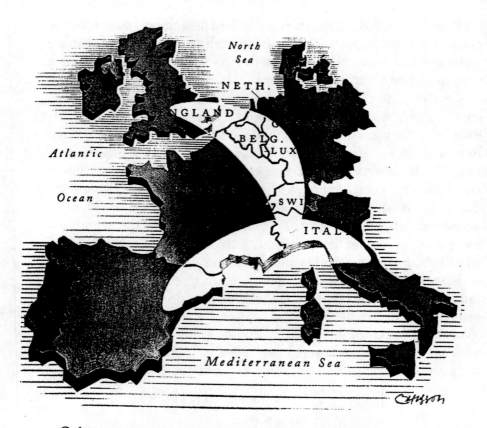

Other potential super-regions include an Atlantic arc stretching from Ireland through Wales and Brittany across the sea into Galicia and Portugal, and a zone that would closely resemble the former Hanseatic League, built around its original Nordic and Baltic membership.

Regionalism's hostility to distant bureaucracies may seem to target the institutions of the EU as much as ministries in national capitals, but it's not that simple. To take advantage of economies of scale and compete globally, the regions need a single market. Pujol and his allies believe the regions and the EU fraternity in Brussels have a common interest: weakening the nation-state. The regional movement, they feel, has been better accepted by EU institutions than national governments. The most important players of the future, they predict, will be the regions and the EU.

Nevertheless, in Germany, France, much of Spain, and most of Italy, there is a curious, perhaps predictable, ambivalence toward the EU; people favor it, by and large, but they reject the proposition that it should exercise power over their lives. They consider Brussels overly bureaucratic and technocratic. In any case, the EU isn't offering what Europeans are looking for: something they can relate to emotionally. The Germans call it *Heimat*, and some say it is the true source of regionalism. In France's 1992 referendum on the Maastricht treaty, the 49 percent who voted against ratification were judged to be largely pro-Europe but anti-Brussels.

Various regionalists see their role as stemming what some of them call the centralizing tide from Brussels. They ask whether it is the EU's job to build highways in Portugal, or to tell farmers how many pigs to slaughter and how big their apples can be, or to ordain a standardized tractor seat for all 15 countries of the union. The system's defenders respond that the EU encourages growth because, for example, instead of having to deal with 15 different sets of standards and regulations, manufacturers of tractor seats for the European market need meet only one.

Brussels also perceives that the single European market will help the regions of Europe by blurring national frontiers. As borders lose their meaning, deeply rooted patterns of commercial and cultural interaction are reappearing in regions where people have more in common, culturally or economically, with neighbors across the border than with their fellow countrymen. Baden-Württemberg, Alsace, and Basel are now one region for employment purposes, and a heavy concentration of both industry and universities is bolstering a regional identity. Saxony, in eastern Germany, is slowly becoming the midpoint of a similar region reaching north toward Berlin, south into the Czech Republic, and east to Poland.

In France, some are concerned that a piece of the southwest will again become part of the Catalan sphere of influence. French cities that were once the cultural centers of Catalonia are watching a lot of Catalan television, and the area around Toulouse is now doing more business with Catalonia than with other regions in France.

The Rhône-Alpes is France's strongest region, and Lyon, its capital and France's second-largest city, is a major international center.

Lyon's commercial policy is gaining independence and extending its European and global reach. Its airport was the first in France to acquire a high-speed rail link. Lyon's plan for growth includes high-speed rail service to Turin, Italy, which will require tunneling 35 miles through the Alps but will cut travel time between the cities to just over an hour. The wealthy triangle formed by Lyon, Turin, and Geneva—known as the Alpine Diamond—has a synergy that few regions of the world can match.

High-speed rail transport will become increasingly important in exploiting that synergy's potential, and will be another equalizer as regions and major cities further detach themselves from national capitals. So-called intermodal transport will move people and goods through a tight network of air, rail, and road links based on joint planning carried out by regional centers in two, three, or four or more countries. The most costly component is the as yet incomplete high-speed rail network; it requires trains of the kind first introduced in Europe as the French *Train à Grande Vitesse*, commonly known as the TGV, along with fully modern terminals linking the rail system to major airports. Germany, Italy, and Spain have emulated France, introducing trains similar to the TGV. Not surprisingly, cities, rather than regions or nation-states, are the strongest advocates of a continental rail system.

In 1988 the regions surrounding Stuttgart, Barcelona, Lyon, and Milan—Baden-Württemberg, Catalonia, the Rhône-Alpes, and Lombardy—formed the Four Motors Association. The idea was that the four would together become the engine for European growth. Thus far the group has not managed to focus attention on the region's knowledge-intensive industries, which was its early purpose. Europe's most prosperous industrial regions are still reluctant to interfere with the methods that have worked so well in the past, even if competing in the global market requires moving as rapidly as possible into technology's upper reaches. Some say the association's real function is to coordinate regional policy with Brussels and work around disputes between EU members over integration issues.

If the larger purpose of the Four Motors Association is wealth creation rather than a conscious return to roots, will the process drive politics in its and other regions to the right, especially as some become richer and others poorer? And who will protect the poor and disadvantaged? Nation-states? The EU? Will new and wider disparities be created? And to what extent is regionalism corrupting local politics? Corruption is already a powerful and debilitating force in numerous European countries, notably France, Italy, and Spain. Increasing the number of decision-makers and the money available to local government increases the opportunities for graft.

A large and unexamined question is the effect of regionalism on European security. Most European members of NATO are scaling back spending for defense, and in more than a few cases self-absorbed regions may insist on smaller commitments of resources for that purpose. Germany is a conspicuous example. When the Berlin Wall came down, some *Länder* leaders wanted to convert military bases into schools and other civilian facilities. Mayors in some of the regions argued for keeping the bases because of the jobs involved. Neither side claimed that the bases were necessary for defense, present or future.

> Europeans no longer think about providing for their security at the level of the nation-state.

Europeans for the most part have lost the habit of thinking about providing for their security at the level of the nation-state. Instead, they have an existential feeling of security from membership in both NATO and the EU. Defense spending by European states is in free fall. But their governments should understand that a diminishing commitment to their own security may weaken support for NATO within the United States, its leader and ballast.

The combination of porous borders and weakened national governments and police forces complicates efforts to combat illegal drugs, organized crime, and hot money. The European Commission says it needs more authority to cope with organized crime syndicates operating across national boundaries and, consequently, existing jurisdictions.

Pondering the effects of regionalism on security raises another question: with regions acquiring separate identities, will some of them tilt against one another, as in the past? The revival of ethnicity brought on by regional resurgence is a concern, and not just in historically volatile areas. Nevertheless, the net effect on security may be positive, at least to the extent that regional power can allay local anxieties and neutralize potentially violent separatist groups. In doing so, regions relieve pressure on national governments. It is not by chance that regional power has grown with the willing assent of the state— although it has grown in some places because national governments could not deter it by any acceptable means.

One way of thinking about regionalism is to recognize that in Western Europe the Cold War was accompanied by vastly successful modernization, which blurred regional cultures. The current revival of those cultures is in part a protest against that process, but in most places a benign one.

THE LÄNDER OF GERMANY

THE REGIONAL current is running strong in most parts of the EU, conspicuously in Germany, Belgium, northern Italy, Spanish Catalonia, southwest France, and the Rhône-Alpes. In Italy, a highly centralized state must cope with a highly decentralized economy and a regionalist north that wants a federal structure. With its even more centralized system, France will have the most trouble coping with regional sentiments. Germany is better prepared, thanks largely to its well-established federal structure. German regionalism also has the strongest roots; tradition and Germany's brief but tumultuous history as a nation-state have strengthened the regional and tribal instincts of its people. Germans today exist comfortably within their federal structure; most of them feel as if they are living once again as Thuringians or Bavarians or Westphalians first, and Germans second. It's easier to say, "I am a Swabian" or "I am a Saxon" than "I am a German," although some (who can say how many?) might add, "I am also a European."

Today's German federalism was not imposed by the victorious Allies of World War II, although they strongly supported it, but by the founders of the Federal Republic in 1948–49. They believed that political life in West Germany should be built around reconstituted *Länder*. In East Germany, Soviet occupation authorities replaced the five eastern *Länder* with 14 military districts. But when the

Berlin Wall came down and unification became a reality, East Germans instantly reclaimed their regional identities. *Länder* flags, not the national flag, were flown.

German federalism is the model for regionalists elsewhere, but it doesn't travel. The *Länder* system requires a large administrative capacity at the state level, which most regions do not possess. The *Länder* governments dominate social policy, including education, and they have a voice in foreign policy through offices they maintain in both Bonn and Brussels. Those offices are used primarily to lobby members of the Bundestag and the diplomatic community and representatives of industry and commerce. Parliamentarians, diplomats, and other lobbyists all agree that the *Länder* offices are the best hosts in Bonn, and more than hold their own in Brussels.

However, the chief source of the *Länder*'s power in Bonn lies not in their lobbying prowess but in their control of the Bundesrat, the upper house of parliament designed to represent the 16 *Länder*. The Maastricht treaty was ratified only after the Bundesrat had bowed to pressure from *Länder* leaders for more authority over EU policy. The Bundesrat must approve more than half of all bills, especially those that concern the financial and administrative affairs of the *Länder*. When the Bundestag and the Bundesrat disagree, a committee is formed to mediate a compromise.

Evidence of the decline of the German state is reflected in the diminished status of various ministries, including even the Finance Ministry. According to Herbert A. Henzler, chairman of McKinsey & Co. in Germany, 40 percent of German public spending orginates on the federal level, 30 percent in the *Länder*, and 30 percent in cities and towns. Federal spending is in continuing decline, he says.

Economic growth in Germany has been concentrated in several rival cities—Hamburg, Munich, Stuttgart, Frankfurt, and Düsseldorf. Regions like Bavaria and Baden-Württemberg rely on their business communities for leverage against Bonn. Their big auto companies, BMW and Daimler-Benz, can threaten to take jobs farther east or across the sea to Puerto Rico or Asia, where costs are not as oppressive. It is politically correct to be involved with the east, but investors in Munich are far less interested in the new *Länder* of eastern

Germany than in the Czech Republic, Hungary, and other East and Central European countries. Siemens, a Munich-based conglomerate that is the third-largest German company behind Daimler-Benz and Volkswagen, has a presence in every East European country, including Bosnia. Siemens reckons that its labor costs in the east are about ten percent of comparable costs in Germany, with productivity at about 70 percent of what it would be at home.

Among the *Länder* of eastern Germany, Saxony is the pacesetter and Dresden the most influential capital city, thanks in part to Saxony's minister-president, Kurt Biedenkopf, who is at least as respected as any of the country's political figures and, aside from Kohl, widely regarded as the most resourceful of them. Biedenkopf's administration is developing productive links with Bavaria and Baden-Württemberg, a task made easier by Biedenkopf's position as a major figure in the Christian Democratic Union, Germany's dominant party. Like many Germans, Biedenkopf feels that the larger interests of both Germany and Europe require further decentralization. Their concern is that a dominant, centralized republic with 80 million citizens and Berlin as its capital will intimidate its neighbors and foster anti-German coalitions.

THE SOUTH OF THE NORTH

SPANISH CATALONIA tends to think of itself as a nation, not a region. It is hard to disagree, even though Catalonia has not known political independence since the late seventeenth century. It was among the early European nations, once a medieval imperium whose maritime power for a time gave it control of Sicily, Corsica, Sardinia, and the Balearic Islands. The Catalan language reached into Provence, and by the fourteenth century most of southwestern France was ruled from Barcelona.

Contemporary Catalans see themselves as charting their course on a similarly large canvas. They not only consider Barcelona the first city of the Mediterranean—which it is—but regard themselves as constituting the north of the south and, more important, the south of the north. They see themselves as belonging to a community of northern European nations and a single market of 400 million consumers.

President Pujol and most politically aware Catalans feel that by any standard criteria, including economic stability, per capita income, population, cultural attributes, history, and outlook, they are more a northern European nation than a region in the less prosperous, less dynamic, more agrarian, and historically divergent mother country. It was Catalonia's entrepreneurial spirit, along with its location, that gave Spain access to the Industrial Revolution. Barcelona's cultured bourgeoisie acted as a magnet for the avant-garde, from Romanticism to Art Nouveau and Surrealism. For Barcelonans, the Castilian capital, Madrid, is a rather provincial city of limited interest. Pujol and his fellow nationalists like to emphasize Catalonia's Europeanness—how it played virtually no part, for example, in the Islamization of Spain, and was always oriented to the north and east. Among the long list of Catalan claims is that in 1359 the Kingdom of Catalonia became the world's first parliamentary government. Pujol is a well-known personality in Western Europe, partly because he is a fervent European, meaning he supports the EU. He uses the union to help him distance Catalonia from Madrid.

Catalan separatism does have its limits. The region's banking and industrial elite are reluctant to rock the boat, aware that Madrid will not surrender complete control of Spain's richest source of revenue and gateway to Europe. Catalonia produces a quarter of Spain's exports and 40 percent of its industrial exports with less than 14 percent of the population. Its renovated port handles nearly a quarter of the entire Mediterranean shipping trade. Like northern Italians, Catalans resent their nation's capital, which they view as sponging up the wealth they create and top-heavy with bureaucracy.

Among Pujol's weapons for distinguishing his putative nation from Spain, none has been more effective than the Catalan language, which he uses to sustain and extend the Catalan personality in Catalonia and beyond. Catalan is the language of instruction in Catalonia's schools, while Spanish is an elective like English and French. A group of parents who sued the state, insisting that children be taught in Spanish, lost. Embittered citizens say that Pujol's Catalonia obliges one to speak his language instead of the mother tongue. Pujol's allies respond that doing otherwise would create two opposing communities; the Catalan language, they say, is the great equalizer in a society where Andalusians and other non-Catalans constitute 40 percent of the population. A different pattern is visible in the media; Barcelona's major outlets for both print and broadcast journalism divide about equally between the two languages.

As imposing as Pujol is, he shares center stage in Barcelona with Pasquall Maragall, the vastly successful and popular mayor. Maragall, an urban planner by training, is said to envisage a resurrection of city-states, some of which would form a metropolitan system stretching across the Mediterranean littoral from Barcelona through southern France and into Italy. He thinks that such a system can function more smoothly and productively than one of nation-states. Maragall envies Milan and observes that Barcelona, too, must be able to sustain an international airport, with nonstop flights to New York and Tokyo. La Scala is another object of his envy; a world-class opera house is high on his list of musts. Still another priority is a high-speed train that would eventually connect Barcelona to Montpelier, Lyon, and northern Italy. There is little else Maragall can do to achieve what he most envies about Milan—its central European location.

DEVOLVING FRANCE

FRANCE IS the world's consummate nation-state. Its uniquely centralized authority dates to the early 1790s, when the country was divided into 88 *départements*, each run by a *préfet* appointed by Paris. In 1964, the *départements* were grouped into 21 regions, all drawn in a way that avoided similarity to the culturally distinct provinces.[1]

But the freewheeling activity in cities and regions along and across France's borders with Germany, Spain, Italy, and Belgium has had a ripple effect. Most major French cities have acquired larger budgets and more authority than ever before. In 1982 the newly arrived regime of President François Mitterand, who saw the *préfets* as a conservative-Gaullist elite, granted fairly broad

---

[1]Christopher Harvie, *The Rise of Regional Europe*, London: Routledge, 1994, p. 58.

powers to regional councils. Since then, the councils and the *préfets*, still appointed by Paris, have coexisted within a complex system of checks and balances.

Last July the government of President Jacques Chirac disclosed plans to delegate more decision-making power to the regions. The minister in charge of the public sector cited "profound archaisms" in the management of the state. Ministries in Paris, he noted, would lose 70,000 jobs, and the number of headquarters functions in Paris would be cut by 30 percent.

> The chief threat to the Paris edifice and Bonapartist tradition lies in the Rhône-Alpes.

The chief threat to the Paris edifice and Bonapartist tradition lies in the largest French region, the Rhône-Alpes, and its capital, Lyon. In its economic strength and versatility, along with the depth of its cultural and educational institutions, Lyon is second only to Paris. The city is home to nine universities with 180,000 students and has a vast technological base. The Rhône-Alpes is as large as the Netherlands, Belgium, and Switzerland combined, stretching from the Rhône River in the north to the Savoie mountains on the Swiss and Italian borders to the east to the rural Ardèche in the south. Other big cities like St. Etienne and Grenoble, one of Europe's premier centers of advanced technology, are collateral sources of regional economic power and reach.

The senior officials and planners in Lyon convey the same awareness of being the hub city of a region on the move as do their counterparts in Barcelona. They compare their projects and goals with those of colleagues there, whom they know well and consult regularly. The chief difference is that the Lyonnais make no claim to nationhood or cohesiveness. The Rhône-Alpes, they recognize, is an artificial construct—an assortment of dissimilar *départements* patched together by the state, against which the region is beginning to turn.

The Lyonnais profess to feel unambiguously French and do not, they say, have the soaring ambition of Catalan nationalists. But they have a similar desire to run their own show and to forge the external commercial links that will help them compete effectively in European and global markets. And Lyon does have some confrontational history. It was once a center of French Protestantism, and became the publishing center—above and below ground—of the Protestant movement. The city was also, in the 1940s, the headquarters of the French Resistance and its greatest leader, Jean Moulin.

Lyon brims with confidence and possesses a powerful entrepreneurial ethos. Along the axis formed by Lyon and Grenoble, the region's main cities, lies a flourishing private sector of over 4,000 companies—exporters in sectors ranging from agriculture to biotechnology that, by and large, have enjoyed trade surpluses with most of the world. Locals like to compare this aggregation with the huge, poorly performing state-owned companies that have long dominated the French economy. The comparison, they feel, helps explain why the Rhône-Alpes began its recovery from the recession of the early 1990s before other regions of France.[2]

Among the Rhône-Alpes' other advantages is Raymond Barre, mayor of Lyon, a deputy in the National Assembly, and president of the city's International Council. Barre, 72, never wanted to be mayor and agreed to run for the job only because the incumbent had been tried and convicted for corruption. Few, if any, other French political figures are as esteemed as Barre; besides having been prime minister for five years, he was also a respected professor of economics. His presence expands Lyon's range of options and aids the entire region, if only because no one in Paris can accuse this statesmanlike figure of promoting the interests of the city or the region at the expense of the country.

Lyon aspires to be the capital of southern Europe, and its claim to the role of southern gateway is strong. Its location and other attributes, including state-of-the-art transportation links, have helped the Rhône-Alpes attract considerably more foreign businesses than any other region of France. Many corporate executives, in deciding where to locate offices and warehouses, discover strong competitive advantages in Lyon's expansive highway system, modern Satolas airport, and links to high-speed rail service.

---

[2]William Drozdiak, "Regionalism on the Rise," *The Washington Post*, October 22, 1995, p. 22.

The city sees itself as the center of Europe's southern arc—a swath that resembles the banana Pujol likes to sketch. However, the Lyonnais configuration also takes in Geneva and stretches across northern Italy to Venice, then later extending to the east to incorporate Vienna and Budapest. Moreover, planners and promoters say, Lyon is establishing the major north-south axis between Frankfurt and Barcelona, and becoming the leading link between Europe's northeast and southwest.

PADANIA RISING?

JUDGING BY the press coverage and commentary, northern Italy would seem to be the caldron of subnational regionalism. In no other part of Europe, except possibly Corsica, is there more intense hostility toward the center, in this case Rome. In no other EU member state is there such an avowedly separatist movement or so much talk of a divided country. No other region harbors so shrill a secessionist, regionalist, or whatever Umberto Bossi, the chief of Italy's far-right Northern League, may be calling himself on any given day. But no part of northern Italy is likely to secede. As is usually the case in Italy, the raucous noises are deceptive and the situation more complicated than it appears.

Northern Italy is a medley of separate regions that have cultural and economic ties to neighboring countries. The Piedmont, Liguria, and Val d'Aoste lie within the French cultural orbit, Lombardy and the Veneto within the German. They are alike in their prosperity: the Veneto, the 7,000 square miles surrounding Venice, probably has Europe's highest per capita income and lowest unemployment. All of northern Italy is also alike in its febrile hostility toward the central government, especially toward what are seen as an intrusive bureaucracy and punitive taxes. Over the last decade taxes on business profits have jumped from 49 to 69 percent. Those who pay them regard them as a tribute exacted by Rome to sustain the idle and feckless of the *mezzogiorno*, the southern part of Italy, where in some areas unemployment hovers around 30 percent.

Northern Italy's regional assertion is bound up with the volatile and unpredictable Bossi, one part rabble-rouser, one part extremist—

"a certifiable loony," in the words of a prominent European ambassador who has observed him closely. But so far, Bossi alone has managed to articulate the grievances of wealthy, disaffected northern Italians. He was not a secessionist at first but soon became one, demanding that Italy be divided into three republics. In the 1992 national elections the Northern League emerged as a major force in the north, with 23 percent of the vote. In the April 1996 elections, the League outpolled all other parties north of the Po River. Nationally, it can claim the support of a tenth of the electorate. It can tilt the balance in national elections, as Bossi proved when he joined with Silvio Berlusconi and his Forza Italia in the 1994 elections and when he withdrew his backing in 1996.

Still, in winning ten percent of the vote in the national election last year, the league lost some parliamentary seats. Two months later its mayoral candidates in three northern Italian cities—Mantua, Lodi, and Pavia—failed to make it past the first round, finishing third behind those of the center-right and center-left alliances.

Bossi's inflammatory rhetoric has become a burden for his movement, as have the memories aroused by the green-shirted militants who surround him. He tells the faithful to stop paying taxes, and he has been pressing for a referendum on secession; on June 2, 1996, the fiftieth anniversary of the Italian republic, he led tens of thousands of people in Lombardy in an oath of allegiance to Padania, a new state that would be composed of the breakaway northern provinces, Italy's economic heartland. Bossi's colleagues, however, do not share the leader's secessionist bias, and, depending on the audience, Bossi himself sometimes disavows secession. The ambiguity about the league's purpose is essential; most of those who vote for league candidates do not favor a split from Rome.

During the campaign last year, Romano Prodi, the leader of the victorious center-left coalition, promised to overhaul Italy's tax system and grant more power to town halls. Now that he is in office, however, Prodi is finding federalism a daunting and distant prospect at best, more an ideal than a goal. Italy has well-developed administrative structures at the municipal level, but its provincial bureaucracies are very weak. When municipal authorities were granted some of the taxing authority they had been crying for some years ago, they subsequently complained; they did not like the added responsibility. Creating a federal system would also mean trying to dismantle a vast, well-entrenched state bureaucracy.

The rich, disaffected northern regions take for granted a robust domestic market and equate the future with their ties to the other side of the Alps. Several firms in the Piedmont are moving into the Rhône-Alpes, where they consider the infrastructure better and the bureaucracy more responsive. Milan and the rest of Lombardy, once an outpost of the Austro-Hungarian Empire, now feel a strong sense of belonging to Mitteleuropa. Milan's architecture matches its attitude. It was the Austrian empress Maria Teresa who pushed for construction of La Scala, the opera house that Maragall envies so. A Milanese planner sees two arcs of prosperity—one stretching from Barcelona to the Danube Valley and enfolding northern Italy, Trieste, Bavaria, and Austria; the other extending from southwestern England through the Rhine Valley to northern Italy. He sees Milan, the region's business and cultural hub, as the axis of the first arc and vital to the second.

BETWEEN BARCELONA AND BRUSSELS

As COMPETITION in the global market gathers force, so does the regional trend. The question many Europeans are asking is whether regions are gradually supplanting nation-states as sources of political authority and custodians of public policy. The answer is unclear, the signs pointing in different directions. For a variety of reasons, European governments no longer seem capable of fulfilling the terms of the social contract—ensuring jobs and prosperity, not to mention absolute security from want, hardship, or inconvenience. But if governments cannot fulfill the social contract, on what basis will they govern? Will they be able to maintain social peace in large cities? Will they guarantee law and order? Will they espouse the exclusion of foreigners, and other populist causes?

Cities and regions can and probably will assume responsibilities that have belonged to central governments. Still, whatever happens, regions are unlikely in most cases to assume responsibility for the social contract, least of all the burden of providing social security.

Equally unlikely is the prospect of an EU built mainly of numerous regions, large and small. So far, the significance of the regions is a good deal more economic than political; the heaviest impact is being made by the super-regions and lesser transnational communities, not least on the global economy. The nation-state is not going anywhere, not anytime soon. Its writ will continue to cover taxation and defense. It retains a solid grip on the EU's institutions. And it remains the only proven instrument for protecting justice, tolerance, and other human values. That said, the signs point to regionalism, not the EU, as constituting the larger threat to the authority of the nation-state.@

Can Europe Work?

A Plan to Rescue the Union

George Soros

The future of Europe has become a very complicated and technical subject, although it really ought to be very simple. We need a strong and viable European Union. Without it, the world would be back where it was at the end of the First World War. Indeed, the map of Europe today looks largely as it did in 1919, but with one big difference—15 countries of Western Europe are linked in the European Union.

Its creators brought a union into existence to prevent a recurrence of war, particularly one between Germany and France. For 45 years it has been successful in this mission. But the collapse of the Soviet empire and the reunification of Germany upset the delicate balance. Chancellor Helmut Kohl wanted to ground a united Germany firmly in Europe, and the French insisted on creating a stronger union to contain a larger Germany. Margaret Thatcher objected and her successor as British prime minister, John Major, exacted heavy concessions, but there was a sense of urgency, a self-

imposed deadline, as leaders of the member states reached a new agreement for Europe. The Treaty on European Union was initialed in the Dutch city of Maastricht in December 1991 and signed two months later.

Maastricht established three pillars for what was now to be styled the European Union: a common currency, a common foreign and security policy, and a common justice and internal policy. Along with this, member states acknowledged that to fulfill its mission the EU must open itself to eastward expansion and admit in a timely fashion countries that qualified. That should have been the end of the story and we should be living happily ever after, with a new institution for a new world. But there is something profoundly wrong in Europe.

The Maastricht Treaty is a flawed document and the European Union we have is not the one we need. The people of Europe barely accepted the treaty in national referendums, and in the five years since it was concluded, dissatisfaction

GEORGE SOROS, sole proprietor of Soros Fund Management, which serves as principal investment adviser to the Quantum Group of Funds, is Chairman of the Soros Foundations, a network of foundations operating in 25 countries.

[8]

with the Union has turned to alienation. Brussels has become a bureaucrat's dream; its legalistic, ever more complicated structure is foreign to the spirit of an open society. High unemployment, a pressing problem across the continent, is widely blamed on the economic convergence criteria Maastricht set for the introduction of the common currency. There is no common foreign policy. Europe's role in Bosnia has become a never-ending source of bickering, failure, and humiliation and a violation of all the principles for which Europe stands. Where has the Union gone wrong? First I shall examine the common currency, then Maastricht's other two pillars and the enlargement process, all of which stand on shaky ground.

E PLURIBUS EURO

Europe needs a common currency. A common market cannot survive in the long run without one because currency markets are notoriously unstable and currency speculation, especially the trend-following variety, can have a destabilizing effect on the economies involved. There are those, particularly in the City of London, who would argue that currency disturbances are short-lived by nature and currency overshoots correct themselves, so that equilibrium is reestablished. But exchange rates do not tend toward equilibrium because they themselves are one of the factors the equilibrium is supposed to reflect. I don't quite know what the equilibrium is, but I do know that it would be different depending on the value of the currencies concerned. Currency fluctuations can disrupt trade relations, as the tensions created by the abrupt fall in value of the Italian lira in 1994-95 demonstrated.

In sum, a single market will prove unsustainable without a single currency.

The method chosen to establish the common currency, however, is fundamentally flawed. The Maastricht Treaty lays out the exact criteria that all countries must meet before they can adopt the euro, and the precise timetable for meeting them. It makes some allowances for the vagaries of reality, but demonstrates a basic lack of understanding of the way economies function and the role economic policy should play. Concerned with specifying the conditions that would ensure the stability of the common currency, Maastricht assumes that these can be attained through a continuous process of convergence among the economies of EU countries. Underlying it all is an erroneous equilibrium theory of economics.

John Maynard Keynes showed that full employment is not the natural outcome of a market equilibrium. To bring about full employment, an economy needs government policies specifically designed for the purpose. Some of these may not be sustainable in the long run. Keynes' favorite prescription, fiscal stimulation through increased government spending, no longer works, since financial markets have developed an allergic reaction to such increases. If he were alive today Keynes would prescribe a different remedy, but he would understand that the invisible hand will not get us to a happy equilibrium.

Consider the specific problem Europe faces. It has once again entered a period of high unemployment, similar to the 1930s. There is general agreement that employment is too heavily taxed and labor markets are too rigid in Western Europe. With employers' social security contributions and personal taxation each at around 50 percent of gross wages, the combined tax burden on net wages of 50 is 100. Severance payments are onerous as well. No wonder employers are reluctant to offer permanent employment and a significant portion of the labor force is out of work.

The stimulation of aggregate demand à la Keynes is no longer practical, but devising other measures would not be too difficult. Almost everyone agrees that labor markets need to be liberalized, the social security system needs to be reformed, and taxation on employment needs to be reduced. It would be best to reduce government expenditures and taxes on employment at the same time. That would stimulate the economy and open the way to a more thoroughgoing reform of the social security system, including an increase in the retirement age as a second step. French President Jacques Chirac should have insisted on such a policy after his election in May 1995, and Kohl ought to adopt one now, as he is trying to put together an economic reform package. But neither is following this path because the Maastricht criteria constrain them: any tax cuts would increase the budget deficit in 1997, the benchmark year under the treaty. It is therefore very unlikely that Europe will see any effective policies to reduce unemployment before the common currency's introduction.

In all likelihood the euro will be introduced in 1999 as specified in the timetable, for the simple reason that Kohl is determined to introduce it and has the political ability to make it happen. His mandate in the March 24 elections in Baden-Württemberg state is likely to carry him through 1999, but he cannot afford any delay. Even the Bundesbank has no stomach for resistance, largely because it now realizes that its present policies have led Germany into a deep recession from which there is no easy way out. But this creates a dangerous situation. People will direct all their anger and resentment over unemployment at the single currency. There may well be a political revolt—particularly in France, notorious for such rebellions— and it would likely take a nationalistic, anti-European direction.

The danger could be averted, but that would require the German and French governments to flout the Maastricht criteria; to be effective, they should do so in tandem. There is nothing in the Maastricht Treaty to prevent a modification of criteria for admission to the new currency regime. And recall that the criteria apply only at the time of admission; afterward, the treaty calls for the coordination of fiscal policies, with penalties for those who violate the rules, but the rules are left to be worked out. Why not start with a coordinated stimulus program right now? The beneficial effects, if such a policy is introduced now, are sure to be felt by 1998, so that the euro would make its appearance against the background of an improving economy.

If leaders wait to try to reduce unemployment until after the currency's introduction, it may be too late, especially if it turns out that the governments are unable to coordinate their fiscal policies. The EU may fall victim to economic orthodoxy, beloved of central bankers, who will wield great influence in the new arrangements. Here too there are disturbing echoes of the interwar period, when, in Keynes' words, the economy of Great

A taste of the single currency: euro coin specially minted for a test run in France this year.

Britain was sacrificed on the altar of the gold standard.

The economy is too important to leave to central bankers. With exchange rates permanently fixed and monetary policy under the European central bank's control, national governments will have few policy instruments at their disposal. If they follow diverging fiscal policies, the monetary union could be endangered by individual governments' pursuit of irresponsible courses. That is why Maastricht set limits on government deficits and the accumulation of government debt. But if those limits are fixed in advance and forever, governments have no room for maneuver.

Economies need to be managed, and economies tied together by a common currency also need a common fiscal policy. The Maastricht Treaty sidestepped that issue by fixing only the entry requirements. But if the governments involved cannot take concerted steps now to combat unem-ployment, it is doubtful they will be able to do so later. In that case, it may be better not to have a common currency at all because mounting popular discontent would likely sweep away present policies, including the single currency.

POLITICS AMONG NATIONS

The second and third pillars of Maastricht—a common foreign and security policy and a common justice and internal policy—have barely begun to function because they have been left to an inter-governmental process and governments always put their own interests ahead of any common interest. Where member countries have delegated their sovereignty by treaty, namely in the Common Market, the arrangements have been effective. But on the second and third pillars of Maastricht there has been little delegation of sovereignty, and cooperation between the member governments does not work.

As for EU enlargement, the Inter-Governmental Conference, which Maastricht set up to handle the issue, instructing it to begin a preparatory review this year, has made little progress. And even with the new Europe's first pillar—economics—leaving common fiscal policy to the intergovernmental process may endanger the arrangements for a common currency.

As currently constituted, the European Union's structure is part of the problem. The EU consists of a central bureaucracy, the European Commission, which is responsible to 15 national bureaucracies and so multiplies the sins of national bureaucracies by a factor of 15. There is a Council of Ministers, where foreign ministers or their deputies represent the national interests of the constituent states. And there is a directly elected European Parliament, which has practically no powers. The net result is an almost complete absence of a common policy and a rising inability to reconcile conflicting interests.

Consider enlargement. The countries of Central and East Europe desperately need to get closer to the European Union. Although communism is well and truly dead, the patterns of thought and behavior learned in a closed society linger, and the institutions and attitudes of an open society are not yet firmly established. Without the prospect of joining the open society of Europe, the countries of the region could fall back on the kinds of arrangements they are familiar with. Since communism is no longer acceptable, they are liable to turn to some form of nationalism. For people to mobilize behind a nationalist cause, the nation must be endangered. If there is no real threat, one must be invented, but there are plenty of genuine grievances to exploit in Central and East Europe because the communist system suppressed all ethnic and nationalist aspirations. Yugoslavia is a case in point.

The way things are going, the terms of admission for formerly communist states will not be decided on before the end of the century. Since it is almost impossible for the Inter-Governmental Conference to make headway working with the present British government, it will probably have to await the outcome of British elections, likely to take place around next April; the conference would then not finish before the end of 1997. Preparations for the introduction of the single currency will consume 1998, so negotiations on the admission of new members will probably start in earnest only in 1999.

Regrettably, the enlargement of NATO is likely to proceed more rapidly. The problems of Central and East Europe require political integration and economic prosperity, not the extension of military alliances. The countries of the region need political, moral, and economic assurance that they are indeed part of the West and the world of open societies. To give them armies and military alliances instead misconstrues the threat. In fact, the expansion of NATO can easily turn into a self-fulfilling prophecy, generating the very dangers against which it is meant to defend.

Enlargement of the EU last year to 15 members has already made the intergovernmental process more unwieldy, and further enlargement will render it completely unworkable. Take only one example. The presidency rotates among the member nations every six months. After enlargement there could be several years in succession when tiny countries like

Luxembourg and Malta hold the presidency; voting rights will have to be modified, because if individual countries or a small group of countries can exercise a veto, reaching any decision will be difficult. But it is also hard for a country to relinquish its sovereign rights to a collection of other countries knowing that those countries are guided by their own interests, not by any common interest.

The Inter-Governmental Conference mechanism entrusts the solution of these problems to the parties responsible for creating them—namely, the member governments. What ought to happen in the EU is for decision-making power to be taken away from the governments. After all, sovereignty rests with the people. Any further delegation of sovereignty should come directly from them, not through the governments. And the EU, as a truly supranational authority, ought in turn to be accountable to the elected representatives of the people rather than to the constituent governments.

There is a Catch-22. People have lost their trust in European institutions because of the way those institutions work. They are less willing to delegate sovereignty, even if that might make the institutions more effective. One might hope for a major reform initiative from the European Parliament, but that body is not accustomed to taking the initiative. One might hope for greater public participation and public debate, but the issues confronting the Inter-Governmental Conference are highly technical and its deliberations are private.

The European Union has the potential to become the prototype of an open society. That is what makes it so desirable, so attractive as an ideal, particularly for the people of Central and East Europe. Open societies are based on the recognition that human understanding is imperfect and all constructs and institutions are flawed to a greater or lesser degree. But the Union has been shaped by bureaucrats, particularly French bureaucrats, and they are not known for their humility. They, better than most, recognize the deficiencies of institutions, which is why they are anxious to impose rigid conditions and a rigid timetable—so that the institutions should move forward, however deficient they are. This method has been effective; starting with the European Coal and Steel Community, bureaucrats with vision have used it to build the European Union brick by brick. But in the effort to meet deadlines and conditions, the basic tenet of open society—that there are bound to be flaws in the design—has gotten lost.

THE END OF THE CIRCLE

It is possible to fix the exact date when the vicious circle of bureaucratic rigidity and public disaffection began: November 9, 1989, the day the Berlin Wall fell. Until then, the European Community bureaucracy could cope reasonably well. For instance, it set a target well in advance for the integration of financial markets in 1992, and the operation was a great success. But the events in Berlin pushed Europe from near-equilibrium into a state of dynamic disequilibrium. It was the triumph of open society over totalitarian ideology. This revolutionary change should have sparked a revolutionary response. But the governments and people of Europe failed to rise to the occasion. Germany was willing to pay for the reintegration of East Germany—indeed, it paid too much—but the rest of

Europe was not. And Europeans were certainly not prepared to make any sacrifice to help the newly independent countries of the Soviet empire make the transition to an open society. If they had been, it would have united Europe in a way the common currency never will.

Matters were left in the hands of bureaucrats, and bureaucrats are notorious for their incapacity to handle revolutionary change. European integration entered a phase resembling the boom-bust so often observed in financial markets. The boom manifested itself in the Maastricht Treaty, and the turning point came half a year later with the treaty's narrow defeat in the June 1992 Danish referendum. Europe could have rallied to the cause, but instead the Danish defeat led to the breakdown of the European Exchange Rate Mechanism that September. Europe has been disintegrating ever since.

The trend toward disintegration, however, may be ready to be reversed. The first sign was the Baden-Württemberg elections in March. Six months ago I would have bet that the introduction of the single currency would be delayed and perhaps deferred indefinitely. I am now willing to bet it will take place on time, even if the convergence criteria have to be modified. A more stable and strongly pro-European government has come to power in Italy, and a Labour government in Britain may soon play a more constructive role in Europe. More important, there is a widespread feeling that the disintegration of Europe has gone far enough. People have been profoundly affected by the tragedy of Bosnia. That is a sentiment on which it is possible to build.

The bureaucratic method of building an integrated Europe has exhausted its potential. The Inter-Governmental Conference should convene a Constitutional Assembly; the people of Europe should be mobilized to bring that about. A Constitutional Assembly would not be empowered to appropriate further slices of national sovereignty without first obtaining the approval of each of the member countries. The new constitution would come into effect only after, say, three-quarters of the national parliaments approved it; in those countries that rejected it, it would be submitted to a referendum. There would be no delegation of powers without authorization. But the Constitutional Assembly would be able to resolve the problems the Inter-Governmental Conference *cannot* resolve, and engage the people of Europe in the process. Only a bold measure, clarifying the nature and identity of the European Union, can stop the gradual disintegration of Europe and prevent a return to the conditions prevailing between the world wars.✿

The Social Question
Redivivus

Tony Judt

Ill fares the land, to hastening ills a prey,
Where wealth accumulates, and men decay.

OLIVER GOLDSMITH

THE LITTLE TOWN of Longwy has a ghostly air. For many years it was an important center of iron and steel manufacturing in the industrial basin of the northern Lorraine and a proud stronghold of socialist and communist unions. Since 1975, however, the local industry, like steelworking everywhere in Western Europe, has been in trouble. Today the steelworks are gone, and so, at first sight, are their workers. At noon on a working day the town is quiet, with empty shops, a few sad-looking bars, and a deserted railway station occupied by a gaggle of drunks. The erstwhile steelworkers, grown old, wait out their lives in bars and cafés, or else stay at home with the television. Their wives and daughters have part-time, nonunion work either in new factories and offices distributed in the fields outside the town or else at commercial centers deposited optimistically at crossroads some 20 miles away. Their sons have no work at all and mill around at these same commercial centers looking at once menacing and pitiful.

There are towns like Longwy all over Europe, from Lancashire to Silesia, from the Asturian mountains to the central Slovakian plain. What makes the shattered industrial heartland of northeastern France distinctive is the political revolution that has occurred there.

TONY JUDT is Director of the Remarque Institute at New York University and author of *A Grand Illusion: An Essay on Europe.*

In the legislative elections of 1978, when the left was defeated nation-wide, the voters of Longwy returned a communist deputy to Paris, as usual. Twenty years later, in the legislative elections of May 1997, the right-wing National Front—which did not exist in 1978—came within 3,000 votes of overtaking the local communist candidate. A little farther east, in the similarly depressed industrial towns and villages around Sarrebourg that abut the German frontier, the National Front did even better: moving ahead of both communists and socialists, its candidates secured more than 22 percent of the vote in half the local constituencies.

The neo-fascist right, whose program constitutes one long scream of resentment—at immigrants, at unemployment, at crime and inse-curity, at "Europe," and in general at "them" who have brought it all about—did better still in the decayed industrial valley of the upper Loire west of Lyons, where one in five voters favored it, and best of all in the towns of Mediterranean France. In the greater Marseilles region nearly one voter in four chose the candidates of the National Front. If France had a system of proportional representation, the front would have not 1 but 77 deputies in the new French parliament (double its number under a short-lived system of proportional repre-sentation introduced for the 1986 elections), and the left would not have a parliamentary majority.

All these regions, and many others where the far right is now the leading local party, were until very recently strongholds of the left. The demographics of most such places have not altered significantly— former communists, not newcomers, are now voting for Jean-Marie Le Pen. The community of these men and women has been de-stroyed, and they are looking for someone to blame and someone to follow. This is not Wigan Pier, the world of British industrial unem-ployment chronicled by George Orwell between the wars. There the economy buckled and the state withdrew from all but its most minimal commitments, but the community held fast and was even strengthened in its shared belief in itself and the justice of its claims. In postindus-trial France (or Britain and elsewhere) the economy has moved on while the state, so far, has stayed behind to pick up the tab, but the community has collapsed, and with it a century-long political culture that combined pride in work, local social interdependence, and in-tergenerational continuity.

THE EXCLUDED

IT IS IRONIC but not mystifying that Le Pen, like other European demagogues, picks up some of his strongest support in frontier districts. Longwy and Sarrebourg are right next to the vanishing borders, once so contested, between France, Belgium, Luxembourg, and Germany. In today's Europe you can live in one country, shop in another, and seek employment in a third. But the free movement of people, money, and goods that is so central to Europe's much-advertised entry into a post-national, global era has not brought prosperity to this region—indeed, the most salient economic effect on the locality has been the loss of jobs in the customs service. The Europe debate, in France and elsewhere, is thus readily cast in terms of security, stability, and protection versus vulnerability and change, with Brussels serving as a lightning rod for a broad range of criticisms directed at globalization and the hegemony of the Anglo-American model of minimal state and maximized profit—what the French nervously and revealingly label *la pensée unique*.

In fact the impact of a global economy on how Europeans, at least, will choose to conduct their lives has been exaggerated. The mantra "global market forces," the latest weapon in the conceptual armory of the forces of change, does duty on a variety of fronts, replacing the superannuated ordnance of progress, inevitability, historical necessity, modernization, and so forth. But like them, it promises and assumes too much. To take the most popular example: when applied as part of a critique of European social policies, global market forces are presumed to require that the high-wage economies of Western Europe rethink themselves, and fast, lest jobs and investment flee the pampered, overpriced European continent in search of cheaper labor and higher rates of growth elsewhere, notably in Asia. But economic growth rates among the Asian "tigers" are slowing down, and understandably; like the high growth rates in postwar socialist countries, they depended on the extensive mobilization and exploitation of resources, human and natural. An indefinitely increasing input of labor and local capital is not sustainable—and this even before we consider that such rates of transformation were only achieved, as in the countries of real existing socialism, by vigorous control and repression.

Moreover, the specific global market force that is advertised as most likely to scupper Western Europe—lower wages in other continents or in Eastern Europe—may not apply much longer. By January 1997, wages in South Korea were approaching two-thirds the level of comparable wages in Germany. Demand for skilled labor in Asian states and in certain countries of Eastern Europe is bringing wages in some sectors close to or even above those earned in the poorest parts of the European Union. Already the majority of foreign direct investment from Western Europe goes to other high-wage countries. Within a few years, wage differentials alone will not be a factor in the case for cost-cutting except for certain industries where comparative advantage will always obtain. And all this ignores the more serious likelihood that Asian and other cutting-edge economies may not long remain a model even for themselves: the social inequalities and political repression that accompany cheap labor and stable investment environments will be vulnerable to comparisons with and disapproval from abroad—global forces in their own right.

But even if global market forces worked as advertised, they could not forcibly transform Europe's public policy because its dilemmas are not essentially economic. There are now more than 18 million officially unemployed people in the European Union. Yet finding jobs for them is not the most serious social question in Europe today—and if jobs were found by significant reductions in wages and benefits, the better to compete with the costs of jobs in other places, the real problems would worsen. Seventeen percent of the present population of the EU live below the official poverty line (defined as an income less than 50 percent of the average in a person's country of residence). Significantly, the highest level of official poverty, after Portugal, is in Great Britain, where 22 percent of the population (over 14 million people) live below the poverty line—and Britain has the best record on job creation in the EU in the past half-decade.

The social crisis, then, concerns not so much unemployment as what the French call the "excluded." This term describes people who, having left the full-time work force, or never having joined it, are in a certain sense only partly members of the national community. It is not their material poverty, but the way in which they exist outside the conventional channels of employment or security, and with little

France's excluded, Paris 1993

prospect of reentering these channels or benefiting from the social liaisons that accompany them, that distinguishes them from even the poorest among the unskilled work force in the industrial economy. Such people—whether single parents, part-time or short-term workers, immigrants, unskilled adolescents, or prematurely and forcibly retired manual workers—cannot live decently, participate in the culture of their local or national community, or offer their children prospects better than their own. Their living and working conditions preclude attention to anything beyond survival, and they are, or ought to be, a standing remonstrance to the affluence of their included fellows. In France, where there are 3.5 million officially unemployed and a further 4 million in precarious work, fully 30 percent of the active population are *exclus*. The figures are significantly lower only in Scandinavia, where the welfare systems of better days are still substantially in place, albeit trimmed. Under any present version of the neoliberal project— budget cuts, deregulation, etc.—the numbers of the precarious, the excluded, and the poor (disproportionately present in communities of recent immigrant origin) are likely to increase because work is disappearing in precisely the places, and at the occupations and skill levels, where most of the vulnerable population of Europe is now concentrated and will remain for the next generation.

In policy terms this is not purely or even primarily an economic conundrum. Rich countries can almost always find the resources to pay for social benefits if they choose, but the decision on how to do so is in the first instance a political one. There have always been two basic ways to finance these benefits. One is for the state to tax work: by charging workers and employers to help it pay for a variety of social services, including unemployment payments to those same workers if they lose their jobs. This makes labor and goods expensive (by adding to employers' costs), but it has the appeal of a certain sort of equity; it also worked rather well in the postwar era of high-wage, full-employment economies, since it padded state coffers when the unemployed and pensioners were in short supply. The alternative, universal, system bills the whole nation, through direct and indirect taxation, for social services that are then made available to those who require them.

Today, with high unemployment, it is tempting to prefer the second, universal option, since governments are trying to reduce the cost of labor to employers (and with less people working there are fewer paychecks to tax). But the political risks entailed in charging every voter for services from which only some (the unemployed, the aged, the infirm) will benefit are high, though perhaps not as high as providing no services at all, since the handicapped, elderly, and jobless can all vote too.

There is now a third option, a version of which has been followed in the United States and now in the United Kingdom—cut benefits and gear unemployment and other compensatory payments to a person's past work record (and income) and his or her continued willingness to find and take work if available. This is now said to be the appropriate social policy for a global economy: it penalizes unwillingness to take a job at the going rate, reduces employers' costs, and limits the state's liability.

This third alternative, however tidily it responds to global market forces, ironically presumes the very spectrum of circumstances whose disappearance has brought it about: the availability of employment, no sustained interruption of work experience by involuntary unemployment, and above all a normal wage high enough so that the percentage of it paid out in unemployment compensation will suffice to keep a person or family out of poverty until work is available. It presupposes the sort of worker and working profile that is now rapidly vanishing in just those places where such policies are being considered or implemented. The result can only be greater poverty, a growing gap between those with steady work and those without it, and ever more men and women excluded from the working, earning, tax-paying community that will understandably look on them with fear and suspicion.[1]

These are the losers—the de-skilled, the unskilled, the part-time, immigrants, the unemployed—all of whom are vulnerable because of the state of the economy but above all because they have lost the work-related forms of institutional affiliation, social support, and occupational solidarity that once characterized the exploited industrial proletariat. It is they who are least able to benefit from the hypothetical added value of a global economy, or even an integrated European one: they cannot read-

---

[1] I am indebted for the above to the work of the sociologist Georg Vobruba of the University of Leipzig, who has done important studies of the impact of varieties of unemployment insurance on the postindustrial work force. See, for example, his "Social Policy for Europe," in *The Social Quality of Europe*, ed. Wolfgang Beck, Laurent van der Maesen, and Alan Walker, Boston: Kluwer Law International, 1997, pp. 105-120.

ily go somewhere else to find work, and even if they did they would not find the social and psychic benefits that once accompanied it but would just be *exclus* somewhere else. Capital can be separated from its owner and move around the world at the speed of sound and light. But labor cannot be separated from its owner, and its owner is not just a worker but also a member of one or more communities—a resident, a citizen, a national.

True, all labor is *potentially* mobile across job skills, space, and time. But it is wildly unrealistic to expect people to change both their working skills and their home every time global market forces dictate it. And in any case the crucial variable here is time: the transformation of an economy may be a rapid affair, but the accompanying social changes cannot be wrought at the same rate. It is the gap between economic change and social adjustment, a gap that has already lasted half a generation and will probably endure for years to come, that is causing the present dilemma and has become, by analogy with the great Social Question of the nineteenth century, the critical issue of our time.

THE SOCIAL QUESTION

IN LATE-eighteenth- and early-nineteenth-century Britain, the visible havoc wreaked on the land and the people by unrestricted economic forces was noted, regretted, and opposed by poets and radicals from Oliver Goldsmith to William Cobbett. The problem of the excluded—landless laborers, pauperized weavers, unemployed bricklayers, homeless children—was attacked in various ways, culminating in the New Poor Law of 1834, which introduced the workhouse and the principle of least eligibility, whereby relief for the unemployed and indigent was to be inferior in quality and quantity to the lowest prevailing wages and conditions of employment, a model of welfare "reform" to which President Bill Clinton's recent legislation is directly if perhaps unknowingly indebted. The conventional arguments against state intervention were widely rehearsed: the free workings of the economy would eventually address the distortions attendant on agricultural enclosure or mechanization; the regulation of working hours or conditions would render firms uncompetitive; labor should be free to come and go, like capital; the "undeserving" poor (those who refused available work) should be penalized, etc.

But after a brush with revolt during the economic depression of the 1840s, British Governments adjusted their sights and enacted a series of reforms driven in equal measure by ethical sensibilities and political prudence. By the later years of the century the erstwhile minimalist British state had set upper limits on working hours in factories, a minimum age for child employment, and regulations concerning conditions of work in a variety of industries. The vote had been granted to a majority of adult males, and the labor and political organizations that the working population had struggled to establish had been legalized—so that in time they ceased to be disruptive to the workings of capitalism and became effective sources of social integration and political stability. The result was not planned, but it is incontrovertible: British capitalism thrived not in spite of regulatory mechanisms but because of them.

> How could economic progress be secured in light of the condition c the working class?

In continental Europe things worked a little differently. There, the impact of economic change, often driven from abroad, was not muted by piecemeal social legislation, both because legislatures responsive to political demands were not yet in place and because farms and factories were unable to withstand foreign competition without protection. In such places, most notably France, there was a long-standing expectation that the state would provide when all else failed, a habit of mind encouraged by the state itself. Those crucial moments when the state (or the king) failed to come through are what we associate with the great crises of the Age of Revolution: 1787-90, 1827-32, and 1846-50, when the response to economic dislocation and social protest all across the continent took the form of a repeated sequence of revolt, reform, and repression.

The nineteenth-century Social Question, as described and interminably debated in the middle decades of the last century, was this: How could the virtues of economic progress be secured in light of the political and moral threat posed by the condition of the working class? Or, more cynically, how was social upheaval to be headed off in a society wedded to the benefits that came from the profitable exploitation of a large class of low-paid and existentially discontented persons?

The response of European states to the problem of managing the social consequences of the early Industrial Revolution owed almost nothing to contemporary theories that purported to describe the inevitable, structural nature of the forces at play. Economic liberalism, whether as a description of the workings of capitalism or as a prescription for economic policies, had little impact on political decision-making or even social policy. That is why we have today, or had until recently, a unique and uniquely stable combination—of market economies, precapitalist social relations and moral expectations (notably our intuitive distaste for extremes of social insecurity), and interventionist states, directly inherited from the enlightened absolutist monarchies of the not-so-distant past—that characterizes the fortunate Western inheritance.

THE PROVIDENTIAL STATE

CRITICS OF the interventionist state today level two convincing charges against it. The first is that the experience of our century reveals a propensity and a capacity, unimaginable in earlier times, for totalitarian regulation and repression not only of people but of institutions, social practices, and the very fabric of normal life. We now know and cannot ignore what the Fabians, the founding theorists of social democracy, the utopian dreamers of collectivist systems of society, and even the well-meaning proponents of paternalist social engineering did not know, or preferred to forget: that the overmighty state, under whatever doctrinal aegis, has an alarming and probably unavoidable propensity to eat its own children as well as those of its enemies.

The other lesson we should have learned from the experience of our age is that, murderous or benevolent, the state is a strikingly inefficient economic actor. Nationalized industries, state farms, centrally planned economies, controlled trade, fixed prices, and government-directed production and distribution do not work. They do not produce the goods, and as a consequence they do not distribute them very well, even though the promise of a more equitable system of distribution is usually the basis of their initial appeal.

Neither of these lessons is entirely new. Eighteenth-century critics of mercantilism knew why state-regulated economies were inefficient and self-defeating. The opponents of autocratic monarchies, from the English Puritans through the French Enlightenment to the great Russian novelists of the last century, had long since itemized the sins and deficiencies of unrestricted central power and its stifling effect on human potential. What the twentieth century teaches is simply an updated version of Lord Acton's dictum: absolute state power destroys absolutely, and full state control of the economy distorts fully. The short-lived disaster of fascism and the longer-lasting tragedy of communism can be adduced in evidence of processes known to our forebears but of which Colbert's system and the ancien régime were but pale anticipations. We now know that some version of liberalism that accords the maximum of freedom and initiative in every sphere of life is the only possible option.

> British capitalism thrived not in spite of regulatory mechanisms but because of them.

But that is all we know, and not everything follows from it. The lessons of 1989 obscure almost as much as they teach, and worst of all they tend to obscure a third lesson: that we no longer have good reason to suppose that *any* single set of political or economic rules or principles is universally applicable, however virtuous or effective they may prove in individual instances. This is not a plea for cultural or moral relativism, but it is not incoherent to believe that a system of economic management might work in one place and not another, or to recognize that, within limits, what is normal and expected behavior by a government in one free society might understandably be thought intolerable interference in another.

Thus the application of neoliberal economic policy in the United States is possible, in part, because even some of those who stand to lose thereby are culturally predisposed to listen with approval to politicians denouncing the sins of big government. The American combination of economic insecurity, social inequality, and reduced or minimal government intervention in the field of welfare legislation, for example, would prove explosive in societies where the state is expected to have a hand in such matters and gets the benefit of the doubt even when it appears to be abusing its power. Thus for reasons that are cultural and historical rather than economic, the U.S. model is not exportable and even across

the breadth of the Atlantic Ocean causes quivers of distaste and anxiety among otherwise sympathetic foreign observers.

The British case, which bears some resemblance to the U.S. one, is in certain respects a little closer to the European norm. The British *state* has never played a very important part in people's lives, at least as they perceive it; it is *society* that binds the British together, or so they had long believed. Reinforced by the myth and memory of wartime unity, British people in the postwar decades were notably sensitive to hints that selfish group claims were being favored by the state at the expense of the common good. Indeed, Margaret Thatcher effected a small revolution in her country precisely by playing on a widespread fear that some sectors of society—the labor unions in particular—had gained access to the state and were using it to sectoral advantage. That she herself expanded the role of the state in other spheres of life—notably justice and local government—and used central authority to benefit other sectoral interests is beside the point. The British were susceptible to the suggestion that their difficulties arose from the omnipresence of an inefficient and vaguely threatening central power, though they had no desire to squander the achievements of state-administered social legislation in the fields of health, welfare, and education, as the Tories' final, ignominious defeat revealed.

But the British example is equally inapplicable to the continental European case—and not just because of the amusing European propensity to speak of Anglo-American neoliberalism as though the British and U.S. experience and examples were interchangeable. There are no doubt many European socialists and liberals who would like to emulate Tony Blair. But the price of that would be to pass through the experience of Margaret Thatcher (without whom Tony Blair would still be an obscure Labour politician with no original ideas of his own), and no European politician of any hue imagines for a moment that his own country could survive *that*. It is not just that Thatcher produced double-digit unemployment and destroyed the traditional manufacturing base of the British economy, while briefly lining the pockets of the middle class with the windfall proceeds from privatization: some of that has already happened in France, Belgium, Spain, and elsewhere. But Thatcher demolished the theory and much of the practice of the providential state, and it is that which is unthinkable across the channel.[2]

In continental Europe the state will continue to play the major role in public life for three general reasons. The first is cultural. People expect the state—the government, the administration, the executive offices—to take the initiative or at least pick up the pieces. When the French demand that their government provide shorter working hours, higher wages, employment security, early pensions, and more jobs, they may be unrealistic but they are not irrational. They do not generally press for lower taxes (in contrast with the U.S. political obsession with tax cuts). They recognize that high taxes are the means by which the state might meet such expectations, and they are indeed highly taxed, which is why they resent it when the state fails to deliver the social goods. Germans, too, expect the state to ensure their well-being. And although, for historical reasons, they are disposed to identify the latter with social compacts and a stable currency, they too expect the state to play an active role in maintaining job security, regulating commerce, and servicing the remarkably generous welfare net with which they have provided themselves.

---

[2]Moreover, in Oxford Professor of Politics John Gray's words, "Neoliberalism in Britain has proved a self-limiting project," *Endgames*, Cambridge: Polity Press, 1997, p. 3. And if it is self-limiting on account of the very ravages it produces (and the electoral backlash that ensues) even in a political culture predisposed to pride itself on individualism and freedom from central restraint, its prospects on a continent where the state is by historical convention the most important and least-contested participant in the political arena are thin indeed. The partial counterexample of the Netherlands illustrates the point. In a small country with no modern history of civil division or conflict, and where central and local government alike are born of discussion and consensus, it has proved possible to manage the reduction of the welfare state and the provision of low-paid and insecure work without social explosion—although note that even the Dutch have not succeeded in squaring the circle of economic transformation: there are as many poor people per capita in the Netherlands as there are in Belgium or France. But the state in the Netherlands has no history of engagement in society and the economy comparable to the state in the Scandinavian states, Germany, Italy, or France. Its example is unlikely to be emulated.

Even in Italy, where the state is weak and much more politically vulnerable, it has played a crucial role in providing employment, transfer payments, regional largess, and an intricate variety of support schemes, all of which have contributed enormously to the social stability of a country whose very unity is in question and that has been prey to more, and deeper, political crises than the Anglo-American experience can begin to conceive of. Let us pose the counterfactual question: where would Italy be now without its huge and inefficient civil service, its overstaffed public services, its dysfunctional and discredited systems of wage-price linkage, its underfunded pension schemes, and its corrupt and abused Cassa per il Mezzogiorno, established in 1950 to channel resources to the backward south but long a feeding ground for the political clients and business associates of the governing Christian Democrats? The Italian state is not all that has stood between Italy as we now see it and some hypothetical Italian miracle of the neoliberal imagination, but between postwar Italy and political collapse. This is not just because the country would otherwise have faced insuperable social conflicts and regional disparities, but because the long-standing cultural expectations of Italians—that the state must do what society and economy, left to their own devices, cannot—would have been unacceptably thwarted. In unsteady and fragmented societies the state is often the only means by which some measure of coherence and stability can be guaranteed. The historical alternative in such cases has usually been the military, and it has been Italy's and Europe's good fortune that *that* route has been taken infrequently in recent memory.

Thus, although the state itself has had a bad press in the recent European past, there has been little loss of faith in the importance of the things it can do, properly led. Only a state can provide the services and conditions through which its citizens may aspire to lead a good or fulfilling life. Those conditions vary across cultures: they may emphasize civic peace, solidarity with the less fortunate, public facilities of the infrastructural or even the high cultural sort, environmental amenities, free health care, good public education, and much else. It is generally recognized that not all of these may be available in their optimal form, but in that case too it is only the state that can adjudicate with reasonable impartiality between competing demands, interests, and goods.

Most important, only the state can represent a shared consensus about which goods are positional and can be obtained only in prosperity, and which are basic and must be provided to everyone in all circumstances.

These are things the market—much less the global market—cannot do. Paradoxically, the idea of an active state today represents an acknowledgment of *limits* on human endeavor, in contrast to its overweening utopian ambitions in the recent past: because not everything can be done, we need to select the most desirable or important among what is possible. The idealization of the market, with the attendant assumption that anything is possible in principle, with market forces determining which possibilities

> Where would postwar Italy be now without its huge civil service?

will emerge, is the latest (if not the last) modernist illusion: that we live in a world of infinite potential where we are masters of our destiny, yet are utterly dependent on the unpredictable outcome of forces over which we have no control. Proponents of the interventionist state are more modest and disabused. They would rather choose between possible outcomes than leave the result to chance, if only because there is something intuitively and distressingly callous about leaving certain sorts of goods, services, and life chances to the winds of fate.

The second case for preserving the state today is pragmatic, or perhaps prudential. Because global markets *do* exist, because capital and resources fly around the world and much of what happens in people's lives today has passed from their control or the control of those who govern them, there is a greater need than ever to hold on to the sorts of intermediate institutions that make possible normal civilized life in communities and societies. We are accustomed to understanding this point when it is directed to the need for voluntary organizations, community structures, small-scale exercises of autonomy in public life, and local civic ventures directed toward issues of common concern such as safety, environment, education, culture. And we understand, or think we understand, the importance of intermediate institutions when we study totalitarian regimes and notice the importance their rulers attached to the *destruction* of anything that came between the isolated, anomic subject and the monopolistic state.

What we have failed to grasp is that, in the late twentieth century, the state is now an intermediary institution too. When the economy, and the forces and patterns of behavior that accompany it, are truly international, the only institution that can effectively interpose itself between those forces and the unprotected individual is the national state. Such states are all that can stand between their citizens and the unrestricted, unrepresentative, unlegitimated capacities of markets, insensitive and unresponsive supranational administrations (of which Brussels is sadly illustrative), and unregulated processes over which individuals and communities have no control. The state is the largest unit in which, by habit and convention, men and women can feel they have a stake and which is, or can be made to appear, responsive to their interests and desires.

Finally, the need for representative democracy—which makes it possible for a large number of people to live together in some measure of agreement while retaining a degree of control over their collective fate—is also the best argument for the traditional state. Indeed, the two are fated to live or die together. Political choices will always be made because politics, as an antithetic activity, is the proper form in which different collective preferences are expressed in open societies. And because the state is the only forum in which politics can be practiced—something that becomes obvious as soon as we envisage the alternatives—it is imprudent as well as unrealistic to seek to reduce or bypass the state. It is because the free flow of capital threatens the sovereign authority of democratic states that we need to strengthen these, not surrender them to the siren song of international markets, global society, or transnational communities. That is what is wrong with the European project as currently practiced, and it is what would be wrong with assigning the policymaking initiative to global market forces.

Just as political democracy is all that stands between individuals and an overmighty government, so the regulatory, providential state is all that stands between its citizens and the unpredictable forces of economic change. Far from being an impediment to progress, the recalcitrant state, embodying the expectations and demands of its citizenry, is the only safeguard of progress to date. Whatever the gains in social legislation on working conditions and hours, education, the dissemination of culture, safeguarding health and the environment, insurance against homelessness, unemployment, and old age, and the limited redistribution of wealth, they are all vulnerable and politically contingent. There is no historical law that says they may not someday be undone. For it is with social advance as with political freedoms: we must always stave off threats to what has been won, rather than presume these gains to be a secure part of some unassailable heritage.

Furthermore, it is not in the interest of proponents of global market forces to seek the dismantling of the providential state. Unregulated markets are frequently self-delegitimizing, as numerous historical examples suggest. Perceived as unfair, they can become dysfunctional and will be rejected even by those who stand to gain from their smooth operation. For social and political stability are important economic variables too, and in political cultures where the providential state is the condition of social peace, it is thus a crucial local *economic* asset, independent of its economic behavior. That is why "the market" has worked well, albeit in very different ways, in situations as distinct as Social Democratic Scandinavia, Christian Democratic Italy, social-market Germany, and providential-state France.

A NEW MORAL NARRATIVE FOR THE LEFT

THE LOSERS in today's economy have the most interest in and need for the state, not least because they cannot readily imagine taking themselves and their labor anywhere else. Since the political left by convention and elective affinity is most motivated to capture the support of this constituency (and had better do so if we are to avoid a selective replay of the 1930s), the present afflictions of the European left are of more than passing concern. And they are serious. Since the late eighteenth century the left in Europe, variously labeled, has been the bearer of a project. Whether this project has been the march of progress, the preparation of revolution, or the cause of a class, it has always invoked the historical process, and history itself, on its behalf. Since the decline of the industrial proletariat, and more precipitously with the end of the Soviet Union, the left in the West has been shorn of its agent, its project, and even its story—the master narrative within which all radical endeavors were ultimately couched, which made sense of their programs and explained away their setbacks.

This is self-evidently the case for communists, but it is no less serious an impediment to moderate social democracy as well. Without a working class, without a long-term revolutionary objective, however benign and nonviolent in practice, without any particular reason to suppose that it *will* succeed or a transcendental basis for believing that it *deserves* to do so, social democracy today is just what its great nineteenth-century founders feared it would become if it ever abandoned its ideological presuppositions and class affiliation: the advanced wing of reforming market liberalism. Now, just as it has been relieved by the death of communism from the crippling mortgage of revolutionary expectations, is the European left to be reduced to defending hard-won sectoral gains and glancing nervously and resentfully at a future it cannot understand and for which it has no prescription?

The reconciliation between the European left and capitalism is still fresh and long overdue. We should recall that as recently as 1981 François Mitterrand's Socialist Party came to power on the promise and expectation of a radical and irreversible anticapitalist transformation. And anyone who supposes that this was a peculiarly and typically French aberration should reread the British Labour Party's 1983 election manifesto—the "longest suicide note in history," in Labour Member of Parliament Gerald Kaufman's felicitous phrase. But today the left is no longer shackled to irrelevant, ineffective, or unpopular policies. On the contrary, the sort of society that the French, Swedish, Italian, and even the German socialists claim to seek is a fairly accurate reflection of the generalized preferences of the majority of their fellow citizens.

The real problem facing Europe's socialists (I use the term purely for its descriptive convenience, since it is now shorn of any ideological charge) is not their policy preferences, taken singly. Job creation, a more "social" Europe, public infrastructural investment, educational reforms, and the like are laudable and uncontroversial. But nothing binds these policies or proposals together into a common political or moral narrative. The left has no sense of what its own political success, if achieved, would mean; it has no articulated vision of a good, or even of a better, society. In the absence of such a vision, to be on the left is simply to be in a state of permanent protest. And since the thing most protested against is the damage wrought by rapid change, to be on the left is to be a conservative.

The brief success story of European social democracy and British Labour over the past half-century can be seen in retrospect to have depended on the same fortuitous circumstances as the welfare states it helped create. Now the left wants to preserve its positions and its hard-won sectoral gains. In defending these acquired rights and supporting those who would add to them—like railway engineers and truck drivers in France who demand retirement on full pensions at 55 or even 50—the left (and sometimes the right) in France, Germany, Spain, and elsewhere confuses and discredits itself and its case by a failure to choose between ultimately incompatible claims. It is not so much fighting the ideological battle against neoliberal heartlessness but seeking to conserve privileges on behalf of the broadest possible constituency of well-organized voters who are anxious at the prospect of reduced income and services.

This paradox, if it is one, is not original. The left was often *socially* conservative—notably during the French Revolution, when some of the most radical moments occurred on behalf of artisans' struggles to preserve established claims and privileges, and again during the early Industrial Revolution. Trade unions, especially those in the skilled trades, were never anything else, even when supporting radical political solutions. But it is an unconvincing posture, and given the impossibility of avoiding *some* unsettling changes in coming years, it is an improvident one.

In these circumstances the dangerous illusion of a radical center has taken hold. Like the French Socialists' 1997 slogan "Changeons d'avenir," Tony Blair's "radical centrism" is an empty vessel, clanging noisily and boastfully around the vacant space of European political argument. But whereas Lionel Jospin's clichés are familiar, those of New Labour are seductively novel at first hearing. Of course there are political advantages to being in the center. In normal times that is where the winning votes are to be found in any binary representative system. But if times become somewhat less normal, as seems likely, the center is quickly evacuated in favor of more extreme options. For the moment, Blairism consists of the successful displacement of the old, discredited left by what might be termed the *bien-sentant* center, the politics of good feeling, in which lightly retouched Thatcherite economics are blended with appropriately well-intentioned social adjustments borrowed from the neighboring liberal tradition. In this way the charge of heartless realism is avoided without any need to imagine alternatives. It is a tempting solution, and one that many of Blair's European socialist colleagues would certainly adopt had some local Thatcher prepared for them a suitably blasted heath.

But it is a mistake. Like the "as if" and "civil society" language of the Czech, Polish, and Hungarian opposition in the 1980s, it is a good and effective weapon in the struggle against insensitive or authoritarian governments. But once those governments have been overthrown or defeated, the morally unimpeachable advocates of anti-politics find themselves confronted with political choices for which their previous experience has not prepared them. They must either compromise and lose their credibility or else quit public life. For most of the past century, the European left has somehow managed to do both. If it is to do better in the future, to avoid repeating its historical pattern of morally redeeming failure, it must return to the drawing board and ask itself these questions: What sort of a society is both desirable and envisageable under the present international configuration? What sort of economically literate policies are required to bring such an objective about? And what sort of arguments will be sufficiently convincing to make people vote to see these policies implemented?

> he left must proceed
> ase by case—cut farm
> rice supports but pre-
> erve public health care.

The fact that the left is in office in most of Europe today is irrelevant to these requirements. Many of the socialists who now govern (in France, Britain, and Italy, for example) got there because of the collapse or division of the local right. In Britain and France a system of proportional representation would have deprived the present Labour and Socialist parties of their parliamentary majority in this year's elections. In that sense they are minority governments without mandates or long-term policies, whose strongest suit is the promise that they can undo some of the damage their predecessors in office did, simply by doing something different. They will not be reelected if they fail to come up with something better than their present offerings.

To begin with, the left might want to make a virtue of the necessity entailed in abandoning the project by which it has lived and died this century. If all history is the history of more than just class struggle, the economic identity of social beings that was so central for nineteenth-century social theorists—whose encumbered heirs we remain—is now distinctly peripheral for ever more people. The disappearance of work—something the nineteenth-century utopians could only dream about!—is a crisis, but it is also an opportunity to rethink social policy. Some members of the European left have latched quite effectively onto the idea of protecting the *exclus*, but they still think of them as just that—excluded from the norm, which remains that of fully employed, wage-earning, socially integrated workers. What needs to be grasped is that men and women in precarious employment, immigrants with partial civil rights, young people with no long-term job prospects, the growing ranks of the homeless and the inadequately housed, are not some fringe problem to be addressed and resolved, but represent something grimly fundamental.

There must, therefore, be a role for the state in incorporating the secular social consequences of economic change, and not merely providing minimum compensatory alleviation. This has two implications. Given the limited range of policymaking initiative in monetary and fiscal matters now open to any one government, the control or regulation of production in all its modern forms is not only undesirable but impossible. But divesting the state of *all* its economic controls is not a good thing; the state cannot run a car company or invent microchips, but it alone has the incentive and the capacity to organize health, educational, and recreational services. It is in the social interest to have a flourishing private *productive* sector, but one whose very existence is the condition for a thriving state service sector in those areas where the state is best equipped to provide the service, or where economic efficiency is not the most appropriate criterion of performance.

The proper level of state involvement in the life of the community can no longer be determined by *ex hypothesi* theorizing. We don't know what degree of regulation, public ownership, or distributive monopoly is appropriate across the board, only what works or is required in each case. Intervention mechanisms inherited from decisions that were appropriate when first made but that have since become anachronisms, like farm price supports or early retirement on full pay for state employees, are indefensible, above all because they inhibit the growth required to provide truly necessary benefits. Conversely, reductions in state involvement in the provision of public housing, medical facilities, or family services—cuts that made demographic, economic, and ideological sense when first introduced in the 1970s and 1980s—now seem perilously socially divisive, when those they might benefit have no other access to such resources.

The modern state still has a striking range of powers over how the economic growth generated in private hands might best be collectively distributed, at least at the local level. If the left could convincingly argue that it had a set of general principles guiding its choices in the distribution of resources and services and could show that those principles were not merely stubborn defenses of the status quo, making the best of someone else's bad job, it would have made a considerable advance. It would need to show that it understood that some must lose for all to gain; that a desire to sustain the intervention capacities of the state is not incompatible with acknowledgment of the need for painful reconsideration of the objects of that intervention; that both "regulation" and "deregulation" are morally neutral when taken in isolation. As things now stand the continental left merely records its (and its electors') discomfort at the prospect of rearranging the social furniture, while Britain's New Labour has come to power on the bankrupt promise that in these tricky matters it has no (unpopular) preferences of any kind.

Such reconsideration of principles is notoriously hard, and it is unfortunate if not wholly by chance that the left finds itself confronted with the need to reimagine its whole way of thought under less than propitious economic circumstances. But there is never a good moment for untimely thoughts. For some time to come the chief burden on the government of any well-run national community will be ensuring that those of its members who are the victims of economic transformations over which the government itself can exercise only limited control nevertheless live decent lives, even (especially) if such a life no longer contains the expectation of steady, remunerative, and productive employment; that the rest of the community is led to an appreciation of its duty to shoulder that responsibility; and that the economic growth required to sustain this responsibility is not inhibited by the ends to which it is applied. What makes all this difficult is that it is a job for the state, and *that* is hard to accept because the desirability of placing the maximum possible restrictions upon the interventionary capacities of the state has become the cant of our time.

Accordingly, the task of the left in Europe in the years to come will be to reconstruct a case for the activist state, to show why the lesson for the twentieth century is *not* that we should return, so far as possible, to the nineteenth. To do this, the left must come to terms with its own share of responsibility for the sins of our century. It was not so long ago, after all, that West German Social Democrats refused to speak ill of the late, unlamented German Democratic Republic, and there are still French and British Socialists who find it painful to acknowledge their erstwhile sympathy for the Soviet project in precisely its most state-idolatrous forms. But until the European left has recognized its past propensity to favor power over freedom, to see virtue in anything and everything undertaken by a progressive central authority, it will always be backing halfheartedly and shamefacedly into the future, presenting the case for the state and apologizing for it at the same time.

Until and unless this changes, the electors of Longwy and Sarrebourg, like their fellows in Austria, Italy, and Belgium (not to speak of countries farther east), will be tempted to listen to other voices, less timid about invoking the nation-state as the forum for redemptive action. Why are we so sure that the far right is behind us for good—or indeed the far left? The postwar social reforms in Europe were instituted in large measure as a barrier to the return of the sort of desperation and disaffection from which fascism was thought to have arisen. The partial unraveling of those reforms, for whatever cause, should not too readily be treated as free of political risks. As the great reformers of the last century well knew, the Social Question, if left unaddressed, does not just wither away. It goes instead in search of more radical answers.

Europe's Endangered Liberal Order

Timothy Garton Ash

THE DREAM IS HERE

LIKE NO other continent, Europe is obsessed with its own meaning and direction. Idealistic and teleological visions of Europe at once inform, legitimate, and are themselves informed and legitimated by the political development of something now called the European Union. The name "European Union" is itself a product of this approach, for a union is what the EU is meant to be, not what it is.

European history since 1945 is told as a story of unification: difficult, delayed, suffering reverses, but nonetheless progressing. This is the grand narrative taught to millions of European schoolchildren and accepted by central and east European politicians when they speak of rejoining "a uniting Europe." That narrative's next chapter is even now being written by a leading German historian, Dr. Helmut Kohl. Its millennial culmination is to be achieved on January 1, 1999, with a monetary union that will, it is argued, irreversibly bind together some of the leading states of Europe. This group of states should in turn become the "magnetic core" of a larger unification.

European unification is presented not just as a product of visionary leaders from Jean Monnet and Robert Schuman to François Mitterrand and Helmut Kohl but also as a necessary, even an inevitable response to the contemporary forces of globalization. Nation-states are no

TIMOTHY GARTON ASH is a Fellow of St. Antony's College, Oxford. His books include *The Magic Lantern, In Europe's Name,* and most recently *The File: A Personal History.* This essay is dedicated to the memory of Sir Isaiah Berlin.

[51]

longer able to protect and realize their economic and political interests on their own. They are no match for transnational actors like global currency speculators, multinational companies, or international criminal gangs. Both power and identity, it is argued, are migrating upward and downward from the nation-state: upward to the supranational level, downward to the regional one. In a globalized world of large trading blocs, Europe will only be able to hold its own as a larger political-economic unit. Thus Manfred Rommel, the popular former mayor of Stuttgart, declares, "We live under the dictatorship of the global economy. There is no alternative to a united Europe."

It would be absurd to suggest that there is no substance to these claims. Yet when combined into a single grand narrative, into the idealistic-teleological discourse of European unification, they result in a dangerously misleading picture of the real ground on which European leaders will have to build at the beginning of the twenty-first century. In fact, what we have already achieved in a large part of western and southern Europe is a new model of liberal order. But this extraordinary achievement is itself now under threat precisely as a result of the forced march to unity. What we should be doing now is rather to consolidate this liberal order and to spread it across the continent. Liberal order, not unity, is the right strategic goal for European policy in our time.

THE PAST AS WARNING

IN THE INDEX to Arnold Toynbee's *A Study of History*, we find "Europe, as battlefield," "Europe, as not an intelligible field of historical study," and, finally, "Europe, unification of, failure of attempts at." Toynbee is an unreliable source, but he raises important questions about the long sweep of European history. The most fundamental point is his second one. Is the thing to be united actually a cultural-historical unit? If so, where does it begin and end? It is, Toynbee claims, a "cultural misapplication of a nautical term" to suggest that the Mediterranean ancient history of Greece and Rome and modern Western history are successive acts in a single European drama. He prefers the Polish historian Oskar Halecki's account, in which a Mediterranean age is followed by a European age, running roughly

By might or money: Europe's would-be unifiers,
Charlemagne, Bonaparte, and Kohl

from 950 to 1950, which in turn is succeeded by what Halecki called an Atlantic age. Today we might refer to our era simply as a global age.

Yet even in the European age, the continent's eastern edge remained deeply ill-defined. Was it the Elbe? Or the dividing line between western and eastern Christianity? Or the Urals? Europe's political history was characterized by the astounding diversity of peoples, nations, states, and empires and by the ceaseless and often violent competition between them. In short, no continent was externally more ill-defined, internally more diverse, or historically more disorderly. Yet no continent produced more schemes for its own orderly unification. So our teleological-idealistic or Whig interpreters can cite an impressive list of intellectual and political forebears, from the Bohemian King George of Podebrady through the Duc de Sully and William Penn (writing already in America) to Aristide Briand and Richard Coudenhove-Kalergi, the prophet of Pan-Europa. The trouble is that those designs for European unification that were peaceful were not implemented, while those that were implemented were not peaceful. The reality of unification was either a temporary solidarity in response to an external invader or an attempt by one European state to establish continental hegemony by force of arms, from Napoleon to Hitler. But the latter also failed, as Toynbee's index dryly notes.

The Cold War's end showed us how much European union owed to superpower tensions.

The attempt at European unification since 1945 thus stands out from all earlier attempts by being both peaceful and partially implemented. An idealistic interpretation of this historical abnormality is that we Europeans have at last learned from history. The "European civil war" of 1914 to 1945, that second and still bloodier Thirty Years' War, finally brought us to our senses. Yet this requires a little closer examination. For only after the end of the Cold War are we discovering just how much European integration owed to it. First, there was the Soviet Union as negative external integrator. West Europeans pulled together in the face of the common enemy, as they had before the Mongols or the Turks. Second, there was the United States as positive external integrator. Particularly in the earlier years, the United States pushed very strongly for West European integration, making it almost a condition for further Marshall Plan aid. In later decades, the United States was at times more ambivalent about building up a rival trading bloc, but in broad geopolitical terms it supported West European integration throughout the Cold War.

Third, the Cold War helped, quite brutally, by cutting off most of central and eastern Europe behind the Iron Curtain. This meant that European integration could begin between a relatively small number of bourgeois democracies at roughly comparable economic levels and with important older elements of common history. As has often been observed, the frontiers of the original European Economic Community of six were roughly coterminous with those of Charlemagne's Holy

Roman Empire. The EEC was also centered around what historical geographers have called the "golden banana" of advanced European economic development, stretching from Manchester to Milan via the Low Countries, eastern France and western Germany. Moreover, within this corner of the continent there were important convergences or trade offs between the political and economic interests of the nations involved—the crucial ones being between France and Germany. None of this is to deny a genuine element of European idealism among the elites of that time. But the more we discover about this earlier period, the more hard-nosed and nationally self-interested the main actors appear. Contrary to the received view, the idealists are more to be found in the next generation: that of Helmut Kohl rather than Konrad Adenauer. There is no mistaking the genuine enthusiasm with which Kohl describes, as he will at the slightest prompting, the unforgettable experience of lifting the first frontier barriers between France and Germany, just a few years after the end of the war.

The national interests propelling closer intra-European ties were still powerfully present in the 1970s and 1980s. Britain, most obviously, joined the EEC in hopes of reviving its own flagging economy and buttressing its declining influence in the world. In a 1988 book entitled *La France par l'Europe,* none other than Jacques Delors wrote that "creating Europe is a way of regaining that room for manoeuvre necessary for 'a certain idea of France.'" (The phrase "a certain idea of France" was, of course, de Gaulle's.) In my book *In Europe's Name* I have shown how German enthusiasm for European integration was nourished by the need to secure wider European and American support for improved relations with the communist east and, eventually, the reunification of Germany. Finally, there was also a growing perception of real common European interests.

As a result of the confluence of these three kinds of motive and those three favorable external conditions, the 1970s and 1980s saw an impressive set of steps toward closer political cooperation and economic and legal integration. Starting with the Hague summit of December 1969, they included direct elections to the European Parliament, the founding of the European Monetary System, the Single European Act, and the great project of completing the internal market in the magic year of "1992."

This dynamic process, against a background of renewed economic growth and the spread of democracy to southern Europe, did contribute directly to the end of the Cold War. One of the reasons behind Mikhail Gorbachev's "new thinking" in foreign policy was Soviet alarm at the prospect of being left still further behind by a "Europe" that was seen as technologically advanced, economically dynamic, and rapidly integrating behind high protective walls. How much more was this true of the peoples of east central Europe, who anyway felt themselves to belong culturally and historically to Europe, felt this with the passion of the excluded—and for whom the prosperous Western Europe they saw on their travels now clearly represented the better alternative to a discredited and stagnant "real socialism." Accordingly, one of the great slogans of the velvet revolutions of 1989 was "the return to Europe." In this sense one could argue, in apparent defiance of chronology, that "1992" in Western Europe was one of the causes of 1989 in Eastern Europe. But the end of the Cold War also ended a historical constellation that was particularly favorable to a particular model of West European integration.

THE PRESENT AS CONFUSION

WE CANNOT judge the period since 1989 in the same way, as history. The case is still being heard, and the evidence is contradictory. On the one hand, we have seen further incremental diminution in the effective powers and sovereignty of established nation-states inside the EU. The Maastricht program, with European monetary union as its central project, is supposed to make a further decisive step to unification by the end of the decade. Yet this decade has also seen the explosive emergence of at least a dozen new nation-states. Indeed, there are now more states on the map of Europe than ever before in the twentieth century. In the former Yugoslavia, these new states emerged through war, ethnic cleansing, and the violent redrawing of frontiers. In the former Czechoslovakia, the separation into two states was carried out peacefully, by negotiation. In the former Soviet Union, there were variations in between.

Nor is this phenomenon of de-unification confined to the post-communist half of Europe. The cliché of "integration in the west, disintegration in the east" does not bear closer examination. It is surprising, for example, to see the progressive dis-integration of Belgium cited as evidence of the decline of the nation-state and the rise of regionalism, for the tensions that are pulling Belgium apart would be entirely familiar to a nineteenth-century nationalist. Each ethno-linguistic group is demanding a growing measure of self-government. My own country, Britain, has for decades been an unusual modern variation on the theme of nation-state: a state composed of four nations—or, to be precise, three and a part. But now the constituent nations, especially Scotland, are pulling away toward a larger measure of self-government.

And what of Europe's central power? Since 1989 Germany has reemerged as a fully sovereign nation-state. In Berlin, we are witnessing the extraordinary architectural reconstruction of the grandiose capital of a historic nation-state. Yet at the same time, Germany's political leaders, above all Helmut Kohl, are pressing ahead with all their considerable might to surrender that vital component of national sovereignty—and, particularly in the contemporary German case, also of identity—which is the national currency. There is a startling contradiction between, so to speak, the architecture in Berlin and the rhetoric in Bonn. I do not think this contradiction can be resolved dialectically, even in the homeland of the dialectic. In fact, Germany today is in a political-psychological condition that can only be described as Faustian, with two souls in one breast. If in 1999 monetary union goes ahead and the German government moves to Berlin, then the country will wake up in its new bed on January 1, 2000, scratch its head, and ask itself, "Now, why did we just give up the deutsche mark?"

What would be the answer? Of course there are economic arguments for monetary union. But monetary union was conceived as an economic means to a political end. It is the continuation of the functionalist approach adopted by the French and German founding fathers of the EEC: political integration through economic integration. But there was a more specific political reason for the decision to make this the central goal of European integration in the 1990s. As so often before, the key lies in a compromise between French and German national interests.

> European monetary union is the price paid for German unification.

In 1990, there was at the very least an implicit linkage made between Mitterrand's reluctant support for German unification and Kohl's decisive push towards European monetary union. "The whole of Deutschland for Kohl, half the deutsche mark for Mitterrand," some wits put it. Leading German politicians will acknowledge privately that monetary union is the price paid for German unification.

Yet to some extent, this is a price that Kohl wants to pay. For he wants to see the newly united Germany bound firmly and, as he himself puts it, "irreversibly," into Europe. Even more than his hero Adenauer, he believes that it is dangerous for Germany, with its erratic history and critical size—"too big for Europe, too small for the world," as Henry Kissinger once pithily observed—to stand alone in the center of Europe, trying to juggle or balance the nine neighbors and many partners around it. So Dr. Kohl's ultimate, unspoken answer to the question, "Why did we just give up the deutsche mark?" will be, "Because we Germans can't trust ourselves." To which a younger generation will say, "Why not?" Many of them see no reason why Germany needs to be bound to the mast like Odysseus to resist the siren calls of its awful past. They think Germany can be trusted to keep its own balance as a responsible, liberal nation-state inside an already close-knit community of other responsible, liberal nation-states. Certainly Kohl's implicit argument will not convince the man in the Bavarian beer tent. In opinion polls, a majority of Germans still do not want to give up the deutsche mark for the euro. So Germany, this newly restored nation-state, will enter monetary union full of reservations, doubts, and fears.

A HOUSE DIVIDED

ECONOMISTS DIFFER, and non-economists have to pick their way between the arguments. But few would dissent with the proposition that European monetary union (EMU) is an unprecedented, high-risk gamble. As several leading economists have pointed out, Europe lacks vital components that make monetary union work in the United States. The United States has high labor mobility, price and wage flexibility, provisions for automatic, large-scale budgetary transfers to states adversely affected by so-called asymmetric shocks, and, not least, the common language, culture, and shared history in a single country that make such transfers acceptable as a matter of course to citizens and taxpayers.

Europe has low labor mobility and high unemployment. It has relatively little wage flexibility. The EU redistributes a maximum of 1.27 percent of the GDP of its member states, and most of this is already committed to schemes such as the Common Agricultural Policy (CAP) and the so-called structural funds for assisting poorer regions. It has no common language and certainly no common state. Since 1989, we have seen how reluctant West German taxpayers have been to pay even for their own compatriots in the east. Do we really expect that they would be willing to pay for the French unemployed as well? The Maastricht treaty does not provide for that, and leading German politicians have repeatedly stressed that they will not stand for it. The minimal trust and solidarity between citizens that is the fragile treasure of the democratic nation-state does not, alas, yet exist between the citizens of Europe. For there is no European *demos*—only a European *telos*.

Against this powerful critique, it is urged that the "asymmetric shocks" will affect different regions within European countries, and these countries do themselves make internal provision for automatic budgetary transfers. In France, it is also very optimistically suggested that reform of the CAP and structural funds will free up EU resources for compensatory transfers between states. (But if we are serious about enlargement, some of these resources will also be needed for the much poorer new member states.) More economically liberal Europeans argue that monetary union will simply compel us to introduce more free-market flexibility, not least in wage levels. None of this makes a very persuasive rebuttal, especially since different European countries favor different kinds of response.

The dangers, by contrast, are all too obvious. EMU requires a single monetary policy and a single interest rate for all. What if that rate is right for Germany but wrong for Spain and Italy, or vice versa? And what if French unemployment continues to rise? As elections approach, national politicians will find the temptation to "blame it on EMU" almost irresistible. If responsible politicians resist the temptation, irresponsible ones will gain votes. And the European Central Bank will not start with any of the popular authority that the Bundesbank enjoys in Germany. It starts as the product of a political-bureaucratic procedure of "building Europe from above" that is even now—as the Maastricht referendum debate in France showed—perilously short of popular support and democratic legitimacy.

In fact, received wisdom in EU capitals is already that EMU will sooner or later face a crisis, perhaps after the end of a pre-millennium boom, in 2001 or 2002 (just as Britain is preparing to join). Euro-optimists hope this crisis will catalyze economic liberalization, European solidarity, and perhaps even those steps of political unification that historically have preceded, not followed, successful monetary unions. A shared fear of the catastrophic consequences of a failure of monetary union will draw Europeans together, as the shared fear of a common external enemy (Mongols, Turks, Soviets) did in the past. But it is a truly dialectical leap of faith to suggest that a crisis that exacerbates differences between European countries is the best way to unite them. The fact is that at Maastricht the leaders of the EU put the cart before the horse. Out of the familiar mixture of three different kinds of motive—idealistic, national-instrumental, and perceived common interest—they committed themselves to what was meant to be a decisive step to uniting Europe but now seems likely to divide even those who belong to the monetary union. At least in the short term, it will certainly divide those existing EU members who participate in the monetary union from those who do not: the so-called "ins" and "outs."

> We fiddled in Maastricht while Sarajevo burned.

Meanwhile, the massive concentration on this single project has contributed to the neglect of the great opportunity that arose in the eastern half of the continent when the Berlin Wall came down. The Maastricht agenda of internal unification has taken the time and energy of West European leaders away from the agenda of eastward enlargement. To be sure, there is no theoretical contradiction between the "deepening" and the "widening" of the EU. Indeed, widening requires deepening. If the major institutions of the EU, originally designed to work for six member states, are still to function in a community of 26, then major reforms, necessarily involving a further sharing of sovereignty, are essential. But these changes are of a different kind from those required for monetary union. While there is no theoretical contradiction, there has been a practical tension between deepening and widening.

To put it plainly: our leaders set the wrong priority after 1989. We were like people who for 40 years had lived in a large, ramshackle house divided down the middle by a concrete wall. In the western half we had rebuilt, mended the roof, knocked several rooms together, redecorated, and installed new plumbing and electric wiring—while the eastern half fell into a state of dangerous decay. Then the wall came down. What did we do? We decided that what the whole house needed most urgently was a superb new computer-controlled system of air conditioning in the western half. While we prepared to install it, the eastern half of the house began to fall apart and catch fire. We fiddled in Maastricht while Sarajevo burned.

The best can so often be the enemy of the good. The rationalist, functionalist, perfectionist attempt to "make Europe" or "complete Europe" through a hard core built around a rapid monetary union could well end up achieving the opposite of the desired effect. One can all too plausibly argue that what we are likely to witness in the next five to ten years is the writing of another entry for Toynbee's index, under "Europe, unification of, failure of attempts at." Some contemporary Cassandras go further still. They see the danger of us writing another entry under "Europe, as battlefield." One might answer that we already have, in the former Yugoslavia. But any suggestion that the forced march to unification through money brings the danger of violent conflict between West European states does seem overdrawn, for at least three reasons. First, there is the powerful neo-Kantian argument that bourgeois democracies are unlikely to go to war against each other. Second, unlike pre-1945 Europe, we have a generally benign extra-European hegemon in the United States. Third, to warn of violence is to ignore the huge and real achievement of European integration to date: the unique, unprecedented framework and deeply ingrained habits of permanent institutionalized cooperation that ensure that the conflicts of interest that exist—and will continue to exist—between the member states and nations are never resolved by force. All those endless hours and days of negotiation in Brussels between ministers from 15 European countries who end up knowing each other almost better than they know their own families: that is the essence of this Europe. It is an economic community, of course, but it is also a security community—a group of states that do find it unthinkable to resolve their own differences by war.

THE CASE FOR LIBERAL ORDER

Now ONE could certainly argue that Western Europe would never have got this far without the utopian goal or *telos* of "unity." Only by resolutely embracing the objective of "ever-closer union" have we reached this more modest degree of permanent institutional cooperation, with important elements of legal and economic integration. Yet as a paradigm for European policy in our time, the notion of "unification" is fundamentally flawed. The most recent period of European history provides no indication that the immensely diverse peoples of Europe—speaking such different languages, having such disparate histories, geographies, cultures, and economies—are ready to merge peacefully and voluntarily into a single polity. It provides substantial evidence of a directly countervailing trend: toward the constitution—or reconstitution—of nation-states. If unity was not attained among a small number of West European states with strong elements of common history under the paradoxically favorable conditions of the Cold War, how can we possibly expect to attain it in the infinitely larger and more diverse Europe—the whole continent—that we have to deal with after the end of the Cold War?

"Yes," a brilliant French friend said to me when I made this case to him, "I'm afraid you're right. Europe will not come to pass." "But Pierre," I replied, "you're in it!" Europe is already here, and not just as a continent. There is already a great achievement that has taken us far beyond de Gaulle's "Europe des patries" or Harold Macmillan's vision of a glorified free trade area. Yet to a degree that readers outside Europe will find hard to comprehend, European thinking about Europe is still deeply conditioned by these notions of project, process, and progress toward unification. (After all, no one talks hopefully of Africa or Asia "becoming itself.") Many Europeans are convinced that if we do not go forward toward unification, we must necessarily go backward. This view is expressed in the so-called "bicycle theory" of European integration: if you stop pedaling, the bicycle will fall over. Actually, as anyone who rides a bicycle knows, all you have to do is to put one foot back on the ground. And anyway, Europe is not a bicycle.

If we Europeans convince ourselves that not advancing further along the path to unity is tantamount to failure, we risk snatching failure from the jaws of success. For what has been achieved already in a large part of Europe is a very great success, without precedent on the European continent or contemporary equivalent on any other continent. It is as if someone had built a fine if rather rambling palace and then convinced himself that he was an abject failure because it was not the Parthenon. Yet the case is more serious and urgent than this. For today it is precisely the forced march to unity—across the "bridge too far" of monetary union—that is threatening the very achievement it is supposed to complete.

> Monetary union threatens the unity it is supposed to complete.

But what is the alternative? How else should we "think Europe" if not in terms of this paradigm of unification that has dominated European thinking about Europe for half a century? How can we characterize positively what we have already built in a large part of Europe, and what it is both desirable and realistic to work toward in a wider Europe? I believe the best paradigm is that of liberal order. Historically, liberal order is an attempt to avoid both the extremes between which Europe has unhappily oscillated through most of its modern history: violent disorder, on the one hand, and hegemonic order on the other—hegemonic order that itself was always built on the use of force and the denial of national and democratic aspirations within the constitutive empires or spheres of influence. Philosophically, such an order draws on the late Sir Isaiah Berlin's central liberal insight that people pursue different ends that cannot be reconciled but may peacefully coexist. It also draws on Judith Shklar's "liberalism of fear," with its deeply pessimistic view of the propensity of human beings to indulge in violence and cruelty, and on a sense that what Shklar modestly called "damage control" is the first necessity of political life. Institutionally, the EU, NATO, the Council of Europe, and the Organization for Security and Cooperation in Europe are all building blocks of such a liberal order.

Liberal order differs from previous European orders in several vital ways. Its first commandment is the renunciation of force in the resolution of disputes between its members. Of course, this goal is an ancient one. We find it anticipated already in King George of Podebrady's great proposal of 1464 for "the inauguration of peace throughout Christendom." There we read that he and his fellow princes "shall not take up arms for the sake of any disagreements, complaints or disputes, nor shall we allow any to take up arms in our name." But today we have well-tried institutions of bourgeois internationalism in which to practice what Churchill called making "jaw-jaw" rather than "war-war."

Liberal order is, by design, non-hegemonic. To be sure, the system depends to some extent on the external hegemonic balancer, the United States—"Europe's pacifier," as more than one author has quipped. And of course, Luxembourg does not carry the same weight as Germany. But the new model order that we have developed in the EU does permit smaller states to have an influence often disproportionate to their size. A key element of this model order is the way it allows different alliances of European states on individual issues rather than cementing any fixed alliances. Another is the framework of common European law. If the European Convention on Human Rights were incorporated into the treaties of the union, as Ralf Dahrendorf has suggested, the EU would gain a much-needed element of direct responsibility for the liberties of the individual citizen.

Liberal order also differs from previous European orders in explicitly legitimating the interest of participating states in each other's internal affairs. Building on the so-called Helsinki process, it considers human, civil, and not least minority rights to be a primary and legitimate subject of international concern. These rights are to be sustained by international norms, support, and, where necessary, also pressure. Such a liberal order recognizes that there is a logic that leads peoples who speak the same language and share the same culture and tradition to want to govern themselves in their own state. There is such a thing as liberal nationalism. But it also recognizes that in many places a peaceful, neat separation into nation-states will be impossible. In such cases it acknowledges a responsibility to help sustain what may variously be called multiethnic, multicultural, or multinational democracies within an international framework. This is what we disastrously failed to do for Bosnia but can still do for Macedonia or Estonia.

Missing from this paradigm is one idea that remains very important in contemporary European visions, especially those of former great powers such as France, Britain, and Germany. This is the notion of

"Europe" as a single actor on the world stage, a world power able to stand up to the United States, Russia, or China. In truth, a drive for world power is hardly more attractive because it is a joint enterprise than it was when attempted—somewhat more crudely—by individual European nations. Certainly, in a world of large trading blocs we must be able to protect our own interests. Certainly, a degree of power-projection, including the coordinated use of military power, will be needed to realize the objectives of liberal order even within the continent of Europe and in adjacent areas of vital interest to us, such as North Africa and the Middle East. But beyond this, just to put our own all-European house in order would be a large enough contribution to the well-being of the world.

Some may object that I have paid too much attention to mere semantics. Why not let the community be called a union and the process "unification," even if they are not that in reality? Václav Havel comes close to this position when he writes, "Today, Europe is attempting to give itself a historically new kind of order in a process that we refer to as unification." And of course I do not expect the European Union to be, so to speak, dis-named. After all, the much looser world organization of states is still called the United Nations. But the issue is far from merely semantic.

To consolidate Europe's liberal order and to spread it across the whole continent is both a more urgent and, in the light of history, a more realistic goal for Europe at the beginning of the twenty-first century than the vain pursuit of unification in a part of it. Nor, finally, is liberal order a less idealistic goal than unity. For unity is not a primary value in itself. It is but a means to higher ends. Liberal order, by contrast, directly implies not one but two primary values: peace and freedom.✪

The Third Way and Liberty

An Authoritarian Streak in Europe's New Center

Ralf Dahrendorf

In many European countries, politicians are trying to go "beyond left and right" to a Third Way. Most of its protagonists have a close relationship to what in Britain is called New Labor, or sometimes, the "Blair project." In fact, the Third Way debate has become the only game in town—the only hint at new directions for Europe's politics in a confused multitude of trends and ideas.

The recent paper signed by British Prime Minister Tony Blair and German Chancellor Gerhard Schröder, entitled *Europe: The Third Way—Die neue Mitte*, begins boldly: "Social democrats are in government in almost all the countries of the Union. Social democracy has found new acceptance—but only because, while retaining its traditional values, it has begun in a credible way to renew its ideas and modernize its programs. It has also found new acceptance because it stands not only for social justice but also for economic dynamism and the unleashing of creativity and innovation."

This document was published a week before the June elections to the European Parliament. Whatever their shortcomings, the European elections undermine Blair and Schröder's assertion that "social democracy has found new acceptance." In 6 of the 15 European Union (EU) countries (Belgium, Denmark, Finland, Ireland, Italy, and the Netherlands), social democratic parties had 20 percent or less of the vote; in two others (France and Luxembourg), they had 22 or 23 percent. In 5 further countries (Germany, Greece, Britain, Austria, and Sweden), the social democratic vote was between 26 and 33 percent. In Spain, 35 percent voted for the democratic Socialists, and in Portugal, 43 percent. In only 4 of these countries were social democrats relatively the strongest party—and this includes France, where the fragmentation of the right allowed Prime Minister Lionel Jospin's Socialists (themselves hardly unified) to have the best showing with just 22 percent.

LORD DAHRENDORF is author of *Reflections on the Revolution in Europe* and *After 1989: Morals, Revolution and Civil Society*. This article is adapted from his address at "Ten Years After 1989," a June 1999 conference in Vienna sponsored by the Institute for Human Sciences in cooperation with Project Syndicate.

[13]

Twenty years ago these parties had twice their current support in Europe. Social democrats are distinctly minority parties in most European countries. Even in Britain, Blair's deceptively large parliamentary majority is based on 43 percent of the popular vote.

The real electoral trend—as underlined by the European elections—is toward nontraditional parties, many of which did not exist 20 years ago. In most European countries their vote adds up to more than the social democratic vote. In truth, voters are confused and uncertain, pulled hither and yon. It is hard to discern any new crystallization of electoral views.

Nevertheless, Blair and Schröder's set of ideas may find widespread support. (It may win as much endorsement outside socialist parties as inside. Blair gets on at least as well with Spain's conservative prime minister, José María Aznar López, as with his French socialist colleague, Jospin.) The key issue confronting all European countries today is how to create sustainable economic improvement in global markets while not sacrificing the basic cohesion of their societies or the institutions that guarantee liberty.

The terminology used in attempts to give this answer is by now familiar. We need market economies with competitive strength, which can be brought about only by loosening constraints and liberating the supply side of economics. We also need societies that include all citizens rather than disenfranchising an underclass. Useful as individual competition is in the economy, it must be tempered by solidarity in social relations.

The Blair-Schröder paper uses a phrase that is misleading, or is perhaps more than a slip of the pen when it says, "We support a market economy, not a market society." What alternative do they prefer? Do they want a command society? Moving in the direction of Singapore would reduce, if not endanger, the third element of the Third Way's program of squaring the circle: that of doing it all "in a free society."

FINDING THE WAY

Anthony Giddens, Great Britain's chief Third Way theorist, places the task of combining wealth creation and social cohesion in several contexts, including the great changes wrought by globalization, the "new dialogue" with science and technology, and the transformation of values and lifestyles. He then identifies six policy areas of the Third Way: a new politics, or "second wave of democratization," from going directly to the people; a new relationship that joins up state, market, and civil society; supply-side policies incorporating social investment, notably in education and infrastructure projects; fundamental reform of the welfare state by creating a new balance of risk and security; a new relationship to the environment evolving out of "ecological modernization"; and a strong commitment to transnational initiatives in a world of "fuzzy sovereignty."

Much can and has been said about each of these policy areas in various books and papers. Overall, the Third Way project has been described as a combination of neoliberal economics and social democratic social policy. That is not entirely fair. In some ways the key feature of this approach is implicit rather than explicit: its optimism. I call this "globalization plus"—accepting the needs of global markets but adding key elements of social well-being. Others describe the underlying approach by reference to the word "risk." Ulrich Beck, another protagonist of the Third Way, has shown that risk is an opportunity as well as a threat to security, an invitation to entrepreneurship and initiative as well as a warning of uncertainties. The same could be argued for another favorite word of this approach, "flexibility."

Perhaps this is where the Third Way actually divides social democrats. Old Labor is threatened by risk and sees flexibility as insecurity, so it tries to hold on to the old certainties. New Labor, on the other hand, emphasizes the new opportunities of individual initiative and the ways people can enhance their well-being by coping with new challenges. Here it becomes evident why the reform of the welfare state is the key area in dispute, and why New Labor exists in Britain and Holland but not in many other countries where the parties of the old right lean more toward the *neue Mitte*. The alliance between Blair and Aznar is not so surprising after all.

The positive, future-oriented sense of opportunity makes the Third Way attractive to those who do not feel threatened, including the new "global class" of people who hope to benefit from changed forces of production. Perhaps it also shows that the Third Way is not likely to inspire a mass movement even if it is, in some cases, useful for winning elections. There is something slightly contrived, almost elitist about the concept, which attracts wider attention only if coupled with evangelistic methods of communication. Spin doctors are therefore essential for the Third Way, as is the strangely religious style of Blair and the brilliant presentations of Giddens and Beck. They all manage to deflect criticism, as if wearing oilskin made of

a curious mixture of diffidence and dogmatism. Skeptical questions are as often answered by reference to what might or even should be as by pointing to real conditions.

The term "Third Way" shows a curious absence of historical awareness among its protagonists—a shortcoming that characterizes the Clinton-Blair type of leadership in any case. It also shows an unfortunate need to have a unified, or at any rate uniquely labeled, ideology. For many of us, by contrast, the liberation from communism in the revolutions of 1989 means that the time of systems has passed. There are no longer even First, Second, or Third Worlds, only varieties of attempts to cope with economic, social, and political needs—and admittedly, also varieties of success. The Third Way presupposes a more Hegelian view of the world. It forces its adherents to define themselves in relation to others rather than by their own peculiar combination of ideas; more often the others have to be invented, even caricatured for this purpose.

In an open world, there are not just two or three ways but an indefinite number. The question—how to create wealth and social cohesion in free societies—may be the same everywhere, since it results from largely global conditions. The answers, however, are manifold. There are many capitalisms, not just that of the Chicago school of economics; there are many democracies, not just that of Westminster. Diversity is not an optional byproduct of high culture; it is at the very heart of a world that has abandoned the need for closed, encompassing systems. Even Third Way politics is quite varied. Nobody expects Schröder to turn Germany into another Britain. The "Rhenish" model of the

Third Way will remain quite different from the "Anglo-Saxon" model, and neither will necessarily be a model for others.

In any case, it is not only cynics who have observed that the best definition of the Third Way is whatever Blair actually does. If he supports a directly elected mayor of London, stands against teenage pregnancies, or favors the privatization of railways, this must be the Third Way. Still, the niggling doubt remains why Blair and his friends need to put it all in one basket. Are the unlimited opportunities of the post-1989 world too difficult to live with? Do the Third Way leaders crave a certainty, at least in their minds, that they deny their peoples in their lives? Is everybody supposed to take risks except those at the top?

AUTHORITARIAN TEMPTATIONS

One word almost never appears—and never in a central place—in all these speeches and pamphlets and books about the Third Way: liberty. There is much talk about fraternity, which, indeed, is one of the movement's central themes. Equality is dispensed with as a goal and replaced by social inclusion and, more recently, justice. (I sympathize on both points.) But liberty? No doubt, Third Way protagonists would say that it is assumed and implied throughout. Consequently it makes a brief appearance in the list of "timeless" values in the introduction to the Blair-Schröder paper: ". . . fairness and social justice, liberty and equality of opportunity, solidarity and responsibility to others." But among *timely* values, liberty has no place.

This is no accident. The Third Way is not about either open societies or liberty. There is, indeed, a curious authoritarian streak in it, and not just in practice. When Giddens speaks of a "second wave of democratization," he in fact means deconstructing traditional democratic institutions. Parliaments are outmoded; referenda and focus groups should take their place. Third Way reforms of the welfare state not only involve compulsory savings but, above all, the strict insistence on everyone working, including single mothers and the disabled. Where normal employment—let alone desirable employment—is unavailable, people have to be forced to work by the withdrawal of benefits.

The Blair-Schröder document contains, among other things, the following curious statement: "The state should not row but steer"—it should not provide the where-withal but determine the direction. It will no longer pay for things but will tell people what to do. Certainly the British experience provides worrying illustrations of what this might mean.

As it stands today, there are too many authoritarian temptations. The internationalization of decisions and activities almost invariably means a loss of democracy. NATO decisions about war and peace, International Monetary Fund judgments about Russia, and even legislation by the EU Council of Ministers are not subject to democratic controls; "private" worldwide financial transactions are even less protected. Decentralization of the state rarely means a gain in democracy and liberty. Especially at the subnational level, it more often empowers militant activists rather than the people and yields to the new nationalism of self-aggrandizing leaders. And at the national level, problems and solutions alike militate against the liberal order. Among the problems, law and order stand out; among the solutions, the proliferation of agencies and quangos (quasi-autonomous nongovernmental organizations) that evade civil control. The Singapore model is in fact not very far from Third Way preferences: let those leaders up there deal with things and leave us in peace! Thus the political class becomes an unchallenged nomenklatura because when those who do not conform are silenced, nobody raises his or her voice.

This is not what practitioners of the Third Way are doing, nor are its theorists advocating this. But the curious silence about the fundamental value of a decent life—liberty (and old, very old liberty if you wish)—may involuntarily make this political episode one further element of a dangerous encroachment. When, in establishing the EU Commission on Wealth Creation and Social Cohesion in 1995, I insisted on adding the words "in a free society," I thought of Beveridge's *Full Employment in a Free Society* but also of the Singapore syndrome.

Today, the temptations of leadership and the comforts of public apathy can combine to form a perilous attack on liberty. Therefore, it is more important than even a few years ago to begin a new political project with the insistence on liberty before we turn to social inclusion and cohesion.☯

Europe's Next Big Idea

Strategy and Economics Point to a European Military

Richard Medley

European military union is fast becoming the successor to monetary union as *the* next big idea for Europe. The dynamic new European Commission president, Romano Prodi, has declared that establishing a unified European military will define his tenure in office, just as his predecessor, Jacques Delors, made creating a European economic and monetary union (EMU) his hallmark. Building a European military capacity is also the first item on British Prime Minister Tony Blair's "to do" list as he tries to make Britain irreversibly a full European partner. Prodi and Blair's center-left counterparts—Gerhard Schröder of Germany, Lionel Jospin of France, and Massimo D'Alema of Italy—are all on board, for both economic and political reasons. American officials have signaled that they, too, are now comfortable with the European military push, having already signed a general agreement to support a European military union at NATO's 50th anniversary summit this April in Washington.

Within weeks of this gathering, Europe's new leaders followed up with a historic decision at their Cologne summit to create an autonomous defense force with the political and military muscle to fight its own battles. They were goaded by the war in Kosovo, which highlighted in vivid and embarrassing detail Europe's dependence on the U.S. military. Far from fostering internal dissension on the continent, Kosovo actually brought the common foreign and security objectives of the European Union (EU) member states into focus. Honing the West's war machine allowed senior European policymakers to score a series of important victories that had eluded their predecessors for decades.

Structurally and symbolically, the most important decision taken at Cologne was to appoint NATO Secretary-General Javier Solana as the first EU foreign policy representative. Finally there will be someone to answer the phone in Europe when Henry Kissinger calls.

The EU leaders also committed themselves at Cologne to creating a fully operational European military, and their concluding communiqué asserted

RICHARD MEDLEY is Chairman and CEO of Medley Global Advisors, a New York–based research and intelligence consultancy specializing in political analysis for international investors and corporations.

[18]

Onward, European soldiers: Integrated rapid reaction force, Florence, Italy, 1996

their intention "to take the necessary decisions by the end of the year 2000" to make European military union a reality. Together, these steps provide a solid foundation for translating the EU's financial muscle into geopolitical clout. And the dynamic works both ways: wealth will breed armed might, and might will breed wealth. Ultimately, moving this military venture forward will yield important long-term economic gains for an increasingly unified Europe.

To see why, consider the three goals that European military union achieves that make it irresistible to the new crop of leaders. First, it assures them of the kind of personal historical legacy that European heads of state still crave. With EMU firmly on track, constructing an EU defense pillar would put them at the center of history in a way that tucking in the corners of monetary union never could. Second, military union moves Europe one giant step closer to political parallelism with the United States. This alone is certain to keep the French fully engaged, come what may. Third, building a military union means building European-based weapons, aircraft, ships, and satellites—and that means jobs for a job-starved continent. Whereas the United States creates three million jobs per year, Europe has not managed to generate that many new jobs over the past decade. Indeed, these economic benefits will be the glue that holds the push toward military union together for its first few years. Europe desperately needs an excuse for a robust employment program, and a "European" defense initiative is a made-to-order solution. Even the miserly European Central Bank would be reluctant to criticize a defense effort designed to bring the EU onto a more level footing with the United States and improve Europe's economy in the process.

SHOW ME THE MONEY

Blair has already begun pushing other EU leaders to build a substantial new capacity to transport troops, equipment, and weapons. This goal was endorsed at a drumbeat of recent summits, including the NATO celebration in April, the Franco-German summit in May, and the Cologne summit in June. The Cologne communiqué explicitly cites the need to expand EU "intelligence, strategic transport and command and control."

Agreements in principle aside, a great deal of work remains to be done on the force-projection front. Luckily, Europe has plenty of room to spend without bumping into the three percent budget-deficit ceiling enshrined in the Maastricht Treaty, particularly if the French proposal of "averaging" the deficits across Euroland is adopted. By any definition, EU defense spending is far less than that of the United States, and the money is allocated in a way that yields far fewer side benefits—from jobs to investment to follow-on research

applications. Larger, more sensibly targeted EU military expenditures would prove a shrewd long-term investment.

Even though the U.S. and EU economies are roughly the same size (around $8 trillion each), the United States spends $290 billion a year on defense, while Europe spends less than $140 billion. Although the historical reasons for this divergence are well known, the effect that Europe's long-term reliance on U.S. defense capabilities has had on continental strategic spending decisions is less obvious. The difference in the U.S. and EU approaches to divvying up their defense budgets is particularly profound. While the United States spends $30 billion per year on advanced research and technology, the EU nations together spend less than $10 billion. And even the relatively paltry sums individual European countries do spend on R&D are largely wasted on projects duplicated elsewhere on the continent, sharply limiting the EU's ability to produce a coherent European military force and destroying any possible side benefits for the union as a whole.

A quick look at the differences between U.S. and European technological and command capabilities during the Kosovo war makes the inadequacy of today's European military glaringly obvious. European forces have no airborne ground-surveillance capacity, no aircraft capable of transporting heavy equipment such as tanks, no long-range cruise missiles, and only one military reconnaissance satellite (which belongs to France, since U.S. officials usually share degraded imagery with Paris). As a result, European forces played a basically insignificant role in the Kosovo air campaign and were largely removed from active engagement after the first few days of bombing.

By moving to close this gap, European leaders can realize important gains that will help both the fledgling European military union and the newly minted euro. As Europe downsizes its standing armies, it can spend much more on procurement and research and much less on personnel, a cost that adds little economic value. Despite severe pressure to cut spending as part of EMU, the EU's leaders understand fully that a more robust European military presence will require both more smartly targeted spending and, perhaps, an increase in overall defense spending. In a *New York Times* op-ed, Blair wrote, "We need to identify the gaps in our capability and plug them. We need to do more to plan our defense together at a European rather than a national level. . . . We need to reconstruct our forces together, and make sure spending on defense matches the need." It is not just the hawkish Blair who supports more spending. German Defense Minister Rudolf Scharping, a stalwart of the Social Democratic Party (SPD), has been fighting pressure to cut his budget and is actively lobbying to spend more on European military transport aircraft. In early July, he told a *Süddeutsche Zeitung* interviewer, "Your question assumes that we pay too much for our security. But the SPD has, like all the experts, strongly proclaimed that the Bundeswehr is underfinanced, particularly in terms of investment. . . . We need information technology and satellites. We need transport capacity." Even Italian Prime Minister D'Alema, the leader of the former Communist Party, said at the April NATO summit, "If this European defense initiative takes off, then Italy will have to spend more on defense."

In fact, the primary reason for the stark disparity between U.S. and EU field capabilities during the Kosovo conflict is that EU countries spend as little as 12 percent of their defense budgets on procurement and research—areas where the United States spends nearly 40 percent of its budget. European military leaders have not yet adapted to an age with no threat of Soviet invasion; Europe's generals still rely on large-scale conscription programs to provide a surplus of bodies to throw in front of invading Soviet tanks. Several European countries have more than one percent of their population in uniform—a complete waste of money and labor.

Large standing armies are not only ill suited to Europe's current military needs but economically counterproductive. To remedy this, European leaders have decided that the first goal of their push toward military union will be to develop a European rapid response force, requiring smaller and far more highly trained military units.

Economic logic should also prod EU leaders to conclude that smaller and more agile professional armed forces are the way to go. Although conscription drives can be viewed as thinly veiled jobs programs for younger workers, they are as economically unsuited to the new global economy as large standing armies are militarily to the new world order. Conscription programs give jobs to people who could be easily employed in other areas while denying the full benefits of military training to those who could use it as a springboard to other, perhaps more permanent, jobs. A smaller professional military would let European governments maximize their current defense dollars on both the employment and procurement fronts. To minimize the impact of a smaller, professional military on already stressed European job markets, total forces should be reduced only as fast as current conscripts' tours of duty end—in most cases, after two years. Since it would presumably take longer than that to recruit an all-volunteer force, the transition could be stretched out to assure that minimum personnel commitments were maintained. That would further ease unemployment totals across the continent.

Ideally, the EU leaders will also agree that their standing armies should be ratcheted back to the same level as in Britain, where only 0.3 percent of the population is in uniform, and use the money freed up by having smaller armies to expand procurement programs first and R&D programs later. Blair and his ministers are pressing other European leaders not to cut their military spending as a percentage of GDP. He is also urging them to view the Cologne communiqué as an important step toward reinforcing Europe's "capabilities in the field of intelligence, strategic transport and command and control"—exactly the areas where major economies of scale and investment returns are present. And the need for more spending is clearly not lost on European officials such as Scharping and D'Alema.

LOOKING FOR RICARDO

If the EU were to match British and American spending proportions for these categories, nearly $70 billion would be spent buying equipment from European manufacturers and directing research toward European labs—a sevenfold increase from the present $10 billion total budget. That would be equivalent to about one percent of European GDP, giving a significant boost to economies groping to find a firm foothold.

Obviously, those benefits would clump in certain sectors. The first beneficiaries of this shift in strategy would be European defense companies, who have been struggling as their governments adopt a "Europe-first" procurement policy even as they are buffeted by a tumultuous wave of mergers and acquisitions. But those benefits would multiply quickly if European leaders follow up on a suggestion made at the Cologne summit to apply a little Ricardian analysis to defense research and procurement.

David Ricardo, the famous nineteenth-century British economist, assumed that countries would use international trade to exploit their natural advantages, and European leaders are now considering whether that kind of proposal could work as military union moves closer. In its most fully realized form—as laid out by Charles Grant of the Centre for European Reform, a London-based Blairite think tank—such specialization would look something like this: Britain would do the R&D for nuclear submarines and fighter planes and build them; Germany would specialize in tanks and diesel submarines; the French would focus on satellites, helicopters, and aircraft carriers; and so on.

Following this model, European industry could maximize the economies of scale that a $70 billion dollar budget should provide. This, in turn, would improve Europe's chances to begin having its share of technological breakthroughs that could be commercialized and fed back into broader technological applications. A unified European military would not only change world politics, it would also change European economies, with benefits that we cannot yet fully imagine. After all, although Al Gore may not have invented the Internet, the Pentagon did. ◈

The Dollar and the Euro

C. Fred Bergsten

THE NEW GLOBAL CURRENCY

THE CREATION of a single European currency will be the most important development in the international monetary system since the adoption of flexible exchange rates in the early 1970s. The dollar will have its first real competitor since it surpassed the pound sterling as the world's dominant currency during the interwar period. As much as $1 trillion of international investment may shift from dollars to euros. Volatility between the world's key currencies will increase substantially, requiring new forms of international cooperation if severe costs for the global economy are to be avoided.

The political impact of the euro will be at least as great. A bipolar currency regime dominated by Europe and the United States, with Japan as a junior partner, will replace the dollar-centered system that has prevailed for most of this century. A quantum leap in transatlantic cooperation will be required to handle both the transition to the new regime and its long-term effects.

The global economic roles of the European Union and the United States are nearly identical. The EU accounts for about 31 percent of world output and 20 percent of world trade. The United States provides about 27 percent of global production and 18 percent of world trade. The dollar's 40 to 60 percent share of world finance far exceeds the economic weight of the United States. This total also exceeds the share of 10 to 40 percent for the European national currencies

C. FRED BERGSTEN is Director of the Institute for International Economics. He was Assistant Secretary of the Treasury for International Affairs from 1977 to 1981 and Assistant to the National Security Council for International Economic Affairs from 1969 to 1971. Copyright 1997© by C. Fred Bergsten.

combined. The dollar's market share is three to five times that of the deutsche mark, the only European currency now used globally.

Inertia is a powerful force in international finance. For half a century, the pound sterling retained a global role far in excess of Britain's economic strength. The dollar will probably remain the leading currency indefinitely. But the creation of the euro will narrow, and perhaps eventually close, the present monetary gap between the United States and Europe. The dollar and the euro are each likely to wind up with about 40 percent of world finance, with about 20 percent remaining for the yen, the Swiss franc, and minor currencies.

Even an initial Economic and Monetary Union (EMU) comprising only the half-dozen assured core countries would constitute an economy about two-thirds the size of the United States' and almost equal to Japan's. The global trade of this group would exceed that of the United States. If the gap between the current market share of the dollar and that of the European currencies were closed only halfway, that would produce an enormous shift in global financial holdings.

Substantial implications emerge for the functioning and management of the world economy. There will probably be a portfolio diversification of $500 billion to $1 trillion into euros. Most of this shift will come out of the dollar. This in turn will have a significant impact on exchange rates during a long transition period. The euro will move higher than will be comfortable for many Europeans. Europe will probably try to defend itself against this prospect by engineering a further substantial weakening of its national currencies between now and the euro's start-up.

In the long run, the dollar-euro exchange rate is likely to fluctuate considerably more than have the rates between the dollar and individual European currencies. This fluctuation could cause prolonged misalignments that would not only have adverse effects in both Europe and the United States but also provoke protectionist pressures on the global trading system. Creation of the euro will raise many policy issues that will require intensive cooperation, both across the Atlantic and in multilateral settings such as the Group of Seven (G-7) and the International Monetary Fund.

Europe has always accounted for a share of world trade comparable to that of the United States. In addition, Europe has had a common trade policy from the outset of its integration process. Trade policy thus has been bipolar for almost four decades, as evidenced by the necessity of Europe and the United States agreeing on all multilateral trade rounds in the General Agreement on Tariffs and Trade and recent sectoral agreements in the World Trade Organization.

The prospective developments on the monetary side would mirror that evolution, equating Europe's market position and institutional arrangements with those of the United States to produce a similarly bipolar regime. The United States, Europe, and global financial institutions are not prepared for these events. The initial blueprints for EMU ignored the issue, and there has been little subsequent discussion in Europe. The United States and the G-7 have failed to address the rise of the euro seriously, as they failed to address EMU's predecessor, the European Monetary System, even when it spawned currency crises with global effects in 1992-93. It is essential that the United States, Europe, and international financial institutions begin to prepare for the euro's global impact.

THE EURO START-UP

THERE IS considerable debate in Europe on when, with whom, and even whether the euro will be created. This analysis assumes that the euro will be introduced on or near the scheduled date of January 1999 and that its membership will quickly, if not immediately, encompass virtually the entire membership of the European Union. The euro's systemic evolution will not be affected by whether the currency is launched in 1999 or 2001, or whether the "Club Med" countries—Italy, Portugal, and Spain—are included at the start or join a couple of years later. The same conclusions apply.

The euro will probably be strong from its inception. The Maastricht Treaty gives the European Central Bank (ECB) a mandate to ensure price stability. The bank will place overwhelming emphasis on establishing its credibility as soon as possible. The ECB will be especially chary of any depreciation of the euro's exchange rate, and is likely to view euro appreciation as an early sign of success. The ECB will be the first central bank in history without a government looking over its shoulder. Since it lacks the 50-year credibility of the

Bundesbank, the ECB will be tougher than its forerunner in pursuing a responsible monetary policy.

Fiscal policy developments are likely to reinforce this outcome. The fiscal criteria of the Maastricht Treaty will probably be interpreted flexibly to enable EMU to start on time and perhaps, largely for political reasons, to include the Club Med countries. The "growth and stability pact" to govern budget positions after start-up seems likely to have large loopholes. If unemployment remains high at start-up, the national governments will probably deploy their only remaining macroeconomic tool—fiscal policy—in an expansionary direction. That would intensify the pressure on the ECB to pursue a tight monetary policy.

Many Europeans believe that fudging the Maastricht criteria would produce a weak euro. On the contrary, combining such budgetary tolerance with a resolute ECB will further strengthen the new currency. The proper analogy is with the Federal Reserve, which produced a sky-high dollar in the early 1980s in the face of Reagan's huge budget deficits, or the Bundesbank, which produced a strong deutsche mark in the face of large deficits in the early 1990s triggered by German reunification. The ECB is likely to out-Fed and out-Bundesbank its most distinguished role models.

The advent of the euro's global role must be considered across three time periods: the run-up from now until 1999, a transition period of five to ten years during which the euro will attain its new position in international finance, and in the long term, when relatively stable structural conditions will have been established.

GLOBAL MONEY

FIVE KEY factors determine whether a currency will play a global role: the size of its underlying economy and global trade; the economy's independence from external constraints; avoidance of exchange controls; the breadth, depth, and liquidity of the economy's capital markets; and the economy's strength, stability, and external position.

On the first two criteria, a unified Europe is superior to the United States. The European Union's GDP was $8.4 trillion in 1996, compared with $7.2 trillion for the United States. Growth of potential output is

similar in the two regions, so their relative position should hold. The European Union also has a larger volume of global trade. EU external trade totaled $1.9 trillion in 1996, compared with $1.7 trillion for the United States.

In terms of openness, the share of exports and imports in total output is now about 23 percent in both the EU and the United States. This ratio has doubled for the United States over the past 25 years while rising only modestly in Europe, but it is also likely to remain broadly similar. Both regions are thus largely independent of external constraints and can manage their policies without being thrown off course by any but the most severe external shocks.

It is almost inconceivable that either the EU or the United States would unilaterally resort to exchange or capital controls. Globalization of capital markets has reached the point where all major financial centers, including many in the developing world, would have to act together to alter international capital flows effectively. Hence the two regions will remain parallel on this key currency criterion as well.

It is less clear when Europe will reach full parity with the United States in terms of the breadth, depth, and liquidity of its capital markets.

The American market for domestic securities is about twice as large as the combined European markets. The European financial markets are highly decentralized. There will be no central governmental borrower like the U.S. Treasury to provide a fulcrum for the market. It may take some time to align the relevant standards and practices across the EU, especially if London is included. Germany may oppose wholesale liberalization, as the Bundesbank has traditionally done in Germany, on the grounds that it would weaken the ability of the ECB to conduct an effective monetary policy.

America's trade position will raise doubts about the future value of the dollar.

On the other hand, the total value of government bond markets in the EU is 2.1 trillion euros, compared with 1.6 trillion euros in the United States. Moreover, international bonds and equities are much more frequently issued in the European markets than in the United States. Futures trading in German and French government bonds, taken together, exceeded that in U.S. notes and bonds in 1995. Expectations over the launch of EMU have already produced a substantial convergence in the yields of government bonds throughout Europe. An integrated European capital market for private bonds shows clear signs of developing. So European parity on this key criterion is likely to occur eventually.

The final criterion is the strength and stability of the European economy. There is no risk of hyperinflation or any of the other extreme instabilities that could disqualify the euro from international status. On the contrary, the ECB is likely to run a responsible monetary policy. On the other hand, Europe may not carry out the structural reforms needed to restore dynamic economic growth. But markets prize stability more than growth, as indicated by the continued dominance of the dollar through extended periods of sluggish American economic performance. Hence the euro should qualify on these grounds as well.

In addition, America's external economic position will continue to raise doubts about the future stability and value of the dollar. The United States has run current account deficits for the last 15 years. Its net foreign debt exceeds $1 trillion and is rising annually by 15 to 20 percent. The EU, in contrast, has a roughly balanced international asset position and has run modest surpluses in its international accounts in recent years. On this important criterion, the EU is decidedly superior to the United States.

The relative size of countries' economies and trade flows is of central importance in determining currencies' global roles. A large economy has a naturally large base for its currency and thus enjoys important economies of scale and scope. A high volume of trade gives a country's firms considerable leverage to finance in their own currency. Large economies are less vulnerable to external shocks and thus offer a safe haven for investors. They are more likely to have the large capital markets required for major currency status.

There is a clear historical correlation between size and currency status. Sterling and the dollar became dominant during the periods when the United Kingdom and the United States were the world's main economies and traders. The only global currencies today are those of the world's three largest economies and traders: the United States, Germany, and Japan.

The relevant comparison for present purposes is between the EU and the euro, on the one hand, and Germany and the deutsche mark on the other. It would be improper to compare the euro, which will meet all of the key currency criteria, with the sum of the individual European currencies, most of which do not. The comparison must be with the deutsche mark, the only European currency that is now used on a global basis.

Hence there will be a quantum leap in the size of the economy and trading unit in question. Germany accounts for nine percent of world output and 12 percent of world trade. The euro core group accounts for 18 and 19 percent, respectively. The full EMU accounts for 31 and 20 percent, respectively. The relevant unit will thus increase immediately by at least 50 to 100 percent. Eventually, the rise will be about 65 to 250 percent.

Crude econometric efforts suggest that every rise of 1 percent in a country's share of global output and trade raises its currency share by roughly the same amount. On this premise, the global role of the euro would exceed that of the deutsche mark by 50 to 100 percent if EMU included only the core group and by 65 to 250 percent if all Europe were included. The deutsche mark, by most calculations, accounts for about 15 percent of global financial assets in both private and official markets. The euro's role could thus reach 20 to 30 percent of world finance if EMU included only the core countries and 25 to 50 percent if the entire EU were involved. The midpoints of these ranges, 25 and almost 40 percent, provide rough indicators of the likely future global role of the euro. If these shifts into the euro came largely out of the dollar, they would eliminate half to all of the present gap between the dollar and the deutsche mark.

> Many agree that the euro will rival the dollar as the world's leading currency.

This evolution could produce a major diversification of portfolios into euros, mainly out of dollars. Official reserve shifts into euros could range between $100 billion and $300 billion. Private portfolio diversification could be much larger. Excluding intra-EU holdings, global holdings of international financial assets, including bank deposits and bonds, are about $3.5 trillion. About 50 percent are in dollars and only about 10 percent in European currencies. A complete balancing of portfolios between dollars and euros would require a shift of about $700 billion. A combination of official and private shifts suggests a potential diversification of between $500 billion and $1 trillion.

Such a shift, even spread over a number of years, could drive the euro up and the dollar down substantially. The extent of the shift will depend on whether the supply of euros rises in tandem with demand. It will also depend on the relationship between the dollar and the European national currencies when the euro is issued. While most Europeans want a strong euro, they also want to avoid an overvalued currency that deepens their economic difficulties. Many believe that their national currencies are already overvalued despite recent substantial declines against the dollar. The only way they can avoid the dilemma is to depreciate the European national currencies further before the launch of the euro. The EMU would then be able to set the initial exchange rate below the fundamental equilibrium exchange rate for the euro. The euro could appreciate modestly without undermining the long-term competitive position of the European economy.

Exchange-market developments from now until the early part of the next century could be a mirror image of the first half of the 1980s. During that period, U.S. budget deficits soared. The elimination of Japanese exchange controls triggered a large portfolio diversification from yen into dollars. Fiscal tightening in Europe and Japan further enhanced the dollar's appreciation. The opposite conditions may apply in the period ahead: further reductions in, or even elimination of, the American budget deficit could coincide with European fiscal expansion and a large diversification out of the dollar triggered by the euro's creation. Substantial euro appreciation and dollar depreciation could thus occur in the transition to EMU.

Many analysts agree that the euro will rival the dollar as the world's leading currency. Most believe, however, that such a shift will take considerable time, since any redistribution of international portfolios occurs incrementally. But there is evidence from the history of major currencies that major shocks can produce rapid changes in portfolio composition. The devaluation of the pound sterling in 1931 permanently reduced the international role of that currency and propelled the dollar into the dominant position. The onset of double-digit inflation in the United States in the late 1970s produced a sharp drop in the dollar's role in just a few years.

These shocks, however, have derived more from poor policy and performance by the lead currency than from the improved position of the new rival. The euro's rise may have to await a serious policy lapse by the United States, as in the late 1970s, or a renewed explosion of America's external debt position, as in the mid-1980s. Even the most successful and best-managed countries undergo occasional setbacks, and the euro's rough parity with the dollar is probably inevitable.

JAPAN AS JUNIOR PARTNER

THE YEN will continue to play an important but smaller role, maintaining its 10 to 15 percent market share. But the world is not likely to see a tri-polar monetary system. The Japanese Ministry of International Trade and Industry's latest report on the topic concludes that "the yen is nowhere near achieving the status of a truly international currency." Japan will need to be included in any new EU-U.S. arrangements but will probably remain a junior partner in the management of the international monetary regime.

Japan's economy is about twice the size of Germany's. Its trade is only slightly smaller, and it has an even better record of price stability over the past 15 years. Yet its currency plays a much smaller role than the deutsche mark, suggesting a significant deficiency when it comes to the other key currency criteria—notably the capabilities of its financial markets. Japan's continued failure to deregulate and modernize those markets is likely to remain a barrier for the yen. Indeed, the fragility of Japan's financial sector is more likely to repel than attract international interest.

Many analysts have hypothesized the emergence of three north-south regional blocs centered around Europe, Japan, and the United States. So far, however, major trade groupings have developed around Europe and the United States but not around Japan. With the Asia-Pacific Economic Cooperation forum linking the United States and Japan, bipolarity may be evolving not only in monetary affairs but in trade as well.

THE NEW TRANSATLANTIC AGENDA

THE EURO'S rise will convert an international monetary system that has been dominated by the dollar since World War II into a bipolar regime. Hence the structure and politics of international financial cooperation will change dramatically.

The exchange rate between the euro and the dollar will pose a significant policy challenge. The United States and the rest of the world should reject any attempt by Europe to substantially undervalue the euro's start-up rate. It would represent a blatant effort by Europe to export its high unemployment and to enable the euro to become a strong currency without any significant cost to its competitive position.

France is running sizable trade and current account surpluses, even adjusted for its high level of unemployment. Germany has the world's second-largest trade surplus and is the world's second-largest creditor country. The EU is a surplus region. By contrast, the United States is the world's largest debtor nation. Its trade and current account deficits are headed well above $200 billion in 1997. These facts hardly suggest that the European currencies are too strong or that the dollar is too weak. The G-7 should, at a minimum, actively resist further European depreciation and dollar appreciation.

	OUTPUT	TRADE[1]
UNITED STATES	26.7	18.3
EUROPEAN UNION	30.8	20.4
CORE EU[2]	18.4	18.9
GERMANY	8.9	12.4
JAPAN	21.0	10.3

[1] GOODS AND SERVICES, EXCLUDING INTRA-EU TRADE
[2] AUSTRIA, BENELUX, FRANCE AND GERMANY

SOURCES: UNCTAND, WORLD BANK, WTO

Portfolio diversification's impact on the exchange rate between the dollar and the euro will also pose a challenge. Unfortunately, there is no way to assess the precise magnitude or timing of that impact, and it is impossible to predict the fundamental equilibrium exchange rate that will emerge for the euro and the dollar. It would, therefore, be a mistake to use target zones or any other predetermined mechanisms to limit dollar-euro fluctuations during the transition period.

However, markets could become extremely unstable. It will be important for the G-7 and the International Monetary Fund to monitor events closely, to form judgments on the likely outcome as the process evolves, and to intervene to limit unnecessary volatility. This monitoring will require much closer cooperation than exists today.

Over the longer run, availability of a more attractive alternative to the dollar could reduce the ability of the United States to finance its large external deficits. With more than $4 trillion in external liabilities and an array of alternative assets available to international investors, however, the United States' policy autonomy already faces considerable limits. Such constraints were felt in Washington in the late 1970s—even though the United States was then the world's largest creditor country—when the dollar's free fall signaled the need to tighten monetary policy and triggered the $30 billion dollar support package of October 1978. They were felt again in early 1987 and early 1995 when the dollar fell sharply against the deutsche mark and the yen.

European countries already pay relatively little attention to fluctuations in their national currencies vis-à-vis the dollar. But external events will play an even smaller role in the larger, unified European economy. Larger and even more frequent changes in the exchange rate of the euro could be accepted with equanimity. The EU might even promote greater currency movements to achieve external adjustment, as the United States has done on occasion.

The euro and the dollar will dominate world finance, but both Europe and the United States will often be tempted to practice benign neglect. If left to market forces, the two currencies will likely experience increased volatility and misalignments. Both outcomes would be destabilizing for other countries and the world economy.

The European Union and the United States must recognize that prolonged misalignments would be costly for their economies too. The United States learned this in the mid-1980s, when dollar overvaluation caused an extended recession in manufacturing and agriculture. Given the pivotal role of the EU and the United States in global trade policy, such lapses would be extremely harmful to the world economy. A structured exchange rate regime should be developed to manage the relationship that will emerge between the dollar and the euro. The EU, Japan, and the United States should negotiate a target zone system with broad currency bands, perhaps 10 percent on both sides of a nominal midpoint, that would avoid large current account imbalances and their attendant problems.

Many Europeans believe that EMU will facilitate such cooperation. Europe will speak with a single voice, enabling it to force the United States to be more cooperative. Some Europeans view this outcome as an important goal of EMU, and one that will offset the continent's enhanced ability to ignore external events.

Trade policy provides support for their logic. The multilateral trading system has been essentially bipolar since the creation of the Common Market in 1958, which has always spoken with a single voice on most trade matters. The united Europe could have chosen to raise barriers against the world, with only modest costs because of its considerable size, but has largely opted to support further global liberalization. Most observers believe that this negotiating structure facilitated the success of the three major rounds of the General Agreement on Tariffs and Trade. It has recently been on display in the forging of the two most important liberalizing measures since the end of the Uruguay Round, the agreement on trade in telecommunications services and the Information Technology Agreement on trade in high-tech goods.

While this pattern may hold, several scenarios can be envisioned. The United States could react defensively to its loss of monetary dominance and seek to create a formalized dollar area, like the United Kingdom's sterling area in the 1930s. The EU could adopt a strategy of benign neglect, arguing that the United States has done so repeatedly and that its turn has now come. Trade protection could result from either course.

When French President Valéry Giscard d'Estaing and German Chancellor Helmut Schmidt decided to create the European Monetary System in 1978, one of their goals was to foster a more stable global monetary regime. The creation of EMU could bring that vision closer to reality. However, in the absence of cooperation between the European Union and the United States, the euro could create greater instability. It is up to the governments of the two regions to achieve a smooth transition from the sterling- and dollar-dominated monetary regimes of the nineteenth and twentieth centuries to a stable dollar and euro system in the early 21st century. The underlying strength and history of the North Atlantic relationship bodes well, but achieving a successful outcome will be a major policy challenge in the years ahead.⊛

EMU and
International Conflict

Martin Feldstein

MONNET WAS MISTAKEN

TO MOST Americans, European economic and monetary union seems like an obscure financial undertaking of no relevance to the United States. That perception is far from correct. If EMU does come into existence, as now seems increasingly likely, it will change the political character of Europe in ways that could lead to conflicts in Europe and confrontations with the United States.

The immediate effects of EMU would be to replace the individual national currencies of the participating countries in 2002 with a single currency, the euro, and to shift responsibility for monetary policy from the national central banks to a new European Central Bank (ECB). But the more fundamental long-term effect of adopting a single currency would be the creation of a political union, a European federal state with responsibility for a Europe-wide foreign and security policy as well as for what are now domestic economic and social policies. While the individual governments and key political figures differ in their reasons for wanting a political union, there is no doubt that the real rationale for EMU is political and not economic. Indeed, the adverse economic effects of a single currency on unemployment and inflation would outweigh any gains from facilitating trade and capital flows among the EMU members.[1]

The 1992 Maastricht Treaty that created the EMU calls explicitly for the evolution to a future political union. But even without that

MARTIN FELDSTEIN is Professor of Economics at Harvard University and President of the National Bureau of Economic Research.

[60]

specific treaty language, the shift to a single currency would be a dramatic and irreversible step toward that goal. There is no sizable country anywhere in the world that does not have its own currency. A national currency is both a symbol of sovereignty and the key to the pursuit of an independent monetary and budget policy. The tentative decision of the 15 European Union (EU) member states (with the exceptions of Denmark and the United Kingdom), embodied in the Maastricht Treaty, to abandon their national currencies for the euro is therefore a decision of fundamental political significance.

For many Europeans, reaching back to Jean Monnet and his contemporaries immediately after World War II, a political union of European nations is conceived of as a way of reducing the risk of another intra-European war among the individual nation-states. But the attempt to manage a monetary union and the subsequent development of a political union are more likely to have the opposite effect. Instead of increasing intra-European harmony and global peace, the shift to EMU and the political integration that would follow it would be more likely to lead to increased conflicts within Europe and between Europe and the United States.

What are the reasons for such conflicts? In the beginning there would be important disagreements among the EMU member countries about the goals and methods of monetary policy. These would be exacerbated whenever the business cycle raised unemployment in a particular country or group of countries. These economic disagreements could contribute to a more general distrust among the European nations. As the political union developed, new conflicts would reflect incompatible expectations about the sharing of power and substantive disagreements over domestic and international policies. Since not all European nations would be part of the monetary and political union, there would be conflicts between the members and nonmembers within Europe, including the states of Eastern Europe and the former Soviet Union.

Conflicts would also develop between the European political union and non-European nations, including the United States, over issues of

---

[1] I have discussed the economic costs and benefits of EMU for Europeans in "The Case Against EMU," *The Economist*, June 13, 1992, pp. 12-19, and in "The Political Economy of the European Economic and Monetary Union: Political Sources of an Economic Liability," *Journal of Economic Perspectives*, Fall 1997, forthcoming.

foreign policy and international trade. While disagreements among the European countries might weaken any European consensus on foreign affairs, the dominant countries of the EU would be able to determine the foreign and military policies for the European community as a whole. A political union of the scale and affluence of Europe and the ability to project military power would be a formidable force in global politics.

Although 50 years of European peace since the end of World War II may augur well for the future, it must be remembered that there were also more than 50 years of peace between the Congress of Vienna and the Franco-Prussian War. Moreover, contrary to the hopes and assumptions of Monnet and other advocates of European integration, the devastating American Civil War shows that a formal political union is no guarantee against an intra-European war. Although it is impossible to know for certain whether these conflicts would lead to war, it is too real a possibility to ignore in weighing the potential effects of EMU and the European political integration that would follow.

THE POLITICS AND ECONOMICS OF MONETARY POLICY

THE MOST direct link between EMU and intra-European conflicts would be disagreement about the goals and methods of monetary policy. The Maastricht Treaty established the ECB and transfers all responsibility for monetary policy after the start of EMU from individual national central banks to the ECB. The ECB alone would control the supply of euros and set the short-term euro interest rate.

Maastricht makes price stability the primary objective of European monetary policy, paralleling the charter of Germany's Bundesbank. The treaty also provides that the ECB would be independent of all political control by the member states and by European-level political institutions. (Although the treaty states that the ECB will report to the European Parliament, this was intended to follow the Bundesbank tradition of an information report rather than any political oversight.) These conditions are very much what Germany wants for the ECB and for monetary policy. Because of its historical experience, the German public is hypersensitive on inflation and fears any monetary arrangement that does not give primacy to price stability and insulate monetary policy from political influence.

But German opinion differs sharply from the opinions about monetary policy in France and other European countries. The notion of a politically independent central bank is contrary to European traditions. Until recently, when Maastricht required all prospective EMU countries to give their central banks independence, most of the central banks of Europe reported to their ministries of finance, and the finance ministers were at least partially responsible for setting interest rates.

The French have been particularly vocal in calling for political control over monetary policy. In a televised speech just before the 1992 French referendum on the Maastricht Treaty, then-President François Mitterrand assured the French public that, contrary to the explicit language of the treaty, European monetary policy would not be under the direction of European central bankers but would be subject to political oversight that, by implication, would be less concerned with inflation and more concerned with unemployment. Mitterrand's statement was a political forecast; France recognizes that the institutions of the EMU would evolve, and continually presses for some form of political body to exert control over the ECB. It has already made considerable progress toward that end.

The December 1996 meeting of the EU Council of Ministers in Dublin emphasized that growth as well as price stability would be an explicit goal of future EMU monetary policy. It also established a new ministerial-level "stability council" described as a "complement" or a "counterweight" to the ECB. Although this body falls short of one that could exercise political control over the ECB, it marked a first French success in establishing that monetary policy should be subject to some counterweight and that growth (that is, short-run macroeconomic expansion) as well as price stability should be a goal of EMU policy. At the European summit in Amsterdam in June 1997, the newly elected French government of Lionel Jospin made further progress. The summit added an employment chapter to the Maastricht Treaty, emphasizing that employment is a parallel goal to price stability. More important, statements by politicians at the Amsterdam summit appear to have redefined the role of the political authorities in making exchange rate policy and, therefore, in managing monetary policy.

German opinion about inflation differs sharply from that in other European countries.

More specifically, the Maastricht Treaty divided responsibility for exchange rate policy between the ECB and the EU Economics and Finance Council, which consists of cabinet ministers of member governments, in an ambiguous way. The drafters of that part of the treaty (the German participants in particular) intended to limit ECOFIN's role to fundamental aspects of the exchange rate system and to leave to the ECB policies that cause short-run changes in the value of the euro. For example, a decision to fix the exchange rate between the euro and the Japanese yen permanently would be a decision for ECOFIN. In contrast, raising or lowering euro interest rates to increase or decrease the exchange value of the euro would be left to the ECB. Although this distinction was the German view, the French expected that ECOFIN would eventually get to give orders about short-run variations in the desired level of the euro exchange rate. The formal rules remain ambiguous, but the government leaders at the Amsterdam summit appear to have accepted a shift of responsibility for short-run exchange rate policy to ECOFIN. Since discretionary changes in nominal exchange rates can be achieved only by changes in monetary policy, this shift would establish a much more fundamental role for ECOFIN, a political body, in the making of monetary policy.

One further recent development relating to the independence of the ECB is noteworthy. Members of the key monetary policy committee of the European Parliament have called for a role for the parliament in supervising the ECB, including its interest rate policies. They have specifically pointed to congressional oversight of the U.S. Federal Reserve as a possible model for such supervision. Although this arrangement may strike a reasonable balance between independence and accountability, parliamentary oversight would clearly be a major shift from the complete independence called for in the Maastricht Treaty, and consequently an area for contention.

At present, individual European governments (especially in France and Germany) are suppressing their disagreement about the control of monetary policy to minimize the risk of political disapproval of EMU in their respective countries. But if EMU proceeds, the independence of the ECB and the goals of monetary policy will become a source of serious conflict among member countries.

INFLATION VERSUS UNEMPLOYMENT

THE ISSUE of who controls monetary policy is closely related to the question of the proper goal of monetary policy. In recent years, because of the Maastricht Treaty's requirements for entering EMU, most countries have resisted the temptation to use monetary policy to reduce unemployment and have followed the Bundesbank in keeping inflation rates below three percent. But once the disciplining example of the Bundesbank is eliminated and monetary policy is made by an ECB in which all member countries vote equally, there is a strong risk that the prevailing sentiment will be for higher inflation. Over the past 12 months, international financial markets have anticipated that outcome by depressing the value of the deutsche mark, the French franc, and the other European currencies that move with them by 25 percent relative to the dollar and the yen.

If the German public sees the inflation rate rise under EMU, it will become increasingly antagonistic toward the EMU arrangement and toward the countries that vote for inflationary monetary policy. Moreover, since an inflationary monetary policy would lower unemployment only temporarily (while leaving the inflation rate permanently higher), the persistence of high unemployment would lead to political pressure for recurring rounds of expansionary monetary policy, causing continuing dissatisfaction among the anti-inflationary countries.

Countries that are more concerned about unemployment than inflation might nevertheless be critical of the ECB for not pursuing an even more aggressive expansionary policy. Although countries have been properly reluctant to attempt such policies in recent years, they can regard their decisions not to do so as decisions they made themselves.

110

But with a single currency, such governments would suffer the frustration of not being able to decide for themselves and of being forced to accept the common monetary policy created by the ECB.

This general conflict about the governance and character of monetary policy would be exacerbated whenever a country experienced a decline in exports or other type of decline in aggregate demand that led to a cyclical increase in unemployment. The shift to a single currency would mean that the fall in demand in a country could not be offset, as it could be with an individual national currency, by an automatic decline in the exchange value of the currency (making its exports more competitive) and a decline in its interest rates (increasing domestic interest-sensitive spending by households and businesses) or by using its own monetary policy to shift interest rates and exchange rates. The ECB would have to make monetary policy with a view to the conditions in all of Europe, not just a particular country or region. The result would be a conflict between the country with rising unemployment and the rest of the EU.

TAXES AND TRANSFERS

WITHOUT THE automatic countercyclical response of financial markets and the ability to use monetary policy to offset a decline in demand, European governments would want to use tax cuts and increases in government outlays to stimulate demand and reverse cyclical increases in unemployment. But the "stability pact" that was adopted under pressure from Germany tells governments that they cannot run fiscal deficits above three percent of GDP after the start of EMU. This restriction creates an important source of tension between countries with cyclical unemployment increases and the other members of the monetary union. The decision at the 1997 Amsterdam summit to weaken the application of financial penalties for violating this deficit ceiling would undoubtedly encourage more violations and, therefore, more quarrels about "irresponsible" fiscal policies.

Since national monetary and fiscal policies would be precluded, the most likely outcome of the shift to a single monetary policy would be the growth of substantial transfers from the EU to countries that experience cyclical increases in unemployment. Financing

111

those transfers would require a significant increase in tax revenues collected by the EU.

The debates about how large such transfers should be and how the taxes to finance them should be collected would exacerbate the more general disagreement that will inevitably arise as the union seeks to restrict the level and structure of the taxes that individual countries may levy. The European Commission is already trying to get countries to move toward more coordination of their domestic tax policies on the grounds that existing differences in tax rates and rules create competitive advantages for some countries. The shift to a single currency would increase the pressure for tax harmonization. As general responsibility for economic policy shifts from national capitals to the European Commission, the European tradition of focusing taxing authority at a single level would be likely to lead to a shift of the exclusive taxing power from the national to the European level. The EU will therefore be disregarding national preferences about redistribution, the size of government, and the structure of taxes. While the pressures for such coordination might be overwhelming once a single currency has been adopted, the loss of national control over taxes and transfers would be another serious source of irritation within the EU.

LONG-TERM UNEMPLOYMENT

As THE decisions shift away from national governments, it will become harder to reach agreement on policy changes to deal with the high unemployment due to excessive regulation and social welfare payments. The shift of policy decisions from national governments to the European level would eliminate the ability to learn from the experiences of individual countries that try different policies and to benefit from the competitive pressures to adopt national policies that succeed. Moreover, the changes in labor market rules and social benefits that have been proposed by certain national governments are now being opposed not only by labor unions within the individual countries but also by other European governments that fear the resulting gains in competitiveness. Thus we hear of opposition to "social dumping" when an inefficient enterprise is closed and witness the imposition of a Europe-wide limit on the number of hours that employees can work. A politically more unified Europe would make it easier to enforce policies that prevent changes in national labor laws or national transfer payments that would reduce structural unemployment and increase national competitiveness.

If EU legislation succeeds in preventing member countries from competing with each other, they will collectively become less able to compete with the rest of the world. The result would undoubtedly be pressure for increased EU trade barriers, justified by reference to differences in social policy between Europe and other countries. European imposition of such protectionist policies would undermine the entire global trading system and create serious conflicts with the United States and other trading partners.

INCOMPATIBLE EXPECTATIONS

As THE monetary union evolves into a more general political union, conflicts would arise from incompatible expectations about the sharing of power. France sees EMU and the resulting political union as a way of becoming a comanager of Europe and an equal of Germany, which has nearly 50 percent more people. In the economic sphere, the current domination of European monetary policy by the Bundesbank would be replaced by that of the ECB, in which France and Germany would sit and vote as equals. As the French contemplate the eventual membership of the economic and political union, they may also hope that their natural Mediterranean allies, Italy and Spain, will give France a decisive influence on European policies. And the skillful international French civil servants might come to dominate the administration of the European government.

Germany's expectations and aspirations are more difficult to interpret. Some German leaders no doubt believe, as Chancellor Helmut Kohl frequently says, that joining a political union improves the prospects for peace by "containing a potentially dangerous Germany within Europe." Other Germans are no doubt less self-sacrificing and simply disagree with the French assessment of the consequences of greater economic and political integration. They see Germany as the natural leader within the EU because of its economic weight, military capability, and central location in an EU that will soon include Poland, the Czech Republic, and Hungary. As Kohl has said, not without ambiguity, "Germany is our fatherland, but Europe is our future."

What is clear is that a French aspiration for equality and a German expectation of hegemony are not consistent. Both visions drive their countrymen to support the pursuit of EMU, and both would lead to disagreements and conflicts when they could not be fulfilled.

The aspirations of the smaller countries to have a seat at the table may be frustrated. As the EU expands from 15 current members to include at least 6 more countries of Eastern Europe, the role that smaller countries will be allowed to play will become more and more limited. Current EU voting rules will give way to weighted voting arrangements in which the larger countries have a predominant share of the votes. This change will frustrate countries that recognize that they have sacrificed the ability to control their own domestic policies and their own foreign relations without having received in exchange an effective say in Europe's policies.

> France aspires to equality, but Germany expects hegemony.

This loss of sovereignty would affect not just monetary and tax policies but a wide range of current domestic policies that will gradually come under the jurisdiction of the European Commission or European Parliament. Rule-making by the European Commission reached a crescendo in 1994 with edicts about such things as the quality of beer and the permissible shape of imported bananas. A fear that complaints about bureaucratic meddling could jeopardize approval of the Maastricht Treaty in national referendums led to a reduction in rule-making by the Brussels bureaucracy and a rhetorical emphasis on Maastricht's principle of "subsidiarity," which asserts that activities will be assigned to whatever level of government is most appropriate—European, national, or local. There is, however, little reason to believe that this vague principle will do much to restrain the substitution of Brussels rules or Strasbourg legislation for what are now domestic policies. Even the Tenth Amendment to the U.S. Constitution, which reserves to the states (or to the people) any powers not delegated to the national government, has not prevented the shift of power to the national government over an enormous range of local issues, such as speed limits on local roads and the age at which individuals may consume alcohol.

A EUROPEAN MILITARY AND FOREIGN POLICY

THE COLLAPSE of the Soviet Union has changed the basis for European foreign policy and military collaboration. Although the United States and the countries of Western Europe have had an extremely close alliance since the end of World War II and continue to coordinate military efforts within the NATO structure, many Europeans in positions of responsibility see their economic interests and foreign policy goals differing from those of the United States with respect to many parts of the world, including Eastern Europe, the Middle East, Africa, and even Latin America. The French and German governments also want to develop an independent military capability that can operate without U.S. participation or consent.

Although the European nations could now more readily pursue an independent foreign policy and military strategy, they are clearly hampered in doing so effectively by the decentralized political structure of Europe. Chancellor Konrad Adenauer summarized the situation in stark terms for French Foreign Minister Christian Pineau on the day in 1956 when England and France gave in to American pressure to abandon their attack on the Suez Canal: "France and England will never be powers comparable to the United States and the Soviet Union. Nor Germany, either. There remains to them only one way of playing a decisive role in the world; that is to unite to make Europe. England is not ripe for it but the affair of Suez will help to prepare her spirits for it. We have no time to waste: Europe will be your revenge."[2] That was a year before the Treaty of Rome launched the Common Market.

The creation of a political union based on the EMU with explicit authority to develop a common foreign and defense policy would accelerate the development of an independent European military structure capable of projecting force outside Western Europe. Steps in that direction are already occurring in anticipation of the stronger political union that will follow the start of EMU. In March 1997, on

---

[2]Quoted in Henry Kissinger, *Diplomacy*, New York: Simon & Schuster, 1994, p. 547.

the 40th anniversary of the Treaty of Rome, France and Germany announced their desire to see a merger of the EU with the existing European military alliance, the Western European Union, so as to strengthen the military coordination of European nations outside the NATO framework. An explicit agreement was reached with the United States that will allow the European members of NATO to use European NATO forces and equipment under European control without U.S. participation.

The attempt to forge a common military and foreign policy for Europe would be an additional source of conflict among the member nations (as well as with those outside the group). European countries differ in their national ambitions and in their attitudes about projecting force and influencing foreign affairs. An attempt to require countries like Portugal and Ireland to participate in an unwanted war in the Middle East or Eastern Europe could create powerful conflicts among the European nations.

THE RISK OF WAR

THERE IS NO doubt that a Europe of nearly 300 million people with an economy approximately equal in size to that of the United States could create a formidable military force. Whether that would be good or bad in the long run for world peace cannot be foretold with any certainty. A politically unified Europe with an independent military and foreign policy would accelerate the reduction of the U.S. military presence in Europe, weaken the role of NATO, and, to that extent, make Europe more vulnerable to attack. The weakening of America's current global hegemony would undoubtedly complicate international military relationships more generally.

Although Russia is now focusing on industrial restructuring, it remains a major nuclear power. Relations between Russia and Western Europe are important but unpredictable. Might a stronger Russia at some time in the future try to regain control over the currently independent Ukraine? Would a stronger, unified EU seek to discourage such action by force? Could that lead to war between Russia and the EU? How would a strong and unified Europe relate to other nations in the vicinity, including those of North Africa and the Middle East, and the Muslim states of the former Soviet Union, which are important or potential sources of energy for Western Europe?

War within Europe itself would be abhorrent but not impossible. The conflicts over economic policies and interference with national sovereignty could reinforce long-standing animosities based on history, nationality, and religion. Germany's assertion that it needs to be contained in a larger European political entity is itself a warning. Would such a structure contain Germany, or tempt it to exercise hegemonic leadership?

A critical feature of the EU in general and EMU in particular is that there is no legitimate way for a member to withdraw. This is a marriage made in heaven that must last forever. But if countries discover that the shift to a single currency is hurting their economies and that the new political arrangements also are not to their liking, some of them will want to leave. The majority may not look kindly on secession, either out of economic self-interest or a more general concern about the stability of the entire union. The American experience with the secession of the South may contain some lessons about the danger of a treaty or constitution that has no exits.

IMPLICATIONS FOR THE UNITED STATES

IF, AS SEEMS most likely, EMU does occur and does lead to a political union with an independent military and foreign policy, the United States must rethink its own foreign policy with respect to Europe. First, the United States would have an opportunity to play a new, useful role within Europe, helping to balance national pressures and prevent the inevitable conflicts from developing into more serious confrontations. The United States should therefore emphasize that it wants its relations with the individual nations of Europe to remain as strong as they are today and should not allow Brussels to intervene between Washington and the national capitals of Europe.

Second, the United States must be aware that an economically and politically unified Europe would seek a different relationship with the United States. French officials in particular have been outspoken in emphasizing that a primary reason for a European monetary and political union is as a counterweight to the influence of the United States, both within European and in international affairs more generally. For the French, American influence is an old issue that frustrated de Gaulle and recurs in attacks on American "cultural imperialism" and U.S. attempts to influence Europe's policies toward countries like Libya, Iraq, and Iran. Such issues would become more widespread in a powerful, independent Europe.

Finally, the United States must recognize that it would no longer be able to count on Europe as an ally in all its relations with third countries. It was safe to assume such support when conflict with the Soviet Union dominated international relations and Europe's interest in containing the Soviet Union coincided with America's. But the global configuration of relations is now more complex. And the Europeans, guided by a combination of economic self-interest, historical traditions, and national pride, may seek alliances and pursue policies that are contrary to the interests of the United States. Although this divergence may tend to happen in any case because of the apparent end of the Soviet threat, the creation of a monetary union that led to a strong political union would accelerate it. If EMU occurs and leads to such a political union in Europe, the world will be a very different and not necessarily safer place.✪

America and Europe: Clash of the Titans?

C. Fred Bergsten

CONTINENTAL DRIFT

THE LAUNCH of the euro offers the prospect of a new bipolar international economic order that could replace America's hegemony since World War II. The global trading system has already been jointly run since the early days of the European Common Market, which enabled Europe to integrate its commerce and exercise power equivalent to that of the United States in that domain. Now Euroland will equal or exceed the United States on every key measure of economic strength and will speak increasingly with a single voice on a wide array of economic issues. The euro is likely to challenge the international financial dominance of the dollar. Moreover, the end of the Cold War has sharply reduced the importance of U.S. military might for Europe and pulled aside the security blanket that often allowed both sides to cover up or resolve their economic disputes for the greater good of preserving the anticommunist alliance.

Economic relations between the United States and the European Union will therefore rest increasingly on a foundation of virtual equality. The United States will either have to adjust to this new reality or conduct a series of rear-guard defensive actions that will be increasingly futile and costly—like the British did for many decades as their leadership role declined. The EU will either have to exercise

C. FRED BERGSTEN is Director of the Institute for International Economics and was formerly Assistant Secretary of the Treasury for International Affairs and Assistant for International Economic Affairs to the National Security Council. Copyright © 1999 by C. Fred Bergsten.

[20]

positive leadership, which it now can do, or become highly frustrated at home and a spoiler abroad.

Partly as a result of these seismic shifts, transatlantic economic interdependence and joint responsibility for global leadership have grown rapidly for both economic superpowers. Europe and America therefore need to devise new strategies and institutional arrangements to manage both their bilateral economic relations and global economic issues. Such strategies can be constructed with or without a "common European foreign policy" that embraces traditional security issues; Europe itself has integrated far faster economically than it has politically. Japan will also be a partner in some elements of this collaboration. But until that country and the rest of Asia recover from their prolonged economic woes—which may take half a decade or more—transatlantic relations will be the crucial pivot for global as well as bilateral economic progress. And since Japan did not play a very forceful international role even prior to the Asian crisis, the timing or even the possibility of its full participation in the core leadership group remains highly uncertain.

The EU and the United States have yet to develop the required new approaches, however. Recent official discourse has focused instead on a range of narrow, highly technical, and even bureaucratic issues: bananas (which the United States as a country does not even directly export), testing procedures for pharmaceuticals, the appropriate representation of Euroland, which international committee should devise reform of the global financial system, and many other relatively minor matters. At their December summit, the two superpowers could agree only to consider new winemaking standards. Although the two sides need to address disputes over lesser issues—which are inevitable given their high levels of trade, finance, and investment—the gulf between policy requirements and operating reality is enormous.

Meanwhile, a long list of serious challenges remains unresolved. America and Europe are at loggerheads over global warming and energy policy. Despite extensive efforts, they have not resolved the bitter dispute over the extraterritorial impact of American foreign policy sanctions and only narrowly averted a collision over antitrust policy in the Boeing–McDonnell Douglas case. While many countries are still reeling from the global financial turmoil, the two economic superpowers snipe at each other about how to share its adverse effects on their own economies and about their competing regional initiatives in other parts of the developing world.

Their greatest failure, however, lies with the looming problems at the heart of the transatlantic economic relationship. America's trade and current account deficits will probably hit $300 billion in 1999. Any slowdown in the U.S. economy could trigger strong protectionist pressure from industries of central importance to Europe, as is already occurring in steel. In addition, the huge U.S. trade deficit and the likely worldwide shifts of capital into the euro could push the euro up sharply against the dollar in the near future. In turn, a stronger euro would hurt Europe's competitive position and seriously exacerbate its unemployment problem, while the weaker dollar would push U.S. prices and interest rates upward, igniting additional tensions across the Atlantic.

A U.S. economic slowdown could trigger protectionist pressures.

The bilateral relationship is thus drifting dangerously toward crisis. In addition, the global superpowers are only partially confronting several key systemic questions. On the monetary side, America and Europe, along with several key Asian countries, seem to be moving toward modest reforms in the "international financial architecture" to incorporate greater transparency in markets, more rigorous adherence to global financial norms, and modest improvements in International Monetary Fund (IMF) procedures. But the two superpowers have failed to propose, let alone implement, fundamental solutions to the unfolding financial crisis that could stabilize capital flows and the international monetary system.

There is little if any discussion of the momentous changes presaged by the creation of the euro—the biggest change in global finance since the dollar surpassed sterling to become the world's leading currency in the interwar period. There has been no U.S. willingness to even discuss Germany's proposals, now endorsed by the other key continental Europeans and Japan, to avoid the destabilizing currency gyrations that have been so disruptive over the past quarter-century. On trade matters, the EU has proposed a Millennium Round of negotiations at the World Trade Organization (WTO) to open markets further and improve the global trading system, while the United

States will host the next WTO ministerial meeting later this year to plan international trade policy for the early 21st century. Until quite recently, however, the United States had resisted the European initiatives and has still offered no detailed proposals of its own. In short, there is no meeting of the minds on how to proceed on either trade or money.

Furthermore, the two sides have not worked out any strategy to respond to the politically potent backlash against globalization already observed around the world, including on both sides of the Atlantic. That resentment could severely impede progress on key specific issues, as Congress has already demonstrated with its refusal to authorize new trade negotiations and its reluctant support for the IMF. The result could be a gradual undoing of the international economic liberalization of the past two or three decades and a profound alteration in policy around the world.

Economic relations between America and Europe are approaching paralysis just when a daunting policy agenda and the advent of full bipolarity require new cooperative initiatives. Officials devote enormous attention to minutiae but none to common strategy or the requisite institutional mechanisms for tackling a growing number of acute challenges. They react on an ad hoc basis to virtually every problem that arises while failing to anticipate readily foreseeable obstacles. To be sure, extensive trade and investment ties limit the probability of the kind of blowups that the United States and Japan have experienced, and transatlantic diplomacy is skilled at keeping problems under wraps. But the economies of America and Europe, not to mention transatlantic relations and the world economy, remain at considerable risk.

THE TRADE DIMENSION

THE UNITED STATES is entering its eighth year of economic expansion. The economy is at full employment. Price inflation is nowhere to be seen. The underlying competitiveness of most American companies is strong. The government budget is in surplus. Although the trade deficit is soaring to record levels, much of this is due to America's superior growth and the Asian crisis; the dollar is not nearly as overvalued as in the mid-1980s.

For these reasons it is particularly worrisome that American trade policy has been stalemated for four years. Despite the strength of the economy, opponents of globalization have successfully stymied any new trade negotiating authority since Congress approved the North American Free Trade Agreement (NAFTA) in 1993 and the Uruguay Round and WTO, which stemmed from the General Agreement on Tariffs and Trade (GATT), in 1994. Congress came close to blocking new U.S. contributions to the IMF—an imperfect but agreed instrument for responding to the global financial crisis that was sweeping the globe.

We know from history that trade policy tends to backslide toward protectionism unless liberalization continues moving forward. Fortunately, multilateral agreements in several key sectors—telecommunications services, information technology, and financial services—followed the Uruguay Round and maintained momentum for several years. (The United States was able to participate on the basis of residual authority from earlier legislation.) Since the failure of the Asia Pacific Economic Cooperation (APEC) forum's sectoral initiative and the flagging talks of the Free Trade Area of the Americas in 1998, however, no significant trade liberalization is under way anywhere in the world. Not surprisingly, the U.S. steel industry has entered the vacuum to seek widespread relief. Top administration officials expect a number of aggrieved bedfellows to follow shortly: machine tools, semiconductors, shipbuilding, textiles and apparel, some agricultural sectors, and perhaps others.

America's bipartisan trade policy of the past 65 years is at risk. This is especially true with a weakened administration that openly acknowledges a huge debt to organized labor for its surprise November 1998 "victory" and shrinks from reopening NAFTA-style splits within the Democratic Party as it eyes the elections in 2000. Even a modest slowdown in economic growth with small upticks in unemployment could tilt the balance toward protectionism. A relapse into recession could unleash substantial restrictive actions and even legislation.

This prospect threatens transatlantic relations for two reasons. First, many of the imports in question are from Europe itself: machine tools from Germany, sweaters and other woolens from Italy and the

United Kingdom, and steel from throughout the region. Even U.S. restrictions on imports from other countries, such as steel from Russia or ships from South Korea, could inflame transatlantic relations if those restricted products are deflected toward European markets already hit by high unemployment and rising imports. The United States is already threatening to retaliate against European restrictions on banana imports and hormone-treated beef, while Europe is threatening to counteract those American steps as well as the U.S. sanctions on European companies operating in Iran and Libya.

Second, even the threat of American restrictions would seriously disrupt the "trade G-2" bilateral relationship between the United States and Europe that has managed global commercial policy for almost 40 years. Europe has spoken with a single voice on most trade matters since the creation of the original Common Market. Hence, it has been able to convert its status as the world's largest trading entity into effective negotiating equality with the United States on trade. The three major GATT liberalization initiatives—the Kennedy, Tokyo, and Uruguay Rounds—ultimately depended on agreements between Europe and America. The more recent sectoral agreements also hinged on their cooperation. A policy reversal by the United States now, or even its failure to overcome the recent stalemate, would undermine the partnership that has been so vital to both regions and to the world trading system.

To its great credit, the EU has recognized the pending threat and proposed a new "Millennium Round" to improve and expand the WTO system, restarting the liberalization process and strengthening the multilateral framework. Such a negotiation would include sectors, notably agriculture and services, that would greatly expand American exports. Indeed, the United States and the EU share an interest in moving as far as possible toward global free trade. They have already eliminated most of their own import barriers, so such an initiative would require the rest of the world to catch up with them, expanding their exports and creating high-paying jobs. The administration failed to endorse the EU strategy until very recently, however, and has still made no specific proposals of its own, despite its role as host of the next WTO ministerial meeting in late 1999. It has failed to convey to Congress or to the American public the huge opportunities for expanding U.S. exports, thereby undercutting the effort to win approval for any new negotiations.

Both sides now run the risk of drift and even paralysis in transatlantic trade policy—with potentially severe repercussions for the rest of the world. A slide into protectionism or even a failure to continue opening new markets would have a major impact on the global trading system. Could we then expect Asian economies, who depend on expanded exports to emerge from their deep recessions, to keep their own markets open? Would the transition economies in the former Soviet Union, Eastern Europe, and Asia stick to their liberalization strategies? With the backlash against globalization already evident everywhere, the ominous inward-looking protectionist and nationalistic policies that the world has rejected so decisively could reemerge once again.

A failure of transatlantic leadership would make such policy reversals particularly likely. The United States and the EU are the only economic superpowers and the only two regions enjoying reasonable economic growth. They created the GATT system and, more recently, the WTO. Despite their own occasional transgressions, they have nurtured and defended the system throughout its evolution over the past 50 years. While Japan has been important on a few issues and the developing countries played an encouraging role in the Uruguay Round, the Atlantic powers built and sustained the world trade order. Their failure to maintain that commitment would devastate the entire regime.

WHITHER THE DOLLAR?

ALTHOUGH THE transatlantic partnership in trade looks shaky, the financial dimension could prove even more disruptive as the euro becomes a major global currency. The euro now represents an economy almost as large as the United States and will be even larger when all 15 EU countries become members. It enjoys considerably larger trade flows and monetary reserves and can boast a far stronger external financial position as a sizable creditor area; in contrast, America's net foreign debt now approaches $2 trillion. As soon as the European Central Bank establishes its credibility, the euro will become a global financial asset and produce a portfolio diversification from dollars into euros by private investors and central banks that could ultimately reach $500 billion to $1 trillion.

The short-term problem is that the shift from dollars to euros could lead to a broad swing in the dollar-euro exchange rate. America's huge trade deficits are certain to produce a sharp fall in the dollar soon anyway, as they have done about once per decade since the early 1970s. The dollar fell 25 percent against the yen during the second half of 1998, and large dollar-yen swings have often preceded general gyrations in the dollar. Europe's unusually large trade surplus, by far its greatest since the mid-1980s, suggests that part of the dollar's decline will be against the euro. The portfolio

> America needs a currency correction to reduce its trade deficit.

shift into the euro could trigger this event and amplify the dollar's decline, already expected on the heels of America's trade deficit. Some European experts have predicted that the euro could rise by as much as 40 percent against the dollar. This is far more than the 10 percent or so that underlying economic conditions suggest but nonetheless is plausible, since currency markets often substantially overshoot their long-run equilibrium levels.

An excessive appreciation of the euro would hurt European competitiveness and push Europe's unemployment up at a time when the new governments throughout the region are determined to get it down. French officials and German industrialists are in fact loath to contemplate any further decline of the dollar, and some even believe that the dollar is now undervalued. Although they will have to accept some fall in the dollar to help correct America's excessive trade deficit and ease U.S. protectionist pressures, the exchange rate could again become another highly contentious issue across the Atlantic.

America obviously needs a currency correction to help reduce its trade deficit. In light of the lag between exchange-rate shifts and trade flows, the administration must hope that it will come sooner rather than later so that results, especially for industrial workers, show before the 2000 election. But a sharp general fall in the dollar could trigger latent inflationary pressures as long as the U.S. labor market remains tight. In turn, the dollar's decline could push up interest rates on inflation fears and foreign demand for higher returns in a falling currency. The stock market could drop and the impending slowdown could even tilt into recession. In short, the result could be an abrupt termination of America's "economic miracle."

The official American position states that the creation of the euro "is good for America if it is good for Europe." This is correct but banal, given the strong impact that the euro could have on the fundamental economic variables on both sides of the Atlantic. At a minimum, the two sides need to agree on a dollar-euro range that would reflect their respective domestic economic conditions. They should then devise new mechanisms, such as clear policy statements and direct intervention in the markets, to keep the rate from straying too far from these underlying fundamentals.

Renewed transatlantic currency instability, and especially a corresponding increase in U.S. interest rates, would also be poisonous for Asian and other emerging market countries trying to recover from the current crisis. Higher American interest rates would increase the cost of servicing their largely dollar-denominated foreign debts and send much-needed capital flows to America instead of to their own needy economies. A failure to manage the dollar-euro relationship effectively could thus have severe consequences worldwide.

These examples only begin to reveal the impact of the new monetary conditions on the United States and the world economy. The existence of a real competitor to the dollar means that the United States will have to pay higher interest rates to attract foreign capital to finance its large external deficits. Such competition will be healthy for the United States over the longer run by providing an incentive to avoid huge budget deficits and double-digit inflation; it might even eventually eliminate its trade imbalance. But the new competition could be quite uncomfortable for a while.

The new monetary environment will also substantially affect the world economy. The dollar and the euro will probably account for roughly equal shares of the great bulk of international financial assets. Prolonged misalignment between them will generate similarly skewed results for other countries that peg their units to either currency. Indeed, the dollar's sharp rise against the yen from 1995 to 1997 partially caused the Asian crisis, since most of the Asian currencies were effectively tied to the dollar. Moreover, misalignments among the major currencies contribute to disruptive protectionist pressures—with particularly large costs for developing and other heavily trade-dependent countries. In addition, considerable dollar-euro instability is likely even without prolonged misalignment because both superpowers will be continental economies with only a modest reliance on trade. Europe may be tempted to emulate America's periodic "benign neglect" of the exchange rate, especially given the European Central Bank's mandate to focus on price stability—but at the cost of hurting smaller countries more sensitive to instability.

As with trade, the two partners bear enormous responsibility for the global monetary system. Despite the high stakes, however, there is still no evidence of serious discussion, let alone strategic preparation or contingency planning against the risks outlined above. Why is there such a gap between the challenges of economic policy and the apparent responses of the United States and the EU? There is certainly no dearth of meetings. The leaders hold semiannual summits and lower-level officials get together constantly. The governments have been quite adept at declaring the launch of new transatlantic "dialogues," "partnerships," and "marketplaces," but the fundamental problems remain unresolved.

CLOSING THE GAP

THERE IS plenty of blame to go around for this lack of preparation. Europe has been preoccupied with regional initiatives, most notably with the euro but also with its enlargement of membership and reordering of regional finances. Its relentless expansion of trade association agreements now encompasses more than 80 countries and raises doubts about its commitment to nondiscriminatory multilateralism (despite its proposal for a Millennium Round). It has failed to design effective procedures to represent Euroland in international financial councils, with member states jealously defending their national prerogatives. This approach has frustrated Americans (and others) who had anticipated more streamlined decision-making. To paraphrase Henry Kissinger, the United States still does not know who to call in Europe when new crises hit. Europe's failure to effectively

C. Fred Bergsten

tackle foreign policy problems in its own backyard, notably Bosnia and now Kosovo, has invited disrespect and even ridicule over the prospect of real partnership.

As I noted above, however, the Europeans have begun to address the transatlantic and global agendas, such as proposing a Millennium Round to restart the trade momentum. They have also floated suggestions for improved exchange-rate management that could reduce the risks of misalignments and instability. Although detailed blueprints for implementing these ideas have yet to be laid out and caution still prevails, the Europeans have nevertheless tried to launch the process.

For its part, the United States has contributed to the lag in two key ways. First, the domestic backlash against globalization adversely affects relations with Europe and the rest of the world. Given its concern for lower-income Americans and the disruptions generated by rapid technological change, the administration has been curiously ineffective in improving the domestic adjustment programs and safety nets that could buffer trade-induced job insecurity and downward pressure on wages. It has failed to work out credible international initiatives on labor standards and environmental concerns, and neither the Republican-led Congress nor the business community has demonstrated the necessary flexibility to foster a political consensus on those key topics. Instead, the administration has mostly backtracked in the face of resistance rather than mounting an effective response, thereby undermining the prospects for tackling the economic challenges ahead. In short, it has failed to reestablish a political foundation for a sustainable foreign economic policy. Europe can understandably view the United States as inward-looking, just as Americans can level that charge at Europeans.

Second, the United States suffers from schizophrenia on the international front. On the one hand, it claims that Europe (and, during better times, Japan) should assert greater international responsibility and "share the burdens of leadership." On the other hand, its revealed preference is to try to maintain American dominance—even while asking others to pay the bill—and to exploit national differences within Europe whenever possible. (The Europeans are also no strangers to this; they continually talk of "a common foreign policy" but almost always act nationally.) One senses that some American officials resist European or other international ideas simply because they originated elsewhere. Whatever the cause, the administration has responded with studied indifference or outright hostility to constructive European trade and monetary proposals.

Regrettably, the Clinton administration has not replied to these European suggestions with any strategic visions of its own. Instead, it has reacted rather than led, whether the challenge was international (like the Asian financial crisis) or domestic (like the antiglobalization campaign). Such a lack of initiative, or even a thoughtful response, costs the United States dearly when confronting major developments such as the advent of a new economic superpower and a challenger currency. Even beleaguered Japan has endorsed Europe's calls for a Millennium Round and new approaches to currency management. The United States must realize that it will be outflanked on economic issues by the other two industrial giants if it continues its passivity.

An important part of the problem is bureaucratic buck-passing. Even though they eventually intervene when forced by events, monetary authorities on both sides of the Atlantic like "freely flexible" exchange rates because they can then blame currency problems on "the market" rather than themselves. Central banks in particular resist any policy framework that might place even the most limited constraints on their cherished independence. Moreover, neither America nor Europe is good at managing the interaction between monetary and trade issues—with different ministries in charge of each domain and little coordination between them—despite the obvious economic linkage.

MANAGED CARE

IT WILL NOT be easy to convert the current transatlantic malaise into an effective partnership. The United States faces significant domestic constraints, both economic and political, and Europe has a full "domestic" agenda. Governments always find it hard to take forceful preventive actions. The turf problems described above represent formidable practical barriers. So what can be done?

There is no need for new transatlantic "grand designs." Instead, the EU and the United States need to install effective working arrangements to address the serious problems ahead, both in their bilateral relations and in the joint challenges of global leadership that will become even more difficult in the coming months and years. They should take separate approaches to financial and trade issues.

The immediate goal on the monetary front is modest: to keep the dollar-euro exchange rate from straying so far from underlying economic fundamentals that it damages their economies, the transatlantic relationship, and the global system. America and Europe should retain flexible exchange rates as the basic paradigm but plan their management preemptively rather than deploying ad hoc measures too late, as at present. Monetary authorities could agree on a fairly wide range, perhaps 10 to 15 percent on either side of an agreed midpoint of € 1.00 = $1.25–$1.30, that would limit dollar-euro fluctuations. Such a band includes the startup rate of € 1.00 = $1.17 but prevents any significant dollar appreciation from that point or any dollar depreciation beyond its previous lows against the constituent European currencies. The authorities should announce their agreed range to convey clearly their official intention to the markets. A qualified majority vote of the EU Council of Economic and Finance Ministers could endorse such an incremental alteration in managing floating rates, while any major reform (like a return to fixed Bretton Woods–style parities) would need its unanimous approval.

Despite their modesty, such new arrangements would provide a helpful operational focus for America and Europe to agree on appropriate exchange rates. They would require close monitoring of the markets and creation of an effective mechanism for joint intervention to protect the ranges. They would also encourage some policy coordination, including of monetary policy, when the exchange rate moves to the edge of the very wide band and something more than direct intervention and official statements is required. They would help stabilize private capital flows by indicating the limits of official tolerance of fluctuations; the absence of government guidance often encourages contagion and destabilizes capital flows when a currency comes under speculative siege. The relative stability of the two major currencies (or three currencies, when Japan reaches comparable agreements for the yen with America and Europe) would be enormously helpful for other countries, who could then peg their unit to one of the key currencies without running the risk of prolonged misalignments.

The scheme would be truly cooperative, based on initial proposals from Europe and Japan and worked out in detail with the United States. The outcome would be a concentric network of largely informal groups to manage international economic and monetary affairs: a core G-2 comprising the United States and Europe; a G-3 including Japan; the existing G-7, G-10, and G-22 to engage the next tier of key countries; and the global institutions, like the IMF, for formal implementation of the more far-reaching reforms. The involvement of the broader groups will ensure that the G-2 does not collude against the rest of the world and promote its own interests at everyone else's expense.

On trade, both sides must restart the process of global liberalization to counter the protectionist tide in the United States and the broader antiglobalization pressures everywhere. The United States and the EU should agree that the 1999 WTO ministerial meeting endorse the early launch of a Millennium Round. The negotiations should aim to produce tangible results every two or three years, to demonstrate progress and broaden market access in countries that still place large restraints on imports. They should also work out key issues of discord, including agriculture, competition policy, the implementation of the WTO rulings (which have been crucial in the banana case), and the rules governing regional arrangements. And they should address the environmental and labor issues that help drive the backlash against globalization.

On the institutional side, the G-2 relationship must be reinvigorated. It should again function as the core of the quadrilateral group with Japan and Canada, and then the full WTO itself. Such a strategy, along with more responsive U.S. domestic policies, should deflect enough protectionist pressure to get the two economic superpowers back on track in managing bilateral trade policy and their global responsibilities.

THE TRANSATLANTIC CENTURY?

NOT TOO long ago, there was much debate over whether the next hundred years would be the "Japanese" or "Asian" century. Now, that looks less likely. The "European century" seems a more likely prospect, or even a "second American century." Some observers have suggested that the 21st century will have a "trilateral" focus on Europe, Japan, and the United States. But the most plausible candidate for economic success and global leadership may instead be the transatlantic partnership. If the United States and the EU can begin to cooperate now as equal partners, even in the economic arena alone, they could resuscitate the vitality of their own relationship and provide effective global leadership. If they fail to do so they will continue to drift apart like tectonic plates, with severe consequences both for themselves and for the world economy.

The economic integration of Europe over the past half-century, culminating in the euro, represents history's most dramatic success in institutionalizing interdependence. It has also been the most sensational instance of nations voluntarily relinquishing their sovereignty in favor of international collaboration. It has assured peace as well as prosperity through judicious economic amalgamation. The countries of the North Atlantic will probably never choose integration as deep as that of Europe and are unlikely to heed the call of former Secretary of State James A. Baker III to keep pace with Europe's course. But the completion of the European economic evolution provides the basis for an effective transatlantic partnership that could herald a similar, if more modest, success story over the next 50 years. It could also presage the next major step forward in managing the world economy.⊛

Misunderstanding Europe

William Wallace and Jan Zielonka

NO RESPECT

EUROBASHING IS back in fashion in the United States. The European visitor to Washington now encounters American economic triumphalism mixed with contempt for Europe's sluggish growth and social protection. American critics castigate Europe for not contributing to regional and global order while demanding that Europeans shoulder more of the cost of leadership. For Europeans in Washington, *Newsweek*'s Michael Hirsh recently noted, "it's hard to get respect."

Anti-European sentiment in America is not new. The United States was built by immigrants who shook off the disappointments of the old world for the hope of the new. Businessmen and politicians in late-nineteenth-century America believed they represented the vigorous future, Europe the enfeebled past. In the two world wars Americans saw themselves as sailing across the Atlantic to sort out European quarrels that the Europeans were incapable of resolving among themselves.

After 1945, the American prescription for Europe was to make it "more like us": to build a United States of Europe that would become America's loyal partner within a broader Western alliance. In the years since, American disappointment at Europe's unwillingness to accept U.S. leadership unconditionally has fluctuated between despair over European political incoherence and fear that the European

WILLIAM WALLACE is a Reader in International Relations at the London School of Economics and the Liberal Democrat spokesman on defense in the British House of Lords. JAN ZIELONKA is Professor of Political Science at the European University Institute in Florence and author of *Explaining Euro-Paralysis*.

[65]

allies might agree on a framework for integration different from what Washington had prescribed.

These days, however, American commentators seem to embrace an exaggerated Euroskepticism. Irving Kristol writes of "the slowly emerging crisis in Europe's economy and society," in contrast to American economic and social vitality. "Europe is resigned to be a quasi-autonomous protectorate of the U.S.," he relates, adding, "Europeans do not know—and seem not to want to know—what is happening to them." Robert Altman and Charles Kupchan have asked whether the United States could help in "arresting the decline of Europe," while Senator Jesse Helms (R-N.C.), in moving the Senate resolution on NATO enlargement, declared that "the European Union could not fight its way out of a wet paper bag." Martin Feldstein has gone so far as to call the collapse of European integration into war a plausible outcome of Europe's economic and monetary union.

Just as European anti-Americanism damaged Western solidarity during the Cold War, so American Eurobashing threatens to unravel transatlantic cooperation in the post–Cold War era. If the United States expects Europe to shoulder a larger burden of global leadership, a decent respect for Europe's opinions is in the American interest. The current approach, combining demands for greater burden-sharing with knee-jerk dismissals of European policies, risks alienating America's most important allies.

THE VIEW FROM AMERICA

SEVERAL DEVELOPMENTS have prompted these new anti-European rumblings. First, Americans remain ambivalent about how far the U.S.-inspired project of European integration should go, for fear it could produce a true global rival. Euroskepticism also stems from the tendency toward hyperbole that characterizes Washington's policy debate. To make matters worse, Americans suffer from dwindling information and expertise on Europe as the American media retreats into domestic coverage and exotic human interest stories and the generation of exiled Europeans teaching in American universities passes on. In the end, American elites are increasingly left with a crude picture of European politics, society, and economic development.

135

As a result, every European move toward greater integration is met by American warnings of the alleged dangers to U.S. interests and even to Europeans themselves. Zbigniew Brzezinski has called for a wider but weaker European Union (EU) to "expand the range of American influence without simultaneously creating a Europe so politically integrated that it could challenge the United States on matters of geopolitical importance, particularly in the Middle East." Yet each time European governments slip back toward disunity, Americans lament the European decline into a continent with "no trumps, no luck, no will," as Stanley Hoffmann put it over 20 years ago. After the exaggerated assertions of Eurosclerosis in the early 1980s came heated charges of a "Fortress Europe" on the heels of the 1986 Single European Act and the 1992 Single Market Program. Lester Thurow predicted a "Head to Head" transatlantic economic confrontation, while more alarmist commentators warned of an emerging "Euroquake," a protectionist economic bloc threatening American trade.

> Eurobashing now threatens transatlantic cooperation.

American responses to the European single currency now follow a similar cycle: first inattention, then assertions that it cannot succeed, then warnings of danger once success appears imminent. American realists simply see the emerging threat of a new economic hegemon, either Germany alone or France and Germany together, rather than recognizing how common policies in the EU emerge from multilateral bargaining among 15 member states. Admittedly, economic and monetary union is a leap in the dark, and its implications for fiscal and economic policies are insufficiently spelled out. But Feldstein's intemperate predictions of doom and Milton Friedman's warnings against this "senseless" venture ignore the benefits that enhanced cross-border integration of European economies has achieved in the past decade. As in the American single market, major companies in Europe now operate across national borders. Hedging operations, accounting in multiple currencies, and currency transfer fees all hold back further integration of Europe-wide production and marketing. Coordination between central banks and finance ministries has tightened considerably in recent years and will tighten further after the launch of

Europe's single currency. Issues of tax convergence, bank regulation, and interregional transfers have all moved up the EU agenda.

American commentary on Europe reflects its own self-image. American warnings in the late 1980s about the threat of economic competition from a powerful Fortress Europe were the flip side of the debate over American economic decline. American denigration of European economic stagnation in the late 1990s mirrors the happy consensus on America's "Goldilocks" economy—the apparent surge toward sustained growth without inflation. But the picture of a European economy in perpetual decline is a caricature. For example, American punditry has ignored the one-time effect of German unification in slowing European growth. The German government borrowed to finance the economic transformation in the former East Germany, forcing the Bundesbank to raise interest rates. Meanwhile, the general squeeze on budgetary deficits imposed by the Maastricht Treaty's criteria for monetary union also temporarily depressed short-term growth. This necessary correction in European fiscal policies should, however, lay the foundation for stronger growth with lower inflation in the future. In fact, the overall EU growth rate between 1985 and 1992, before the unification-induced rise in

German interest rates, was higher than that in the United States. Faster American growth between 1993 and 1997 may reflect different stages in the business cycle rather than long-term changes in competitiveness.

American observers also seem to ignore the European recovery this year, which will see the EU catching up to the United States. The Organization for Economic Cooperation and Development forecasts that Europe will grow even faster than America in 1999. American leadership in information technology is unchallenged, but in pharmaceuticals and new materials Europe is not lagging far behind. Sluggish domestic demand in Germany has been accompanied by the rapid development of exports to central and Eastern Europe. While France has struggled through a painful adjustment of economic and social policies with stubbornly high unemployment, the Netherlands achieved a higher growth rate than the United States in 1997 (4.2 percent versus 3.7 percent). Ireland's growth rate was an astounding 10.5 percent, Finland's a technology-driven 5.9 percent. Airbus is keeping up with Boeing; Daimler-Benz, now with Mack Truck and Chrysler in its group, is not far behind General Motors. Transatlantic trade, in overall balance for much of the past 20 years, has recently shifted toward a robust European surplus.

American denunciation of Europe's costly welfare systems, extensive social regulation, and sluggish labor mobility also project on Europe the domestic American debate. Proponents of free markets and welfare cuts hold a vested interest in portraying Europe as chronically uncompetitive. But the German economy is a standing rebuke to neoliberal critics; according to their theories it should have imploded years ago. Several times during the past two decades Anglo-Saxon economists have written obituary notices for the German model, only to watch it bounce back on high-quality exports, a well-trained and productive workforce, and adjustments in social and economic policies negotiated among managers, employee representatives, and federal and state authorities.

The various models of social regulation and welfare observable in Western Europe do carry heavy costs, most evident in their current failure to create full employment. All models suffer from demographic changes as populations age and pension and health care costs rise; all are forced into painful adjustments to welfare payments. But a sturdy safety net also delivers tangible benefits. Life expectancy throughout the EU is higher than in the United States, infant mortality lower. European societies maintain a much smaller gap between rich and poor than does the United States. Bringing jobs to communities rather than compelling workers to tear up their roots and move hundreds of miles maintains social cohesion. Europe's cities are vibrant and safe, and crime rates are sharply lower than in the United States. America jails over one percent of the working-age male population, a proportion eight times higher than the European average. Were this figure added to calculations of the unemployment rate and the cost of the American prison system to the U.S. welfare budget, one would get a more balanced comparison between American and European approaches to economic and social regulation.

BEASTS OF BURDEN

AMERICAN CRITICISM of European incoherence in foreign and defense policy is better justified, notably in the Bosnian tragedy. European rhetoric in 1991 that "the hour of Europe" had come would soon ring hollow, as did the 1992 Maastricht Treaty's assertion that "a Common Foreign and Security Policy is hereby established." Tragically, domestic pressures in Germany forced a hasty recognition of Slovenia and Croatia without any accompanying plans to help consolidate their independence, protect minority rights, or address the bloody ramifications for Bosnia. The Balkan crisis provided a painful lesson in the problems with collective foreign- and defense-policymaking for the EU, with Germany ultimately agreeing to send troops outside its borders on a mission in Europe for the first time since World War II. With less success, France and Britain developed a bilateral defense dialogue without creating an effective multilateral framework for joint European action. Nevertheless, EU foreign policy remained so fragmented that U.S. Bosnia envoy Richard Holbrooke charged European governments with "sleeping through the night" while American policymakers imposed a compromise settlement.

What America really demands is that Europe pay for U.S. hegemony

Here again, however, American criticism masks an underlying ambivalence. Successive U.S. administrations have called for political and security partnership while obstructing moves toward a "European caucus" within or outside NATO. One telling example was the Senate resolution on NATO enlargement, which reasserted "an ongoing and direct leadership role for the United States in European security affairs" while demanding that "the responsibility and financial burden of defending the democracies of Europe ... be more equitably shared."

For European governments this story is wearily familiar. Henry Kissinger's response to Western Europe's first steps toward foreign policy coordination, at the Helsinki Conference on Security and Cooperation in Europe in 1972–73, was to demand that American representatives sit in on all consultations among European nations. He felt particularly concerned that Western European governments might develop an autonomous policy toward the Middle East. More recently, the U.S. response to European negotiations on common foreign policy at the 1991 Maastricht Intergovernmental Conference signaled that the transformation of the Western European Union, the defense arm of the EU, into an autonomous grouping within NATO would be unacceptable to the United States. The British and Dutch governments took the hint and weakened their proposals for closer European cooperation while the French stiffened their resistance to what they saw as the re-emergence of American hegemony. As a result, the EU to this day remains a civilian power, an effective global actor in economic policy, aid, and international institutions but without comparable political clout or military capacity. Having helped produce this dilemma, U.S. officials now criticize it.

American Euroskeptics accuse the European allies of being free riders on American-provided security. But that charge is sustainable only within the narrow confines of military capability and expenditure. True, European NATO members together only spend the equivalent of 66 percent of the U.S. defense budget. By any broader definition of security, however, the European contribution is far higher. In the five years after the Berlin Wall fell, three-quarters of Western economic and financial assistance to Russia and the countries of central and Eastern Europe came from the EU. Over half the international aid to the West Bank and Gaza from 1994 to 1997, designed to boost the Middle East peace process, came from Western Europe, in contrast to only 10 percent from the United States. European contributions to international organizations and economic development in the poorest states of Africa and South Asia far exceed the shrinking U.S. share. This is equitable burden-sharing by any honest calculation. Constant repetition of the claim that Europe should pay more—without letting those who pay the piper have some say in choosing the tune—is one of the most corrosive elements in American criticism. Western European governments, deeply conscious of the value of the American-led NATO framework, are far from breaking the transatlantic link. But there is increasing irritation that what Congress and the administration really demand is that the Europeans pay for U.S. hegemony.

THE VIEW FROM EUROPE

FOR EUROPEANS, American confidence in the vigor of the U.S. economy contrasts oddly with American protests that the United States can no longer afford to support its share of international responsibilities. This incoherence is one result of American politics being projected onto transatlantic relations. Years of partisan wrangling over the U.S. deficit, taxation, foreign aid, and contributions to international organizations have created a consensus that Americans cannot pay more and resentment that the European allies appear to be paying less. A review of the U.S. debate on transatlantic relations prepared by the Council on Foreign Relations was peppered with the terms "resentment" and "resentful," reporting anger at the European allies for not pulling their economic weight and not giving the United States full support on every aspect of its diplomacy.

European governments, which have struggled to publicize to Congress and the American media their substantial financial contributions to Russia, Eastern Europe, the Middle East, and Africa, are annoyed by the failure of American political leadership to recognize this reality. From the president downward, U.S. leaders happily lecture their allies on their responsibilities but flinch from warning Congress of how inaccurate its perceptions truly are. The confident expectation of America's foreign policy elite that Europeans will sweep aside their own domestic constraints when the United States needs their support contrasts painfully with the timid hesitancy when this same foreign policy elite approaches its own domestic audience. Many of the most internationalist of administration officials feed rather than combat congressional resentment. In one example, at the NATO foreign ministers' meeting in December 1997, Secretary of State Madeleine K. Albright protested that the United States was providing 90 percent of the funds for a new training program for the Bosnian police. "In key areas such as this," she admonished her colleagues, "other members of the alliance need to do much, much more." Her European audience, conscious that they were already providing over 70 percent of the total budget for peacekeeping and civilian construction in Bosnia and 80 percent of the peacekeepers on the ground, could only worry about the impact on audiences in Washington of such selective statistics.

While American foreign-policy makers complain about the chaos of different institutions in Brussels and clashing national interests among European states, Europeans have to grapple with the confusion of competing power centers in Washington. Europeans see American foreign-policy making crippled by the wide gap between the professional elite and Congress and by another comparable gap between Congress and public opinion. Such gaps emerged partly from the post-Vietnam and post–Iranian Revolution traumas that still hang over American politicians, and partly from the power that lobbies wield in Washington politics. As a result, the United States will launch unilateral actions to satisfy a domestic interest group and expect that other nations play obedient multilateral-minded partners. America disregards international law and institutions while insisting that other states accept the rulings of international bodies when convenient for the United States.

The Washington elite is fond of sharply contrasting the clarity of American strategic leadership with the bumbling confusion of European allies. But Europeans, struggling to balance their own domestic interests against those of their partners without antagonizing the United States, see a similarly confused alliance leader: a nation driven off track by domestic politics, trapped in a political cockpit where the constant pursuit of campaign contributions and specific lobbies threatens to overtake wider Western interests. Washington's approach to NATO enlargement—reversing its elaborately prepared Partnership for Peace initiative—produced major changes in American policy declared without warning in speeches to Polish-American and Baltic-American groups, while wildly differing estimates of enlargement costs became ammunition for interagency politicking. Much of the funding for the U.S. Committee to Expand NATO was provided by armaments companies that hoped to sell U.S. weapons systems to new member states. Parochialism came to drive policy.

DOING IT OUR WAY

DAMAGE TO transatlantic relations also comes from the distortion of American foreign policy through the power of domestic lobbies and the arrogant unilateralism of congressional leaders. Two-thirds of the world's population is now covered by some form of U.S. sanctions imposed by Congress or state and local governments—a messier tangle of overlapping and incoherent laws than anything the EU can offer. The powerful Cuban lobby has discredited America's policy toward Castro, while U.S. policy toward the Middle East is distorted by the influence of the strong pro-Israel lobby. European governments understand that it made sense in domestic politics for President Clinton to unveil increased sanctions against Iran at the World Jewish Congress in New York and why Senator Alfonse D'Amato (R.-N.Y.)

has pushed for the Iran-Libya Sanctions Act (ILSA). But these moves still make Europeans cynical about such policies and make all the more questionable the Clinton administration's insistence that European allies categorically accept American leadership in Middle East policy.

Even greater damage results from the way some congressional leaders, and even a few administration officials, address their European partners. Any European parliamentary leader who treated American representatives in the style of the Senate's current foreign relations chairman would provoke outrage in Washington. Jesse Helms walked out when the British foreign secretary disagreed with him on burden-sharing in a May 1997 meeting. "To hell with international law," *The San Francisco Chronicle* reported that D'Amato told a European ambassador who suggested that ILSA contravened it. D'Amato further added, "You've got a choice to make: you're either with us or against us, and I only hope for your sake you make the right decision." European diplomats and politicians are particularly galled by White House officials who assure them that the policies resulting from such rhetoric are nevertheless part of a rational global strategy that Europe must support.

In one telling example of U.S. ambivalence toward international law, American policymakers have called on European states, institutions, and private actors to support the restitution of Jewish property and investments stolen during the Holocaust. This transatlantic appeal to international justice, backed by threats of unilateral sanctions, roughly coincided with the American refusal to accept that the jurisdiction of the International Criminal Court (ICC) might apply to the United States. European governments are painfully aware of the dark periods in their history, but they find it hard to accept the claim that America is entirely exceptional. "Everyone knows that the United States is a righteous nation," Joshua Muravchik of the American Enterprise Institute boldly declared to a surprised European audience. For Europe, it is not self-evident that the United States, with its own historical demons, has earned the right to be outside and above the disciplines of international law. In the end, Europeans were left scratching their heads when American delegates voted against all their European allies and sided with Iraq, Libya, and China in opposing the ICC.

The American approach to international organizations is now evident: unilateral abrogation of its own financial obligations combined with the insistence that other states observe theirs, all while demanding that the organization in question follow Washington's commands promptly and fully. Few Europeans can understand the deep roots of American antagonism toward the United Nations, and European governments feel no sympathy for America's failure to pay its U.N. dues. The United States depends on U.N. inspection teams to probe Iraq's weapons program and needed the United Nations to assemble the coalition that forced Iraq out of Kuwait. Watching the United States selectively exploit the United Nations when necessary and disrespect it the rest of the time, European governments are hard pressed to persuade their citizens to follow U.S. policy wherever it may lead. European officials are similarly dismayed when the United States assumes that the International Monetary Fund and the World Trade Organization will follow American preferences.

PARTNERSHIP WITHOUT ILLUSIONS

To THIS DAY, the United States calls for greater collective European action but insists on American approval before any joint European initiative, especially in security matters. American policymakers decry the European culture of dependency on U.S. leadership while insisting in the same breath that it continue. Without defending that dependency, the confusion of Brussels institutions, or the ever-irritating differences of style among leading European governments, one must address the inconsistencies in

145

American thinking rather than rehash the familiar deficiencies of European cooperation.

American think tanks offer prolific proposals for transatlantic redesign. Few, however, address the changes that are needed in American policy to reinforce this partnership. There is a sad parallel between this failure and the EU's treatment of the post-socialist governments of central and Eastern Europe between 1990 and 1996. The EU set out a series of tasks and targets that the applicant states were required to accept without admitting that it would itself have to adjust to a transformed Europe. Not until the summer of 1997, when the European Commission issued its *Agenda 2000* report, did the EU spell out the reforms that it needed to prepare itself for eastern enlargement. But an equally introspective American report on the adjustments that the United States must make to accommodate a changing Europe has yet to appear.

For example, a 1997 RAND report, *America and Europe: A Partnership for a New Era*, still views the relationship as one that the United States will lead in the Cold War style. One proposal, closely echoing Kissinger's 1973 demands, suggests that Europe inform and consult the United States before making EU decisions. "This will be awkward for EU members and institutions, but it is essential for an effective partnership," the report insists. And yet the same report dismisses the idea that U.S. policymaking should take European interests into account as "illogical . . . because the United States is a sovereign country." In a similar vein, Charles Kupchan's 1996 *Foreign Affairs* manifesto for "an Atlantic Union" concentrates on what the Europeans must do to adhere to American preferences, not the other way around.

Transatlantic relations in the late 1990s are characterized by intense economic relations but weak political contacts. Yet an effective U.S.-European political partnership across a wide range of policy areas is essential to global order and the world economy. Those in Washington who depicted the Asia-Pacific region as representing America's future and Europe its past must recognize after the eruption of the Asian crisis that the European allies—with all their evident flaws and weaknesses—are the United States' only dependable partners, sharing America's values and burdens.

William Wallace and Jan Zielonka

A MATTER OF TRUST

THE SURVIVAL of the transatlantic partnership forged under the exceptional circumstances of the Cold War should not be taken for granted. For most of American history, relations with Europe have been cool. If Europeans were to apply to America the same realist logic that John Mearsheimer of the University of Chicago applied to post–Cold War Europe, they would predict a return of American isolationism or transatlantic rivalry. But a productive transatlantic relationship cannot be sustained without a firm base of domestic support within both the United States and Europe. Sadly, American foreign-policy makers have failed to provide the necessary domestic leadership.

There is a danger that American elites will continue to react to the successful launch of the European single currency with a mood swing comparable to ten years ago, from proclamations of Europe's decline to complaints of European threats to American interests. Monetary union will indeed alter the balance of the Atlantic relationship and force further political integration among EU member states. Smaller steps toward integrating EU foreign policy—such as the reorganization of the European Commission's directorates-general for external relations into a coherent group and the transformation of the role of the EU Council's secretary-general into a post akin to that of the NATO secretary-general—may also appear to strengthen Europe and threaten American interests. Detailed negotiations for eastern enlargement of the EU are bound to involve compromises that some American enterprises will see as adversely affecting their interests. Different domestic constraints will pull European and American policymakers in opposite directions on issues ranging from global warming to food additives to genetically modified crops.

As Europe's unwieldy confederal mechanisms lumber forward, however, American elites must avoid alarmism. They will do more for the future of Atlantic relations if they focus on how American government and politics should best adjust to ensure that Congress and the public gain an accurate picture of European developments. The United States does not need grand transatlantic redesigns. Instead, it must integrate its relations with the EU and NATO and accept that a European caucus within NATO is in America's long-term interest. On this point, the RAND study correctly observes, "American resistance to the formation of an EU identity within NATO will only rekindle European interest in an eventual EU military alliance outside NATO." As a start, the United States could consolidate its huge missions to the EU and NATO and appoint a senior political figure to represent the United States as a whole to the European institutions.

A long-term partnership requires mutual accommodation and two-way communication. Americans who understand the critical importance of the Atlantic relationship in a disordered world must also recognize the adverse impact that Washington's self-absorbed but noisy debate has on its European listeners. They must exert themselves not only to listen more carefully to European concerns but also to convey them accurately to political opinion makers in the United States. Europeans who understand the central importance of the transatlantic relationship already recognize the many obstacles presented by disjointed European institutions and do their best to overcome them. An end to Eurobashing from across the Atlantic would help them in their task.

Germany's New Right

Jacob Heilbrunn

LIBERATING NATIONALISM FROM HISTORY

WHEN THE Berlin Wall collapsed in 1989, a number of observers predicted that a reunited Germany would begin experimenting with its newfound power and revert to the bellicose habits of the past. The Bonn political elite, however, has been remarkably resistant to change. While Chancellor Helmut Kohl has flirted with attempts to "normalize" Germany's Nazi past and create a self-confident nation, and the Bavarian Christian Social Union has bucked the pro-Europe course, he and his Christian Democratic Union (CDU) have not deviated from their efforts to submerge a unified Germany in a federal Europe that boasts a common currency. Nor have any of the other major political parties, from Kohl's coalition partner, the liberal Free Democratic Party (FDP), to the Social Democratic Party (SPD). Even the antinomian Greens embrace the idea of a centralized Europe as a means of diluting German economic and military power. In his new book, *The Wrong Path of Nationalism*, Heiner Geissler, former general secretary of the CDU, expresses the conventional wisdom: "Germany has achieved its great successes in economic, social, and foreign policy not as a classical nation-state, but rather as a democratic, cosmopolitan, and European-oriented country."[1] Konrad Adenauer's famous campaign slogan, "No Experiments!" remains the unofficial motto of postwar Germany.

Since 1989, however, this doctrine has begun to be challenged by the elite that first created, in the nineteenth century, the idea of a unified German nation: German intellectuals. A change is taking place in Germany, not at the political but at the intellectual level. Whether or not it turns into a political movement or is taken up by

---

JACOB HEILBRUNN is an Associate Editor at *The New Republic.*

one of the established political parties, the change will have a serious impact on Germany's redefinition of its identity and interests in the new Europe. Fought largely over the lessons of the past, today's and coming battles about national pride could well shape Germany's future. In modern Germany politics does not make history; history makes politics.

A profound move to the right has been taking place among Germany's best-known novelists, such as Hans Magnus Enzensberger and Martin Walser. Bonn University political scientist Hans-Peter Schwarz, the biographer of Adenauer, has recently written a book entitled *The Central Power of Europe*, calling for a recognition of German power. But no heretics have attacked the dogmas of the old Federal Republic of Germany more passionately than the nationalist intellectuals who lead what has become known as the *Neue Rechte*, or new right. The German new right consists not of skinheads in jackboots but journalists, novelists, professors, and young lawyers and business executives. Its champions include former Chancellor Willy Brandt's widow, Brigitte Seebacher-Brandt, the filmmaker Hans Jürgen Syberberg, the playwright Botho Strauss, the historian Ernst Nolte, CDU parliamentarian Heinrich Lummer, and sympathizers such as the self-described "German-Jewish patriot" and historian Michael Wolffsohn. Paradoxically, the new right is made up of nationalists from both ends of the political spectrum. Nationalists on the left hope to remake the SPD; nationalists on the right, the Free Democratic Party. Everyone from former Social Democratic Chancellor Helmut Schmidt to Heiner Geissler has denounced the movement, and dozens of alarmist books with such titles as *Is the Republic Capsizing?* have appeared in the past two years.

Underlying new right positions is a deep hatred of the westernization of Germany under the influence of the United States over the last five decades. The advent of an American-style multicultural society is perceived to pose a great threat to Germanness. Hatred of the United States is what binds the right nationalists and defectors from the left who make up the movement. But above all, whether the topic is World War II or current immigration, the new right

---

[1]Heiner Geissler, *Der Irrweg des Nationalismus*, Weinhem: Beltz Athenäum, 1995, p. 9.

seeks to rehabilitate German nationalism by seizing on communist and leftist excesses to elide Germany's own misdeeds.

1968 AND ALL THAT

THE NEW RIGHT calls itself the generation of 1989, and its main foe is the leftist generation of 1968. The '89ers do not seek to become a mass movement. They hope to emulate the tactics of the '68 generation, which "marched through the institutions," as the '60s phrase had it, to win influence in newspapers and magazines like *Die Zeit* and *Der Spiegel*, in think tanks, and in the SPD. Such figures as Rainer Zitelmann,

Rainer Zitelmann

an editor at the conservative newspaper *Die Welt*, accuse the '68 generation led by left-wingers including the philosopher Jürgen Habermas, the novelist Günter Grass, and the historian Hans-Ulrich Wehler of having infiltrated the media and universities where they wield a "fascism cudgel," enforcing a moralistic and "politically correct" version of history that emphasizes the uniqueness of Nazi crimes so as to suppress German national pride. The stranglehold this self-accusatory history has on Germans, they say, makes it almost heretical to attack the Maastricht Treaty on European Union or the influx of immigrants. In a kind of rhetorical jujitsu, they depict themselves as revolutionaries seeking to overthrow a "totalitarian" society ruthlessly run by an ossified '68 generation.

Ultimately, the struggle between the '68ers and '89ers might be dubbed one between the antifascists and the anti-antifascists. Both define the past in terms of the present. Antifascists see the Bonn republic as a vibrant liberal democracy that broke with the *Sonderweg*, or anti-Western German special path that ended in Nazism. The antifascist '68ers have created what is known in Germany as a *Betroffenheitskultur*—a culture of contrition in which every conceivable political issue is viewed through the prism of the Nazi past.

Anti-antifascists will have none of this. In their version of history, the real historical detour was the creation of a westernized Bonn republic that substituted self-flagellation for an assertion of German national interests and honor. Anti-antifascists do not deny the reality of the Holocaust; instead, they seek to depict Nazism in a milder light by portraying Hitler as a social modernizer and harping on the crimes of Stalin. The anti-antifascists argue that the self-effacing Bonn republic that based its identity on antifascism must be replaced by a self-confident Berlin republic that returns to nationalist doctrines respectable before the Nazi regime took power. A "normal" Germany freed of the albatross of the Nazi past will be able to assert its interests like any other nation. With the collapse of the self-proclaimed East German antifascist utopia, the way has been cleared for a return to German nationalism.

ADENAUER'S GERMANY

THE SOURCES of the postwar German right actually lie on the left. The westernized Federal Republic was shaped by two forces: Chancellor Konrad Adenauer and the 1968 generation of student revolutionaries. Adenauer's great accomplishment was breaking with the radical conservatism espoused by such Weimar intellectuals as the Nazi jurist Carl Schmitt and the writer Ernst Jünger to found a new political tradition called West German conservatism. It was the SPD, led by Kurt Schumacher, a survivor of 12 years in Nazi concentration camps, that espoused continuity with the German past. The SPD rejected Adenauer's efforts to anchor Germany in NATO and the European Community in the hope of creating a neutral and unified nation. Schumacher, who memorably described Adenauer as "Chancellor of the Allies," saw Adenauer's policies as betraying German interests—a theme that the new right has revived in returning to the Weimar-era tactic of jockeying between East and West that Adenauer jettisoned.

If Adenauer grounded Germany in the West politically, the successor generation in the SPD led by Willy Brandt completed Germany's cultural westernization. Brandt supported the efforts of the '68 student revolutionaries to break with the stern, patriarchal style of the Adenauer years. The '68 generation confronted the crimes of the Nazi past that their parents had suppressed and produced an overdue cultural revolution. Jürgen Habermas, among others, imported American and European exile social thought into Germany to legitimize a

Ernst Jünger

Kurt Schumacher

break with the established German order. But part of the '68 movement degenerated into the terrorism of the Baader-Meinhof Red Army Faction, and others went on from anti-Nazism to pacifism and anti-Americanism, on the one hand, and to denouncing "consumer terror" on the other. They claimed that the Federal Republic was not a real democracy but, in some ways, a continuation of the Nazi regime. The '68ers consolidated their ideological revolt in the universities, schools, churches, trade unions, and the media. Schoolchildren who refused to attend peace demonstrations were given lower marks, and in 1977 one in five professors reported being attacked in some form—personal violence, classroom disruption—by the radical left.[2] Berlin, which was exempt from the military draft, became a hotbed of left-wing anarchists who took over entire sections of the city. Instead of facing down the new left, Brandt and his éminence grise Egon Bahr adopted it, compounding the mischief. They presided over an SPD and an Ostpolitik that abandoned the idea of reunification and blurred the moral boundaries between democracy and communism.

In the mid-1970s such figures as the philosopher Hermann Lübbe and the historian Michael Stürmer led a neoconservative backlash. In dismissing the idea of a single Germany and embracing permissiveness, argued Stürmer, a gifted historian and later a speechwriter for Chancellor Kohl, the '68ers had left Germany without a sense of pride in its past. When in 1986 the historian Ernst Nolte followed up Stürmer's writings with an essay in the mainstream *Frankfurter Allgemeine Zeitung* entitled "The Past that Will Not Pass Away," the *Historikerstreit*, or historians' dispute, was born. Centered on the uniqueness of the Holocaust, the *Historikerstreit* adumbrated the themes that have preoccupied Germany since 1989. In the essay, Nolte

---

[2]Jeffrey Herf, *War by Other Means: Soviet Power, West German Resistance, and the Battle of the Euromissiles*, New York: Free Press, 1991, pp. 102-103.

depicted Lenin's Red Terror as a dress rehearsal for the Holocaust and the Holocaust itself as a defensive response to "Asiatic terror."

At that time Nolte spoke for a small minority in maintaining that the Holocaust was simply one among a number of horrific historical events. His violation of the taboo in Germany on depreciating the uniqueness of the Final Solution outraged liberal West German sensitivities particularly because he had been on the left in 1963 when his seminal book, *Three Faces of Fascism*, was published. Today Ernst Nolte is nothing less than the *spiritus rector* of the new right.

The passions seething beneath the patina of Nolte's scholarship became manifest when he explained to me, in the beautifully refined German of an older generation, that the nation's identity crisis revealed itself in the way Germany was whipping itself into a lather over the fire-bombings of shelters for Third World refugees seeking asylum. "When someone throws burning material into a house, they don't necessarily want to kill a human being, but could have completely other intentions," he maintained. They might simply be expressing social frustration, just as left-wing anarchists had expressed their dissatisfaction with the state of affairs in the 1960s. Dropping his voice to a whisper, he concluded, "And to characterize it as attempted murder—our justice system has done that—seems highly questionable to me." To Nolte and the new right, the danger is that Germany will be swallowed up in a larger Europe filled with alien races. The United States has inflicted the notion of a multicultural society on Germany—one that is designed to "root out the classes and groups in Germany to whom the responsibility for the First World War and the victory of National Socialism are ascribed."[3]

THE WAR OF MEMORIES

FEW TOPICS bring into relief the tactics of the new right as clearly as the traumatic one of foreign immigration. The rash of neo-Nazi attacks on refugee shelters in the early 1990s delivered a black eye to the Federal Republic's efforts to present a new Germany to the outside world.

---

[3]Ernst Nolte, *Streitpunkte: Heutige und künftige Kontroversen um den Nationalsozialismus*, Berlin: Propyläen, 1993, p. 428.

Although the American media exaggerated the extent of the violence, the response of the Bonn government was tardy and flaccid. In January 1996 the torching of a shelter in Lübeck ripped open the German psyche once again. The fire, which killed ten and injured dozens more, took place on the same day that Israeli President Ezer Weizman addressed the Bundestag as part of the new Holocaust Remembrance Day, which German President Roman Herzog had inaugurated to demonstrate that Germany would continue to mark the liberation of Auschwitz even though its 50th anniversary had passed. The country went into a state of collective shock. Mass demonstrations took place, the mayor of Lübeck called for "civil disobedience," and Herzog announced that his patience was "finally coming to an end." Then came a fresh surprise: police suspicions shifted from the neo-Nazis to a disgruntled resident of the shelter.

Firebombing a house, says historian Ernst Nolte, is not always attempted murder.

There the matter would have rested in the old Federal Republic. But this time the German right went on the offensive. Konrad Adam, a journalist sympathetic to the new right, editorialized in the *Frankfurter Allgemeine* that Germans' rush to condemn themselves as Nazis epitomized the hold of the "guilt mythology." Figures such as former President Richard von Weizsäcker, the paper said, were members of a "moralizing caste" and "emissaries of a culture of contrition." CDU parliamentarian and former West Berlin Interior Minister Heinrich Lummer wrote in the nationalist weekly *Junge Freiheit* (Young freedom) that it was time to start asking, "How often are Germans the victims of foreign assailants?"

In January the Charlottenburg town hall in Berlin afforded me a ringside seat for what one *Die Zeit* editor called "the war of memories." Meeting there, led by the young historian Rainer Zitelmann, was a faction of the FDP seeking to transform the liberal party into a right-nationalist one, as Jörg Haider did with the Austrian Freedom Party in the mid-1980s. Under the charismatic 46-year-old chairman, who has described immigrants as "social parasites" and concentration camps as "punishment camps," the Freedom Party increased its electoral support from about 10 percent in 1986 to 22 percent in 1995. The immediate occasion for the Berlin meeting was the publication of a collection of new right essays entitled *For Freedom*. Echoing Haider, the speakers rose to denounce European monetary union, a multicultural society, and a German obsession with the Nazi past. The most unbuttoned speaker was Klaus Rainer Röhl. Formerly a communist married to a Red Army Faction leader, Röhl now exemplifies the move to the right among many German intellectuals. He fired up the audience of several hundred young Berliners with the news that the "danger comes from the left. We've had enough of this stigmatizing, of this media dictatorship, of this political correctness." After pausing foppishly to finger the pocket watch in the vest of his designer suit, he bellowed, "It is President Herzog who should be apologizing to the inhabitants of Lübeck since everyone presumed that they were Nazis."

Once the meeting ended tumultuously, with the audience hooting down a representative of the mainstream Berlin FDP, we trooped into the beer hall adjoining the meeting room. I sat next to Alexander von Stahl, former attorney general of Germany. After Stahl ordered a round of beers, I asked him about the popular German reaction to Lübeck. "This people is sick! This people is sick!" he erupted. The reaction to Lübeck is incomprehensible, he said, for anyone who is not a German. At the end of the table a young man was explaining how he had taken over FDP meetings in the Spandau and Tempelhof sections of Berlin. "Those boys in Tempelhof are great," a middle-aged woman told me excitedly. "The Germans lie to themselves about their nationhood. These boys are ready to shed their blood for the fatherland." As the evening wound down, I found myself talking to Ansgar Graw, 34, a historian and official at Radio Free Berlin, who ordered a round of schnapps. "In four minutes an Austrian has his birthday at midnight," he said. Glasses clinked to toast Jörg Haider.

THE PAST IS OUR COUNTRY

THE GERMAN new right does not have a politician like Jörg Haider. What it has are intellectuals like Rainer Zitelmann of *Die Welt*, founded by newspaper magnate Axel Springer. Zitelmann is the impresario of the new right. Like Nolte, he has twice had his car firebombed by left-wing anarchists. His notoriety is such that when I attended a Bonn conference on the economy, he had merely to rise to ask a question to set some five hundred attendees whispering furiously. A Maoist in high school, he aims to use the tactics of generational conflict and cultural war on behalf of the right. Zitelmann is an indefatigable publicist who has written a score of books on German history and politics. His Ph.D. dissertation transformed the Führer into a social revolutionary deeply influenced by the American New Deal.

> For most people, argues Karlheinz Weissmann, everyday life in the Third Reich was normal.

Zitelmann's goal is to normalize German nationalism by first normalizing the Nazi past. When I met him outside the Ullstein Building—Springer built it so that it would tower over the Berlin Wall during the Cold War—Zitelmann brandished an article from Germany's biggest tabloid, *Bild Zeitung*. "Here's an article on the average German," he said. He began reciting the statistics on weight, height, and hobbies, declaring triumphantly after each, "That's me!" At lunch, Zitelmann painted a dire portrait of Germany. Daily politics, he explained, should no longer be determined by the memory of National Socialism. What is popularly known as a *Schlussstrich*, a line under the past, did not need to be drawn. Rather, "a line has to be drawn against this permanent self-flagellation and self-hatred, which produces neo-Nazis in the end. We must become normal." According to Zitelmann, the '68 generation has prevented this from occurring: "The ideology of the '68ers has settled like fine dust . . . into every nook and cranny of society."[4] Zitelmann was previously an editor at the mainstream Ullstein publishing house, where he presided over the publication of a seemingly endless stream of books by young German historians that make for eyebrow-raising reading.

The most vivid example so far of how the new right would palliate the Nazi past is *The Way Into the Abyss*. Because it was published in 1995 as part of the distinguished Propyläen German history series, it created a furor. For weeks the pages of German newspapers were filled with analyses and denunciations of the book. Its author, Karlheinz Weissmann, a high school teacher in Göttingen, had previously written

---

[4]Rainer Zitelmann, *Wohin treibt unsere Republik?* Frankfurt am Main: Ullstein, 1995, p. 37.

a book called *Recall Into History* that attacked both the Soviet Union and the United States for dismembering Germany after World War II. *The Way Into the Abyss* builds on that "insight."

The theme of the book is that in neither its intentions nor its actions did Nazi Germany differ from its enemies. In his introduction, Weissmann explains that a moralistic '68 generation has refused to allow historians to depict the Nazi era as it was actually experienced by the German people. After the demise of communism and with the reunification of Germany, the moment has arrived for a demystification of Nazism and a "normalization of historical understanding." While Weissmann never shrinks from depicting the horrors of the concentration camps, he devotes as much space to discussing sports in the Third Reich as he does to the murder of Jews. The constant emphasis is on how everyday life in Germany remained unaltered under the Nazis: the population outside the camps supposedly had full access to foreign newspapers, went dancing, and listened to the radio. Hitler's rise to power was the result of "completely comprehensible political decisions." The entire Nazi era is described in coldly neutral terms, the conclusion being that since some seven million Germans died in World War II, "no people had done so much penance for the deeds that it carried out, or that were carried out in its name."

When I spoke with Weissmann, he went still further. Sherman in Atlanta and the British in South Africa, he said, had engaged in wartime massacres. The Germans were no exception. Anyway, it was not so much ordinary Germans who were at fault during World War II as the Allies. Their failure to aid the German resistance during the July 20, 1944, plot against Hitler, he explained, "completely discredits them." The "Habermas faction" had propagated a version of history that shamed Germans into thinking that they now must accept foreigners and hand out welfare benefits. But economic pressures, coupled with a more objective history, were changing things. No longer would Germans be tyrannized into putting up with an American version of a multicultural society. They would return to their traditional values. "It's all going much more quickly than people realize," he crowed.

For Weissmann's new right followers, his book has become a sacred text. Criticism of it is dismissed as a new instance of political correctness. One young historian defended the book to me as we ate dinner in a steak house; waving his knife in the air, he complained, "The German left always accuses us of counting numbers. But they count how many pages Weissmann writes about the Holocaust. If German historians could determine that we killed eight rather than six million Jews, they would jump for joy."

GERMANY AND THE WEST

THE NEW RIGHT is shot through with self-pity. The ambition of Weissmann, Zitelmann, and others is to construct a lachrymose history in which Germans are victims of the United States as much as of the Soviet Union. This became obvious in the first programmatic statement of the new right, *Ties to the West*. A volume of essays edited by Zitelmann, Weissmann, and Michael Grossheim, its appearance in 1993 created something of a sensation in Germany. In the introduction, the editors coyly stated that they were posing questions, not advocating that Germany abandon NATO and the European Union. They even interspersed a few Atlanticist contributors, but it was crystal clear that the new right was less anti-Eastern than anti-Western.

The editors boasted that only a "younger generation" freed of the burdens of the past that bedeviled both conservative Atlanticists and liberal '68ers could objectively assess the drawbacks as well as the benefits of Germany's Western alliance. They envisioned a Germany that would return to old-fashioned geopolitics to maneuver, as it had in the past, between East and West. In a play on Joseph Goebbels' famous 1943 speech in the Berlin Sportpalast calling for "total war," the editors bemoaned the "utopia of a *Totalwestintegration*," or integration with the West that has assumed a totalitarian character.

Reunification, according to the book, provides a second chance. Jochen Thies, a former assistant to Helmut Schmidt, observed that "in terms of power politics the Federal Republic finds itself . . . in a cloaked, half-hegemonic position like the Bismarckian Reich of 1871 or the Weimar Republic in 1922 after the conclusion of the Rapallo pact [which established relations with the Soviet Union]." Yet in his view, the Bonn political elite remains an emasculated one that cannot summon up the courage to exploit new possibilities.

Instead, traumatized by the crimes of the Nazi past, it is bent on handing over sovereignty to the European Union.

At the core of the book is the notion that despite Auschwitz, Germany must recognize that it is once again a great power in the middle of Europe. "One precondition is coming to terms with history, whose dark sides cannot be forgotten, but which also cannot determine daily politics," writes Ansgar Graw. There is nothing particularly objectionable about this statement, but it is part of a pattern of equivocation that employs what might be called the "but" technique. Auschwitz was a terrible event, but . . .

The barely suppressed anger that underlay the book spilled over in spectacular fashion in an advertisement signed by several hundred prominent Germans in an April 1995 issue of *Frankfurter Allgemeine*. Appearing on the 50th anniversary of the end of the Second World War, the ad, drafted by Zitelmann, Weissmann, and Heimo Schwilk, stated that the liberal German media's "one-sided" focus on the German surrender as an act of liberation from the Nazi dictatorship obscured the fact that May 8, 1945, was the "beginning of the expulsion, terror, and new oppression in the East and the division of our nation." Insidiously employing the traditional language of German approaches to the history of Nazism, it concluded that "a conception of history that is silent, represses or relativizes these truths cannot serve as the foundation of the self-understanding of a self-confident nation, something we Germans must become within the family of European peoples if we are to prevent similar catastrophes from occurring in the future." Among those attacking the advertisement were Rita Süssmuth, the CDU president of the Bundestag, and Ignatz Bubis, the leader of the Central Council of Jews in Germany, the country's principal Jewish cultural and religious organization. In response, Zitelmann, Weissmann, and Schwilk ran a second advertisement in the *Frankfurter Allgemeine* denouncing the "opinion terror of political correctness." The advertisements caused such a furor because they shifted the emphasis from German culpability for World War II to what Germany suffered at the hands of the Red Army, ending up with the Germans as the real victims of the war.

> Remembrance of the Holocaust is equated with leftist oppression.

The ambiguous character of the new right, its skillful maneuvering in what is called in Germany the "gray zone" between conservatism and the radical right, exasperates the German liberal media. Members of the new right claim that they are simply adding a long-suppressed voice to the political spectrum, and that they are only saying Germany needs to rethink its relationship to Europe and the United States. No new right outlet strives harder to project a democratic image than the newspaper *Young Freedom.*

As its spiffy offices attest, *Young Freedom* has strong financial backing from German industrialists. It is attractively designed and publishes a variety of authors writing on everything from foreign policy to rock music. To buttress its democratic credentials, it tries particularly hard to give space to authors on the nationalist left. Its editorials praise Ignatz Bubis' denunciations of anarchists. ("They want to co-opt me," Bubis told me.) The paper, which recently celebrated its tenth anniversary, is a prime target of leftist anarchists, who have firebombed its printing plant in Weimar. Kiosks in Berlin that carry it have received similar treatment. Thus the new right can depict the left, with a grain of truth, as the real repository of authoritarian German tendencies.

With his close-cropped brown hair, jeans, and windbreaker, the 29-year-old editor in chief, Dieter Stein, could pass for an American college student. But Stein, who founded *Young Freedom* while a high school student in Freiburg, has followed in the footsteps of his father, a revisionist military historian. He and his publication have close ties to Jörg Haider and the Austrian Freedom Party; one of Haider's lieutenants sits on the board of the paper. For Stein, as for most other members of the new right, it is German subservience to the United States that provokes ire. The West Germans, he told me, are dishonest. They wish to appear harmless to foreigners. They have a despicable bearing. They lie about their own nationality. East Germans, by contrast, did not suffer from these hang-ups. Whereas the Soviets "chopped off Nazi heads in Leipzig and then stopped," Stein explained, the Americans put the entire nation under "suspicion." West Germans were deprived of their Germanness. "Every West German had to fill out a questionnaire on their activities during World War II," sputtered Stein. "Everyone had to lie."

THE SELF-CONFIDENT NATION

A PERSISTENT theme of the new right is that Germany must become not only normal, but self-confident. New right history holds that the pliant political class installed by the Western allies after 1945 was replaced by an even more "degenerate" and self-loathing one in 1968. The '68ers have created a politically correct version of history that they enforce through the media with totalitarian efficiency. The idea is that the Bonn republic is as illegitimate as the Weimar Republic or the German Democratic Republic.

GERMAN INFORMATION CENTER

Botho Strauss

The '68ers who have defected to the new right and former East Germans disillusioned with the Federal Republic enunciate these themes most vociferously. One such defector is Botho Strauss, a poet and Germany's leading playwright, winner of the Georg Büchner Prize, the nation's most prestigious literary award. In 1993 Strauss sent shock waves through intellectual and political circles with an essay in *Der Spiegel* entitled "The Swelling Song of the Billy Goat"—the goat being the symbol of the new right in France and Germany. The "Strauss controversy," as it became known, succeeded the *Historikerstreit*. Strauss defended the neo-Nazis as the inevitable product of a deformed '68 generation and attacked the "sinister aeries of the Enlightenment." The Germans, Strauss lamented, had become a deracinated people. They had exchanged a sense of nationhood for rampant consumerism. The neo-Nazis understand that it is necessary to protect German ethnicity, but "that a people wishes to assert its legal customs against another and is prepared to sacrifice blood we no longer understand, and, in our liberal-libertarian self-delusion, view as false and damnable." Strauss concluded by asking whence the next Führer.

Strauss' defection sent the '68ers into a frenzy. For more than a year German papers and magazines were filled with discussions of Strauss and his polemic. "Botho Strauss is a dangerous madman. . . . One had hoped that this kind of farrago had been washed away by the blood-bath of 1945," former SPD General Secretary Peter Glotz wrote. Strauss allowed his essay to be used as the lead in a new right manifesto, *The Self-Confident Nation*. Like *Ties to the West,* it consisted of essays by intellectuals and journalists and provided further evidence of the extent to which the new right is made up of former leftists. One contributor, the editor Ulrich Schacht, was born in a women's prison in the German Democratic Republic and later extricated from the east by Willy Brandt. A noted poet, Schacht first joined the SPD, then grew disgusted with its close relations with the regime in East Berlin. Other contributors to the volume include Brigitte Seebacher-Brandt and Wolfgang Templin, a leader of the pro-democracy citizens movement in the GDR.

Like Strauss, these writers view the westernized Bonn republic and the liberal media with contempt. For them Bonn was a deviation from the true course of German history, an excrescence to be replaced by a self-confident Berlin republic. "The time has disappeared, the time from which sorrow, shame, and timorousness arose," wrote Seebacher-Brandt. "It does not exist, and it never has existed—the 'Bonn republic.'" Klaus Rainer Röhl portrays the Bonn political class as quislings who sold out to the United States. Röhl maintains that Jewish emigrants such as the philosopher Theodor Adorno carried out these reeducation efforts. The message is clear.

Underlying this contempt for the Bonn republic is fury at the failure of Willy Brandt's 1968 *Enkel,* or grandchildren, in the SPD to embrace reunification in 1989. In her book *The Left and Unity,* for instance, Seebacher-Brandt excoriated the antipathy toward the German nation among the '68ers: reunification revealed that the "soul of the people" and its "dreams, instincts, and moods" run far "deeper than a superficial left-wing rationality" can comprehend. Tilman Fichter, chief educator at the SPD party school in Bonn, echoes Seebacher-Brandt. In his book *The SPD and the Nation,* Fichter attacks his own '68 generation for suppressing the theme of "national identity" and clinging to the Bonn republic. He calls for a "modern social-democratic understanding of the fatherland." Among former East Germans, the hatred of the westernized Federal Republic is even more pronounced: Frank Castorf, a leading theater director in East Germany, revealed his sympathies for "fascist ideas" in an interview with *Junge Welt.*

While we waited for the subway at the cavernous Friedrichstrasse station, I asked Jens Falk, a former East German and an editor at *Young*

Freedom, about life in the GDR. "Some things were better," he replied. "Things were regulated." The strapping six-footer pointed at an iron catwalk and laughed. "I probably would be up there patrolling the border. Today no one cares about anybody." He paused. "If I beat you to a pulp here," he said, "no one would lift a finger. There was a feeling of solidarity in the GDR, just as there was in the Third Reich." I looked curious. Was there such a feeling of solidarity? Jens snorted. "Of course, just look at the Wehrmacht, at what kind of men we had there."

WILL IDEAS HAVE CONSEQUENCES?

THE EXTENT to which these anti-Western ressentiments gussied up in the language of the new right have penetrated the mainstream is the concern of Heiner Geissler and other Atlanticists in the CDU. Geissler remains a CDU parliamentarian and in *The Wrong Path of Nationalism* warns against a recrudescence of new right doctrines. The 36-year-old Friedbert Pflüger, who studied at Harvard and served as an assistant to former President Weizsäcker, is a member of the Bundestag and a CDU spokesman for disarmament. In 1994 Pflüger wrote a book warning against the inroads the new right was making into traditional conservatism. He called it *Germany Is Drifting.*

Pflüger believes that his warnings helped take some of the wind out of the sails of the new right. When I met him in the spacious, airy new quarters of the Bundestag in Bonn, which seemed to epitomize the liberal spirit of postwar Germany, it was hard to imagine that Germany could drift anywhere. But Pflüger noted that a change has taken place in the political landscape. "In the 1970s," he explained, "he who was for the West and NATO was on the right. Today in the *Frankfurter Allgemeine* there are people who say, 'Let's not make an ideology out of the West.'"

The *Frankfurter Allgemeine,* Germany's most distinguished newspaper, plays a key role for the new right. The paper is as ambiguous in its approach to the new right as the movement is about its own intentions. Writers such as Zitelmann and Weissmann sometimes write for it. One of the paper's editorial writers, Eckard Fuhr, contends, "The almost libidinous attachment to the guilty history of Germany . . . directs itself negatively against anyone who views 'ties to the

West' as a simple and sensible fact, not as the basis for a new thera-peutic national cult. . . . There is no reason to carry 'the West' around like a monstrosity."[5]

Perhaps the most important figure at the paper is Frank Schirrmacher, the editor of its feuilleton section. The 40-year-old Schirrmacher is the cultural doyen of Germany. A thoughtful intellectual whose pol-itics are those of Chancellor Kohl, Schirrmacher is no friend of Zitelmann and Co., but, as he put it, "if they write something we like, we'll print it." But as our talk stretched into three hours, it took on an

DPA/PHOTOREPORTERS

Frank Schirrmacher

increasingly metaphysical cast, and it became clear that a yearning for an unbroken German tra-dition is scarcely confined to the fringes of the new right. Schirrmacher too seemed to represent a new, younger generation in Germany, impatient with the verities of the Cold War.

Germany, Schirrmacher told me, exists "in a situation where it is actually the hegemonic power of Europe. The whole political scene does nothing else but say that we aren't. Even though we are." Schirrmacher had a point. The refusal of the Bonn political class to face up to Germany's new posi-tion was creating an opening for the new right. The strategy of the new right, he pointed out, was to usurp traditions, and it was first off the mark in "thematizing" the question of a united Germany's position in Europe. Schirrmacher's hope, as he expressed it, is that Germans will return to the texts of such Weimar oracles as Carl Schmitt and Ernst Jünger and "confront" them. Germans need to think in terms of power again as they did in the past, he argued. Schmitt's work on geopolitics, *Land and Sea,* was the "greatest literature." "There was the age-old dream of a fusion between the Roman-Spanish world and the Slavic-German world," he said, "and I could imagine that a new cultural flowering might emerge."

This is the sort of language that troubles Ignatz Bubis and other op-ponents of the new right. Bubis' affability, tolerance, and directness have made him one of the most popular figures in Germany. His refusal to

---

[5] *Franfurter Allgemeine Zeitung,* "Westen, was sonst?" June 8, 1994, p. 1.

exaggerate the extent of neo-Nazism and his defense of Jews who have chosen to remain in Germany have earned him laurels across the political spectrum. A few weeks before our interview, Bubis was shouted down as, of all things, a Nazi by left-wing anarchists at the University of Hamburg when he admonished students not to assume that neo-Nazis had firebombed the shelter in Lübeck. Yet he fears the right more than the left. To Bubis, the new right is a growing menace that must be confronted. "I see it as a real danger, a very real danger," he said. Bubis stressed the "elegant manner in which they proceed. They do it on an intellectual level." In his view, the danger is a relativization of the Nazi past and a trend toward populism in the major parties. In both the CDU and FDP, he noted, there are "elements that would be happy to make a coalition with new right figures."

Some on the left experience a cathartic bliss in denouncing Germany.

Nevertheless, the criticisms of Bubis, Pflüger, and others mean that an unsavory whiff still clings to the new right. The political future of the movement is murky. For all his ingenuity when it comes to garnering publicity, Zitelmann will not be able to take over the FDP at the federal level. The attempt of Manfred Brunner, the former leader of the Bavarian FDP, to create a new citizens party opposed to European monetary union flopped. The SPD's attempt to campaign on anti-Europe themes in state elections in Baden-Württemberg was no more successful. The CDU, for now, remains fixed on the pro-Europe politics of Chancellor Kohl. Officials at the federal chancellery say that what is most disturbing are the "diffuse anti-Western sentiments in the East."

To think of the new right as a new mass party, however, is a mistake. The new right is no cause for panic. It can be seen as a natural development in Germany after 1989. Perhaps the Germans need to rouse rather than suppress the demon of nationalism in order to exorcise it. Nor does the new right's contention that a moralistic left-wing media dominates the German cultural landscape miss the mark. There is an excessive preoccupation with the Holocaust in Germany, which the left, a little unwittingly, exploits for present political purposes. Some Germans experience a kind of cathartic bliss in denouncing themselves and their nationality.

But the new right represents the other extreme. It too exploits the Holocaust—although in a more pernicious fashion—by scanting its importance. Its most likely accomplishment will be to push the boundaries of what is considered permissible in German political discourse. The rapidity with which new right themes are being taken up by members of the CDU's youth movement, for example, is a source of concern to party officials of the Konrad Adenauer Foundation, the CDU's leadership organization. The FDP is already moving toward a more austere economic program, and the issue of foreigners' rights looms large. Kohl's likely successor, Wolfgang Schäuble, indulges in new right rhetoric, asserting that Germans gain their identity "not from commitment to an idea, but from belonging to a particular nation, a *Volk*." He has written about returning to the "emotional, connective power of the nation."[6]

"What do these revisionists really want, these shrewd, sturdy young lads that one sees everywhere," asks the journalist Harald Martenstein in the February 11 *Der Tagesspiegel*, based in Berlin. For the moment, they seem to want a rethinking. Robert von Rimscha, a young editor and coauthor of a new book, *'Political Correctness' in Germany*, gave me an answer. "In the next 20 to 30 years," he cheerfully proclaimed, "there will be a flood of revisionist books. I am sure of it."

In February 1996 *Der Spiegel* ran a cover story on the war on the eastern front written by its publisher, Rudolf Augstein. One of the revisionist books Augstein reviewed was *Stalin's War of Annihilation*. Written by Joachim Hoffmann, a former director of the military history research division of the Bundeswehr, the book claimed that Stalin, not Hitler, was responsible for World War II. A few weeks earlier *Young Freedom* had gone into ecstasies over the book. The *Der Spiegel* cover showed Hitler squaring off against Stalin. The article's title asked, "Aggressor Hitler, Aggressor Stalin?" *Spiegel* was hardly endorsing the book, but a new soft revisionism has begun putting question marks after what were once certainties.✿

---

[6]Wolfgang Schäuble, *Und der Zukunft zugewandt*, Berlin: Siedler, 1994.

Responses

Mr. Heilbrunn's Planet

On Which the Germans Are Back

Josef Joffe et al.

Jacob Heilbrunn's account of the rising New Right in Germany reminds you of those prefab tales that America's European detractors like to serve up to the choir back home after a quick sweep through the country ("Germany's New Right," November/December 1996). Grab a few income statistics purporting to show that the rich are getting richer while the poor, what else, are getting poorer; visit a public school in the Bronx and conclude that nobody can read but everybody packs a piece; turn a pile of garbage into a towering symbol of urban decay; use a panhandler on 42nd and 8th as Exhibit A for America's mounting homeless crisis; finally, add some quotes from a leftish U.S. columnist inveighing against bigotry and injustice, and what do you get? A cheap indictment of the United States that "proves" what readers in your target audience have always "known": the United

States is barbaric. Pandering to prejudices, such a piece will cast as much light on America's central realities as a trip to the garbage dump will teach people about a country's museums, colleges, literature, and economic system.

The events and names Heilbrunn uses are part of a tale that just might have had a sliver of reportorial credibility three years ago. But to a reader who knows a bit about Germany, these 19 pages about Rainer Zitelmann, Botho Strauss, or the *Historikerstreit* now seem like 9,000 words on the 1993 Kentucky Derby. If you are an aficionado, you may still remember a few of the losing horses, but reading about them today as if they were the grandsons of Secretariat leaves you scratching your head.

What does Heilbrunn want us to believe about post-reunification Germany? "A change is taking place in

JOSEF JOFFE is Editorial Page Editor and a columnist at *Süddeutsche Zeitung* and an associate at Harvard's Olin Institute for Strategic Studies.

[152]

Germany, not at the political but at the intellectual level . . . A profound move to the right has been taking place among Germany's best-known novelists . . . The German new right consists not of skinheads in jackboots but journalists, novelists, professors, and young lawyers . . . Underlying new right positions is a deep hatred of the westernization of Germany under the influence of the United States," and so forth. Naturally, this is perfect fodder for those who will always worry about Germany. Never mind that "Greater Germany," seven years after reunification, remains the Federal Republic writ large: placid, sluggishly centrist even in the face of Depression-level unemployment; embodied in all its normality by the heavy, slightly oafish figure of Helmut Kohl, chancellor since 1982; a state that instead of throwing its weight around keeps insisting on *more* European integration while walking very softly when it comes to carrying the stick of military power in places like Bosnia. In short, Germany is boring. But since so many suspect it, there must be another, the *real,* Germany hiding behind this implausibly friendly giant—a country secretly polishing ye olde jackboots, dreaming of lost glory and new power, and ready to claim its No. 1 position loudly and insistently, with an Erich von Stroheim accent, of course.

SMALL FRY

Enter Heilbrunn. Whom does he trundle out to prove or insinuate the more enticing story? Let us take his favorite in the rogues' gallery of the German neo-right, a certain Herr Rainer Zitelmann. "The German new right," Heilbrunn writes, "does not have a politician like [the rightist Austrian populist] Jörg Haider. What it has are intellectuals like Rainer Zitelmann of *Die Welt,* founded by newspaper magnate Axel Springer. Zitelmann is the impresario of the new right."

What Heilbrunn either does not know or fails to tell us is that Mr. Big, which he never was, is strictly yesterday. In 1993, when Heilbrunn apparently conducted, and concluded, much of his research—you never quite know when the conversations he quotes took place—Zitelmann might have *looked* like an "impresario." He was head of *Die Welt's* weekend culture section, which he purposely and insistently used as a platform for neo-rightist lore—his own stuff and that of his comrades in the Fatherland-saving business. Too bad for the American reader that Heilbrunn does not bring the story up to date. For, alas, Zitelmann, the master intellectual, proved too much even for the editorial staff of the right-of-center daily. After 50 editors signed a petition against the paper's "slide to the right" under Zitelmann, the "impresario" was dismissed from his editorial position.[1]

---

[1] For those who remember *Die Welt* as Germany's *New York Times* of the 1950s and 1960s, it is worth noting that this moderately right-of-center daily, a loss-maker for 20 years, is now the least important of Germany's quality papers, with a circulation less than half that of the liberal *Süddeutsche Zeitung* and the conservative *Frankfurter Allgemeine Zeitung.* On the petition, see "Revolte gegen Rechtsausleger," *Süddeutsche Zeitung,* March 12, 1994, p. 17. On Zitelmann's dismissal, see "'Geistige Welt' sucht nach einem neuen Chef," *Süddeutsche Zeitung,* May 6, 1994, p. 13.

Kulinarische Reise durch deutsche Lande

GERMAN EMBASSY

Kohl's worldview: his 1996 cookbook

In due time, Manfred Geist, the editor in chief who had brought Zitelmann to *Die Welt*, was also relieved and replaced by a centrist, Thomas Löffelholz. Heilbrunn's "impresario" of the new right was not fired outright, which is very hard to do under German labor law, but shunted into a staff position; when last heard from, he was apparently selling insurance on the side.[2] So much for the multiplying tentacles of the new right.

Nor does the story end here. Like a metastasizing cancer, Heilbrunn wants us to believe, Zitelmann allegedly used his position in the media business to implant the right authors and their books into Germany's collective consciousness. Before his disastrous move to *Die Welt*, Zitelmann was an editor at Ullstein

Verlag, a sterling name that goes back to the Jewish publishing family of the Weimar Republic. But in another misreading, Heilbrunn calls Ullstein Publishing at the time "mainstream"—which is correct, if you are willing to call *The Washington Times* mainstream, too.

What Heilbrunn again either does not know or does not tell, lest it ruin his indictment, is that Ullstein was then co-owned by Herbert Fleissner, a rightist-conservative Sudeten German publisher who, in 1985, had fused his Langen-Müller with Springer's Ullstein in a joint holding called Ullstein-Langen-Müller Verlag. Deliberately testing the waters after reunification in 1990, Fleissner had allowed Zitelmann and his henchmen to publish a series of neo-nationalist, revisionist, and anti-left books—as Fleissner had in 1981 published the glorification of the Waffen ss by memoir-writing "paleorightist" Franz Schonhüber, who would later become mini-führer of the tiny right-wing Republikaner party. Here, in the middle of this budding *trahison de clercs*, we also find Karlheinz Weissmann, another central figure in Heilbrunn's panopticon of would-be Alfred Rosenbergs and Joseph Goebbelses, "young German historians" producing "a seemingly endless stream of books . . . that make for eyebrow-raising reading."

With Zitelmann's active connivance, Weissmann was indeed invited to write a book on the Nazi period for the distinguished Propyläen German History series (Propyläen, please note, had also been acquired by Fleissner in the Ullstein deal). The main thrust of the book is, as

---

[2] "Keine Sorge, Rainer Zitelmann!" *Die Woche*, August 9, 1996, p. 40.

[154]   FOREIGN AFFAIRS · *Volume 76 No. 2*

170

Heilbrunn correctly points out, that "in neither its intentions nor its actions did Nazi Germany differ from its enemies." Moreover, Weissmann declared that it was high time to "demystify Nazism" and to reach a "normalization" of historical understanding—a German code word for finally burying the Nazi past. Naturally, this raised a storm of indignation in the press and among historians, but that was not the main moral of the tale.

The real point, again, one that Heilbrunn ignores lest it ruin his case, was the German reaction to the "re-reeducation" shenanigans of Zitelmann, Weissmann, et al. If this was a cancer, the German body politic soon unleashed powerful antibodies. In this case, the soi-disant right-wing Axel Springer Verlag, undoubtedly irked by the nasty publicity, took back both Ullstein and Propyläen from Fleissner, effective January 1, 1996, dissolving the joint holding. A few months later, the Weissmann volume, which, according to Heilbrunn, had become a "sacred text" to the author's "new right followers," was expelled from Propyläen's backlist.

STILL SELF-FLAGELLATING

So much for the attempt of the Zitelmanns to take over Germany. Nor does any of the other evidence Heilbrunn marshals buttress his indictment—although the Zitelmann episode is his most grievous misreading of reality. He thinks that a new periodical, *Die junge Freiheit* (Young freedom), is the latter-day yuppie equivalent of *Das Reich*, the journal of the ss intelligentsia. According to Heilbrunn, the magazine has "strong financial backing from German industrialists." This will probably be news to its publishers and editors since *Die junge Freiheit*, in spite of its hip packaging of the neo-rightist message, is on the verge of bankruptcy. It is a bad bet to make it through 1997.

Let us move from these dreary details to the general point. It will take a lot more to budge present-day Germany from its sluggish centrist position than the Zitelmanns and *Young Freedom* fighters. Just look at the reception that greeted Harvard scholar Daniel Goldhagen in Germany last year. For 700 pages in the German translation of his book, *Hitler's Willing Executioners*, Goldhagen told the Germans, in so many words, that the Holocaust could only have happened in Germany because they were the way they were—infected, alone among nations, by the bacillus of "eliminationist anti-Semitism," which turned annihilationist when the time was right. If Heilbrunn were even half right, 80 million Germans should have risen in violent protest against the impudent American Jew who would once more stick them with the notorious "German national character" thesis. Actually, much of the historical profession and many pundits tried to kill *Hitler's Willing Executioners* as early as April—months before the translation would arrive on the German market in August. The critics branded it as "unoriginal," "sensationalist," "old hat"—in short, "don't read."

But when Goldhagen showed up in Germany in September, his book promotion tour turned into a "triumphal procession," as the weekly *Die Zeit* called it.[3]

---

[3] I have written a more thorough discussion of the book's German reception, "Goldhagen in Germany," *The New York Review of Books*, November 28, 1996.

People came to blows over tickets to the panel discussions in which Goldhagen participated; the last one, in Munich, had to be moved from a medium-sized theater to the 2,500-seat hall where the Philharmonic performs. By Christmas, 165,000 copies had been sold—more than in the United States, a market over three times as large.

THE BORING TRUTH

Let's restate the basic point. Apart from not doing his homework, Heilbrunn is so utterly wrong on Germany because the old—and admittedly very compelling—theories on Germany no longer work. Germany, that enigmatic and brooding Bismarckian construction that belonged to neither East nor West, that tottering powerhouse that went off on a pathological course at the beginning of the twentieth century, that Germany is no more. Germany is now of and in the West, with a political system more liberal than France's and more decentralized than Britain's. It is ultra-stable and yet more capable of reform than France, Spain, or Italy. It is normal, and it is boring. And thank God for that.

To convict on Heilbrunn's indictment, a very different set of exhibits would have to be brought into court. First, where in Germany is a significant right-wing party—like Haider's Free Democrats or Le Pen's National Front? It does not exist. The cynically misnamed Republikaners have been languishing for years around the two percent mark—despite relentlessly rising unemployment.

Second, who is trying to make hay of Germany's alleged oppression by sinister forces that would exploit the country's Nazi past? Every once in a while, some politician pops up from this or that part of the legitimate party spectrum and tries to raise a flag against Brussels or the euro. The message from the voters, over and over again, is this: Neo-nationalism does not pay, no matter how skeptical we are about the monetary union or the European Union's banana regulations.

Third, where is the soil on which such parties and politicos might flourish? That is the most important usual suspect who cannot be rounded up. The pied pipers' tunes of the 1920s and 1930s simply do not resonate in modern Germany because the underlying reality, the humiliation of 1919, is missing. How can anybody say "Brussels" and mean "Versailles" when European integration is the very framework of Germany's legitimacy and influence? How could anybody invoke "discrimination," as after 1919, when the world outside does not try to hold down German military power but positively *begs* Bonn to contribute forces for duty in Somalia, Bosnia, Zaire . . . How could anybody even begin to preach national reassertion in a world where 30 percent of Germany's GDP goes into exports and two-thirds of those go to the European Union?

The politics of resentment and nationalism does not work in a society that has come away with a powerful double lesson from the catastrophe of 1914-1945 and the benign 50 years that followed. When Germany went it alone, it reaped ever worse disaster; when Germany voluntarily accepted the ties of community and integration, it flourished beyond belief.

PANGS OF DOUBT

To his credit, Heilbrunn does not completely evade this rather basic insight. At the end of his piece, he writes: "To think of the new right as a new mass party, however, is a mistake. The new right is no cause for panic." But why does he spend the preceding 18 pages stoking panic with such insubstantial kindling? Why does he try to build an indictment on the basis of evidence that is so woefully out of date? If he had published this article as a piece of reportage in *The New Republic* in, say, 1993, it would still have been off the mark, but not as wildly errant as it was in late 1996.

An essay like Heilbrunn's should set off alarm bells in any editorial office. The story tries to reverse established wisdom on the basis of arbitrary, shoddy, indeed bizarre evidence (Who is Mr. Zitelmann?) that cannot quite be nailed down in time and space. Nor does the story discuss, let alone try to disprove, contrary evidence; instead it ignores the mountain in favor of the ugly little molehill. Yes, Germany could turn neo-nationalist and revisionist, but then Bill Clinton could take a vow of chastity, and Newt Gingrich could demand a 30 percent increase in welfare spending. In each case, the supporting evidence should, at a minimum, be equal to the enormity of the claim.

Apples and Oranges
MARK LILLA

By focusing his attention on books like *Die selbstbewußte Nation*, newspapers like *Junge Freiheit*, editors like Rainer Zitelmann, and writers like Botho Strauss, Heilbrunn has performed a real service for his English-speaking readers. But perhaps in an attempt to inflate the new right's influence, he has misled his readers—and

perhaps himself—by associating the movement's leaders with a number of other thinkers and writers who not only have nothing to do with the new right but actually represent an alternative to it.

Heilbrunn correctly links nationalist mystagogues like the dramatist Strauss to film director Hans Jürgen Syberberg and historian Ernst Nolte. But what conceivable connection can there be between these figures and writers like Hans Magnus Enzensberger and Martin Walser, let alone philosopher Hermann Lübbe, journalist Frank Schirrmacher, and—most absurd of all—the late social democratic politician Kurt Schumacher?

The first group represents a very old and deeply anti-Western element of German culture that was revived by the '68 left and is now being manipulated by the right. But the second group is highly critical of this old German mysticism, in whatever contemporary form it might take. Its members have made their peace (some later than others) with the idea of the German nation, not out of romantic inspiration but out of the sober realization that national feelings are a fact of political life, however unpleasant, and must be recognized if they are to be kept in check. None are anti-American.

Simply put, these two groups represent different historical, political, and—this being Germany—moral phenomena. To insist on distinguishing them is not to split hairs; it is absolutely essential to understanding the real political stakes in Germany's current intellectual debates.

MARK LILLA *is an Associate Professor of Politics at New York University.*

Kohl's Right

MICHAEL MERTES

Heilbrunn's task was hardly simple. Describing the new right is like grabbing a wet bar of soap—and a shrinking one at that. Never large to begin with, the movement's inner circle seems to have collapsed since its zenith in 1995. Although I agree with many of Heilbrunn's claims about the new right, he is wrong to state—or even insinuate—that Brigitte Seebacher-Brandt, Michael Wolffsohn, and Frank Schirrmacher are among its ranks.

Those who form the new right's inner circle are strongly opposed to Helmut Kohl's pro-Western foreign policy. In his 14 years in office, Kohl has made it clear that he stands for the irrevocable integration of the Federal Republic into the European-Atlantic community of nations. His firm commitment to European Monetary Union (EMU) is but the most recent example of his decidedly antinationalistic approach.

The problem facing the true core of the new right is that they lack everything required for political success: attractive personalities, a minimum of team spirit, a coherent party program, an effective party organization, and—last but certainly not least—voters. As far as I know, Manfred Brunner is the only true member of the new right ever to run for parliamentary office, and he failed miserably; running for the European Parliament as the leader of a party that fought, on nationalist grounds, against the imminent "abolition of the deutsche mark by the Euro," Brunner received only 1.1 percent of the vote—hardly impressive.

Heilbrunn points to such facts with unmistakable clarity. Whatever his survey's shortcomings, it should not be interpreted as an argument that the second German Republic—as so often alleged in past years and decades—is preparing for the coming of the Fourth Reich. Such ugliness often lies not in the truth, but in the eye of the beholder, and I find no such ugliness in Heilbrunn.

MICHAEL MERTES *is Director-General for Political Analysis and Cultural Affairs at the Federal Chancellery in Bonn.*

Falsely Accused

MICHAEL WOLFFSOHN

I have always thought that *Foreign Affairs* deals with fact rather than fiction. I may have been wrong. The way Jacob Heilbrunn described my own political positions and convictions had nothing to do with fact. It was pure fiction.

Heilbrunn calls me a "sympathizer" of people whom he describes as having "a deep hatred of the westernization of Germany under the influence of the United States." Those who have read my books or articles or know of my German-Jewish-Israeli biography are well aware of my bridge-building activities between Germany and the United States. My bi-weekly columns in *Bild Zeitung*, Germany's largest daily newspaper, stand as proof of this German-American-Jewish involvement.

DR. MICHAEL WOLFFSOHN *is a Professor at the Historisches Institut at Universität der Bundeswahr München in Munich.*

Witch Hunt

MICHAEL STÜRMER

Heilbrunn's article is based on sloppy research and comes to flimsy conclusions revealing little or no understanding of who's who in today's Germany. Instead of wondering why there is no significant German right, he concocts a conspiracy theory. And as he cannot prove his point through marginal figures, he adds some respectable names. I was not amused to find myself, along with Wolfgang Schäuble, Hermann Lübbe, Michael Wolffsohn et al. accused and condemned as sympathizers of people whom Heilbrunn describes as being driven by "a deep hatred of the westernization of Germany under the influence of the United States."

I take exception to such nonsense inspired at best by hearsay, at worst by an attempt at moral assassination. I was interested to learn, for example, that Ernst Nolte, already well established when I was still a doctoral candidate, should have needed my tutoring and "followed up" my writing. I should also like to know precisely when and where, in the "mid-1970s," I fired broadsides against '68ers, permissiveness, and loss of pride in German history.

The reality was very different: Herman Lübbe and a few others, myself included, tried to save some sense and knowledge of history against the wilder proposals for school curricula pronounced, at the time, under the flag of anti-capitalism and anti-Americanism.

While Germany is struggling with unification and globalization, and promotes NATO expansion, EMU, and European integration, Heilbrunn is searching for sinister forces working behind the scenes to set the country adrift.

MICHAEL STÜRMER *is a Professor at Stiftung Wissenschaft und Politik in Ebenhausen, Germany.*

The Older Right

NORMAN BIRNBAUM

It is difficult to understand why Heilbrunn attaches so much importance to the supposed antecedents of today's new right. Moving away from younger enthusiasms has characterized many generations since 1641, 1792, and 1917. Today's younger Germans are exceedingly unlikely candidates for steadfastness. Perhaps more could be learned by asking about the political choices of their parents—and grandparents.

In any event, the peculiar combination of historical vacuity, narcissistic chauvinism, and provincial *ressentiment* they voice may not be quite as new as Heilbrunn supposes. The editorials on the right side of the *Frankfurter Allgemeine Zeitung's* front pages have, for the past four decades or so, frequently expressed the same sentiments, if in rather less strident tones. Finally, Heilbrunn is a younger scholar and his trips to Germany have clearly been commendably ascetic. Had he spent much time in the front cabins of airliners talking with German business executives, he would have derived a rather more nuanced perspective of the originality of the views propounded by Germany's self-proclaimed new thinkers.

NORMAN BIRNBAUM *is University Professor at the Georgetown University Law Center in Washington, D.C.*

Heilbrunn Replies

Josef Joffe is frantically defending something I never attacked. Nowhere in my article did I say that German democracy was in peril or that figures such as Rainer Zitelmann would "take over Germany." On the contrary, in my first paragraph I emphasized that despite numerous warnings after the fall of the Berlin Wall that a reunified Germany would begin to flex its muscles, the "Bonn political elite . . . has been remarkably resistant to change." Far from issuing an "indictment" of Germany, as Joffe puts it, I attempted to place the followers of the new right in their proper context by calling them "heretics." And far from wanting readers to "believe" anything about post-reunification Germany, I stressed the ambiguous character of the new right and attempted to offer a dispassionate account of the impassioned intellectual debates over national identity and pride.

Joffe will have none of this. To expose my story as hopelessly outdated and based on inept research, he singles out my depictions of Zitelmann and Karlheinz Weissmann. Joffe would have us believe that Zitelmann is a cowed figure. But when I spent the month of January 1996 researching my article, Zitelmann continued to write for *Die Welt*, attracted attention in newspapers such as the *Frankfurter Allgemeine Zeitung* and *Die Zeit*, and remained a guru for members of the new right. I find it difficult to share Joffe's description of the Ullstein publishing house as ever having been beyond the "mainstream"; the firm has always published hundreds of books on a variety of topics. Joffe also maintains

that the deletion of Weissmann's book, *The Way Into the Abyss*, from the Propyläen list has put paid to his revisionist pretensions. But Weissmann's efforts were recently defended by Germany's leading political scientist, Arnulf Baring of the Free University Berlin, who has himself moved from the left to neoconservatism, in an essay in the right-wing weekly *Welt Am Sonntag*.

I would argue that the public profile of the new right remains higher than Joffe is willing to acknowledge. Indeed, though Joffe claims the new right was finished in 1993, the movement had its most spectacular success with a publication of an appeal in April 1995 in the *Frankfurter Allgemeine Zeitung* denouncing the liberal German media for its "one-sided" focus on German surrender on May 8, 1945, as an act of liberation.

Finally, Joffe invokes the popular reception in Germany of Daniel Goldhagen's egregious book to argue that if I were "even half right," the German people should have risen en masse in protest against it. Once more, Joffe grossly exaggerates the depth of nationalist sentiment that I attributed to most Germans. If Goldhagen's tour of Germany showed anything, it was that German youths were all too ready to place themselves retroactively on the "good" side of history by embracing an American Jewish author's blanket condemnation of their forefathers and by transforming him into a media star.

As Michael Wolffsohn's letter indicates, the last thing most German neoconservatives want is to be linked in any way with the new right. But what is one supposed to think when this self-described "German-Jewish patriot," writing in the July 17, 1994, *Hamburger Abendblatt*, announces that "no smelly old-right stench wafts around Karlheinz Weissmann, Brigitte Seebacher-Brandt . . . Botho Strauss and others. . . . They are not resigned and defensive. They are unbelievably and unusually offensive, rebellious conservatives. . . . The spirit today is on the right: right-democratic."

I am, however, sorry to see that Michael Stürmer, who has been criticized by new right figures for his staunch Atlanticism, took umbrage at my reference to his calls for a robust German national identity. To take just one example, in an essay in the *Frankfurter Allgemeine Zeitung* on April 25, 1986, entitled "History in a history-less land," Stürmer observed that "loss of orientation and the search for identity are brothers. But anyone who believes that this has no effect on politics and the future ignores the fact that in a land without history whoever supplies memory, shapes concepts, and interprets the past will win the future."

Stürmer was right. A battle has begun to take place on the intellectual level over German national identity. To describe this battle is not tantamount to blotting the escutcheon of the Federal Republic. What is Joffe so frightened of? German democracy is strong enough to survive the new right.

JACOB HEILBRUNN *is an Associate Editor at* The New Republic.

Germany's Choice

Timothy Garton Ash

A HISTORIC MOMENT

THE GREAT FOREIGN policy debate in Germany has only just begun. In fact, the very nature of the foreign policy actor—Germany—is still disputed. Is this a new Germany or just an enlarged Federal Republic? After the first unification of Germany in 1871 it was clear to all that Europe had to deal with a new power. For all the underlying continuity of Prussian policy, the new German empire, or second Reich, was not just Prussia writ large.

Following the second unification of Germany, the change has been much less immediately visible. Externally, this unification was achieved by telephone and checkbook rather than blood and iron. Internally, the constitutional form of unification was the straight accession of the former German Democratic Republic to the Federal Republic. The larger Federal Republic continues to be integrated in the European Union (EU), NATO and other leading institutions of Western internationalism. Nor has much changed on the surface of everyday life in western (formerly West) Germany. Last but not least, there has been the emphatic continuity of government policy so massively embodied by Chancellor Helmut Kohl—in all senses one of the largest figures in European politics today.

This year Germany has no fewer than 19 elections, culminating in the national election on October 16. The present conservative-liberal

TIMOTHY GARTON ASH is a Fellow of St. Antony's College, Oxford, and author most recently of *In Europe's Name: Germany and the Divided Continent*.

[65]

coalition—composed of the Christian Democratic Union, the Christian Social Union and the Free Democratic Party—is not certain to return to office. Yet Kohl's Social Democrat rival for the chancellorship, Rudolf Scharping, is going to extraordinary lengths to reassure German voters and the outside world that there will be almost no change in German foreign policy if his party comes into power.

In time, however, the deep underlying changes in the country's internal and external position must affect Germany's foreign policy. Even if foreign policy is not itself a major election issue, the elections will catalyze the process.

WHAT'S IN A NAME?

WITHIN GERMANY, analysis and prescription are inextricably intertwined. Claims about what Germany is are also assertions about what Germany should be. The state in question continues to be called Bundesrepublik Deutschland, which is officially translated as "the Federal Republic of Germany," but is literally "Federal Republic Germany."

Some argue passionately that what really matters in the name is still the "Federal Republic": a post-national democracy with constitutional-patriotism in place of nationalism and state sovereignty devolved both downward to the federal states and upward to "Europe," meaning the EU. Others say that what really matters now is the "Germany," which should aim to become a "normal nation-state" like Britain or France, with all the traditional attributes of sovereignty, a great capital called Berlin, plain unhyphenated patriotism and the responsible but determined pursuit of national interest. Most fall somewhere in between, both seeing that Germany has and feeling that it should have a new mixture of the two, as the state name implies. But what mixture?

This Germany is larger, more powerful and more sovereign, and it occupies a more central geopolitical position than the old Federal Republic. Some German commentators have sweepingly asserted that Germany is now back in the old *Mittellage* of the Bismarckian second Reich: that fateful monkey-in-the-middle situation to which a long line of conservative German historians have attributed the subsequent, erratic and finally aggressive foreign policy of the Reich. Others say that Germany is again a central European state, or even the center of Europe. Such striking claims need to be examined skeptically.

The leaders of the old Federal Republic were always deeply conscious of Germany's Cold War position as the divided center of a divided Europe and Berlin's position as the divided center of the divided center. The foreign policy of the Bonn republic was made under constant tension between its western and eastern ties. The Bonn government was vulnerable to blackmail from Moscow and East Berlin. Today Germany has no such dependency on the East. The last Russian soldier will leave Germany by the end of August 1994. In terms of its constitutional order and international ties, Germany is now more fully in the West than it was throughout the Cold War.

Many German politicians like to say that Germany's integration into the West, and specifically into Europe—that is, EU-rope—is irreversible. Since European history offers few examples of the irreversible integration of states into larger entities, and since the years following the end of the Cold War have been rich in examples of the opposite, this claim is bold, if not foolhardy. To observe that the West sorely misses the Soviet negative integrator has become a truism. Nonetheless, the single market and political institutions of the EU, the integrated command of NATO and all the associated habits of permanent cooperation are different in kind from earlier alliances between European states.

Geographically, this Germany also lies more to the west than did the Bismarckian Reich. A glance at the historical atlas shows Germany sprawling across east-central Europe, with Prussia stretching into what is now Lithuania and the Russian territory of Kaliningrad (formerly Königsberg). Today's political map shows a compact territory west of the Oder and Neisse rivers and the diamond wedge of Bohemia. Germany still faces sensitive special eastern issues, but the country's center lies westward.

In 1967 Federal Chancellor Kurt Georg Kiesinger observed that a reunited Germany would have a "critical size . . . too big to play no part in the balance of forces and too small to keep the forces around it in balance by itself." Exactly so. Germany is now the most powerful country in Europe. But it is not a superpower. It has great assets in each of the three main dimensions of power—the military, the economic and the social. But it also has special liabilities in each department.

Militarily, Germany has some of the largest and best-armed forces in Europe. However, in the "2 plus 4" unification treaty, the new Federal Republic solemnly reaffirmed the old Federal Republic's commitment not to acquire atomic, biological or chemical weapons. This may change.

> The Bundesbank has made foreign policy by not making foreign policy.

One cannot take post-Hitler public abhorrence for national military power as a permanent given. If Germany were not, in the longer term, to seek enhancement of this dimension of its power, to complement or buttress the other two, it would be behaving differently from most large states in history. But for the moment, several statements can be made with confidence. Germany is not in the world super league of military power. It is still virtually unthinkable that a German government would use force or the threat of force unilaterally to achieve a national goal, except the defense of its own territory. Any qualitative upgrading of its military power, including some form of control over nuclear weapons, would almost certainly come in a multilateral (probably European) context.

Economically, Germany is in the super league, and this power has been actively deployed, although in two distinct ways. First, economic instruments and incentives have been liberally and skillfully used by the German government to achieve its foreign policy goals. Second, the Bundesbank's single-minded pursuit of domestic monetary and fiscal policy objectives has had a direct impact on the economies of Germany's neighbors and trading partners, and hence on the country's foreign relations. The Bundesbank has, as it were, made foreign policy by not making foreign policy.

However, Germany is now afflicted by a double economic crisis. There is, obviously, the massive cost of incorporating and reconstructing the former East Germany. But there is also, less obviously, the crisis of the old West German "social market economy," which was already beginning to lose its competitive edge before unification.

Experts differ on how far and how fast Germany will surmount this double crisis, but for the next few years the consequences for foreign policy are clear. If Germany is still most unlikely to use guns as an instrument of foreign policy, neither will it be so ready to use butter. All decisions, including those inside the EU, will be scrutinized more closely for their impact on German budgets and competitiveness in European and world markets.

The third dimension of power has to do with the overall attractiveness of a particular society, culture and way of life. Its crudest measure is the number of people inside a country who want to get out compared to the number outside who want to get in. (One might call this the Statue of Liberty test.) In the 1980s this was a vital component of German power. Germany, seen in 1945 as a threat and a synonym for horror, had by 1985 become a model and magnet (West Germany, that is). When in 1989 people east of the Iron Curtain spoke of returning to Europe and normality, West Germany was a central part of the liberal, democratic, civil and bourgeois "normality" they had in mind.

But this achievement too is under stress. The exemplary openness and civility of the old Federal Republic have not yet been restored across its larger territory. This failure is not simply a case of easterners exhibiting the pathologies of post-communism. It is as much a problem of the condescending and at times frankly neocolonial attitudes of westerners toward easterners. There is more than a grain of bitter truth in the joke that when in 1989 the East Germans started chanting, "We are one people," the West Germans replied, "So are we."

The seemingly open, tolerant, civil society of the old West Germany has, in the last four years, too often looked like a spoiled, defensive consumer society, both demanding and assuming perpetual economic growth while yearning for the lost comfort of living with one's back to the Berlin Wall. Where easterners and westerners have found common ground, it has sometimes been in scapegoating the foreigners who have been admitted to the country in large numbers but given citizenship less liberally. At times, it seems as though the Federal Republic has grown in size but shrunk in spirit. These strains and the extreme voices they breed on the right and left will play into the political process through this year's elections. A nation still preoccupied with becoming one nation may have less time and patience, as well as less money, for foreign policy.

The Random House Dictionary of the English Language, published in 1968, memorably defined Germany as "a former country in Central Europe." Today Germany is a country in west-central Europe. In fact, together with Austria, it is west-central Europe. It is a Western state, but one directly confronting many of the problems characteristic of the former communist East. A troubled, medium-heavyweight power—and a nation in its perennial condition of becoming.

PROCESS, TRADITION AND CHOICE

WHAT FOREIGN POLICY will be made on these substantial but shifting foundations, and how will it be made? It is sometimes suggested that Germany lacks a political class or internationalist elite such as can be found in Paris, London or Washington. Yet Germany does not want for highly sophisticated, knowledgeable, multilingual practitioners and analysts of foreign affairs (including many of those who make this criticism).

It is true that a middle generation of politicians is coming into power with little experience beyond the professional party politics of the Federal Republic. But the same could be said of Kohl when he came to Bonn and of many American presidents. Some learn on the job. It is true that no one in Germany expected or was prepared for the quantum leap in Germany's power and responsibilities following unification. But neither were American elites prepared for the United States' quantum leap in the second half of the 1940s. They rose to the occasion.

Germany has a much less clear preponderance of wealth and power than the United States did a half-century ago, and a far more difficult geopolitical situation. But something of the human challenge for leadership, and the excitement that goes with such a challenge, is palpably there in Germany (and palpably not in France or Britain). Besides the question of personal qualities, however, there are those of process and tradition.

The foreign policy process in Germany labors under some disadvantages familiar to other Western democracies. As in all television democracies, German politicians often seem to be following public or published opinion rather than leading it. (It was this, and not any subtle or sinister calculation of national interest, that prompted Germany's initiative for the diplomatic recognition of Croatia in 1991.) The fact that responsibility for foreign policy is divided between a chancellor and a foreign minister from different political parties can on occasion make for more heat than light. And both the Bundesbank in Frankfurt and the constitutional court in Karlsruhe have become— rather against their will—important institutions in foreign policy.

Nonetheless, Germany has over the last 30 years pursued one of the most consistent foreign policies of any Western power. As a result, it has a well-formed foreign policy tradition. This tradition, a blend of Adenauerian Westpolitik and Brandtian Ostpolitik, has several distinctive features. Besides the renunciation of force and the pursuit of reconciliation with former foes, there is what one might call attritional multilateralism. German diplomacy has excelled at the patient, discreet pursuit of national goals through multilateral institutions and negotiations, whether in the European Community, NATO or the Helsinki process.

> Germany has pursue[d] one of the most consi[s]tent foreign policies of any Western powe[r]

Closely related to this is the habitual conflation of German and European interests. In the German case, this policy has not merely been the familiar old European game of pursuing national interests in Europe's name. In postwar German politics there has also been a great deal of genuine idealistic commitment to the process of European integration. But for that very reason, German policymakers have sometimes found it difficult to distinguish between the one and the other.

At the same time, running like a leitmotiv through the history of the Federal Republic has been the effort, under all chancellors, to widen the bounds of German sovereignty and power. Certainly, German chancellors were at the same time busily and demonstratively surrendering elements of sovereignty to Europe. But the paradoxical effect of this readiness to surrender sovereignty was to convince Germany's key allies and partners that Germany could again be trusted with full sovereignty. It was by laying on the golden handcuffs

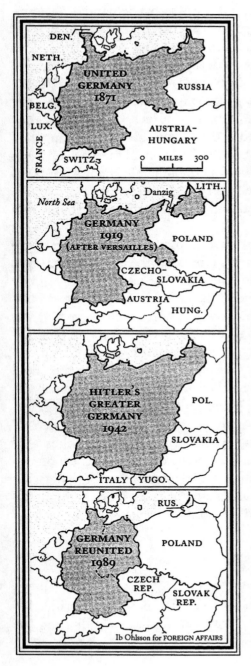

Ib Ohlsson for FOREIGN AFFAIRS

that Germany set itself free.

Also ingrained in this tradition are the politics of *sowohl-als-auch*: not either-or, but as-well-as. The essence and great achievement of Genscherism was to maintain and improve Germany's ties with a wide range of states, which were themselves pursuing quite different and contradictory objectives. This complex balancing act involved saying somewhat different things in different places. Fudge was the hard core of Genscherism. This may not always have endeared Bonn to its more plain-spoken friends, but such an approach was well-suited to the achievement of Germany's aims in the last two decades of the Cold War.

This foreign policy culminated in a success beyond the dreams of those who made it. So it is not surprising that the first inclination of German policymakers was to stick with it. Even after the retirement of Hans-Dietrich Genscher in 1992, the motto of the foreign ministry was, "Herr Genscher is gone, long live Genscherism!"

Yet the policy that served the old Federal Republic so well is less appropriate for the new one. The state's external dependencies have been decisively reduced, but the external demands on it have significantly increased, and the resources to meet those demands have not grown commensurately. In the short term they have shrunk. The conclusion should be plain: the Federal Republic can and should make clearer choices than in the past. These are not absolute "either-or" choices—to some extent, all major states have to genscher—but choices of priorities: between the demands of its special relationship with the United States and those of its special relationship with France, between deepening the existing European Union around the Franco-German core and widening it to include Germany's immediate eastern neighbors, between relations with east-central Europe and those with Russia. Not all these things are compatible. Certainly not all can be done at once.

The obvious starting point for determining such priorities would be a definition of the national interest. However, the German national interest is particularly difficult to define when the nation itself is still in the making. Moreover, in Germany merely stating that one should define the national interest is controversial. Those who believe that the Federal Republic is or should be a post-national democracy on the path to a genuine European union regard the very notion of defining the national interest as suspect, retrograde, even reactionary. On the other hand, those who wish to see Germany become a normal nation-state use the idea of defining the national interest almost as a campaign slogan.

Yet this argument is itself a sign that a major foreign policy debate is slowly getting under way. In newspaper columns, speeches and Germany's ubiquitous television talk shows one can hear echoes of some of the great debates of the 1950s and 1960s—the Charlemagne school of West European integrationists, the German Gaullists, the Atlanticists, the Ludwig Erhard economic *mondialistes*—as well as snatches of much older tunes.

FOUR OPTIONS

To SHARPEN THE debate let us consider four possible priorities for German foreign policy after 1994, with several factors militating for and against their adoption.

Carolingian Completion

For this school, the top priority would be a decisive further deepening of the existing European Union around a Franco-German core. Germany, France and the Benelux countries would go ahead of other member states, in the variable-speed Europe for which the Maastricht treaty in fact allows. Monetary union would be achieved in this core group around the end of the century, and prove a decisive step—as it was in German unification—toward political union. In ten years one would have, if not a United States of Europe, then at least a Confederal Republic of North-Western Europe—Charlemagne's empire in a new form.

For: This has been the personal top priority of Helmut Kohl and seems to be high on the personal list of Rudolf Scharping. (Not accidentally, both men have been prime minister of the western state of Rhineland-Palatinate, a region with close historical ties to France.) The Paris-Bonn axis has a 30-year track record and personal and institutional momentum. This simplistic version of Europe as an answer to the German question still has some appeal: it looks like somewhere for Germany to go. Maastricht, wrote President Richard von Weizsäcker, offers Germany "the chance of being delivered from the *Mittellage.*"

Against: The Franco-German relationship has been rocky since German unification. It is far from certain that the Euro-idealism of the middle and younger generations in Germany is as widespread or deep as that of the immediate postwar generation. In this respect Helmut Kohl begins to look like a magnificent dinosaur. His likely successors have a more hard-nosed view of the EU. So do many of Rudolf Scharping's colleagues in the leadership of the Social Democrats.

More broadly, over the last two years Germany has experienced the popular reaction, also seen elsewhere in Europe, against the Messina-to-Maastricht model of functionalist, bureaucratic European integration from above. An appeal to the constitutional court against the Maastricht treaty meant that Germany was actually the last country in Europe to ratify it. The court produced a complicated judgment that nonetheless drew a clear line against any automatic progress to monetary union. As German budgets are squeezed, there is growing resentment of the outsize German contribution to the EU's budget. The outspokenly Euro-skeptical Bavarian Prime Minister Edmund Stoiber, sometimes jovially dubbed "Edmund Thatcher," is an extreme case, but not simply an aberration.

German banking and business circles are also far from enthusiastic about European monetary union. By and large, they think a single market can operate perfectly well without it. Further steps toward economic, monetary and social policy harmonization in the EU are not calculated to sharpen Germany's competitive edge in other markets.

Underneath, there is the deeper matter of sovereignty. It is one thing to surrender sovereignty in order to regain it. But has Germany now regained sovereignty only to surrender it? Even for the world's most dialectical nation, this may be a twist too far.

Wider Europe

Whatever anyone says, there is a day-to-day tension between concentrating on deepening or on widening the EU. This brings us to a second possible priority: widening the EU and and NATO to include Germany's eastern neighbors. Germany would do everything in its power to ensure that within ten years the Czech Republic, Poland, Hungary, Slovakia and Slovenia would follow Austria, Sweden, Norway and Finland (the "EFTANS") into the European Union, the West European Union and NATO. Beyond this it would try to help the Baltic states, Romania, Bulgaria, Albania and, if they really became peaceful democracies, Croatia, Serbia and Bosnia, to prepare themselves to follow over the next decade. Europe would be built from EU-rope out.

Naturally, this approach would involve further derogations from the idea of the single *acquis communautaire*, with long economic transition periods for new member states and further special provisions of the kind seen in every earlier round of enlargement. Nonetheless, Germany would aim to preserve, in this Europe of more than 20 states and 400 million people, the present historically unprecedented level of permanent, institutionalized interstate cooperation, with major elements of economic and legal integration.

For: Germany has already shown a major interest in enlargement. Foreign Minister Klaus Kinkel was instrumental in pushing the negotiations with the EFTANs to a successful conclusion. Building on the achievements of a quarter-century of Ostpolitik, Germany has over the last four years played a leading and constructive role in east-central Europe (some problems connected with present or past German minorities notwithstanding). It has an obvious vital interest in having peaceful, stable democracies at its eastern frontier. Poland is now less than an hour's drive from Berlin—or a few minutes by fighter plane. It is no accident that the German defense minister, Volker Rühe, was the only senior Western minister to come out clearly in favor of a rapid enlargement of NATO to include Germany's eastern neighbors.

Perhaps there is still a little gratitude for what brave Poles, clever Hungarians and principled Czechs did to make German unification possible. The (exaggerated) fear of mass immigration from the east has also concentrated minds on this issue. Enlargement would expand the internal European market for German goods. German manufacturers are already taking advantage of the much cheaper skilled labor to be found just over the border by relocating production there. Last, but by no means least, Germany would be at the center of this wider Europe.

Against: This option would have substantial short-term costs. Unlike the EFTANs, these new members would definitely not be net contributors to the EU budget. Cheaper imports from east-central Europe could also undercut more expensive German products. In the short term, keeping industrial jobs in Bohemia could mean losing them in Bavaria. In the long term, such a bracing wind of competition would be good for the German economy, just as the North American Free Trade Agreement will be good for the American economy. But tell that to German trade unions and to voters already peevish about not getting richer.

Such an opening to the east would also be resisted by some of Germany's less economically developed EU partners. (Keeping agricultural jobs in Polish Galicia can mean losing them in Spanish Galicia.) As now constituted, the EU aggregates rather than transcends national, sectoral and regional special interests. Hence its continued overt and covert protectionism against eastern goods. Thus far, Germany's key European partner, France, has been extremely reluctant about enlargement, preferring to keep a smaller Europe with France still at its center.

There is no major lobby for this option in Germany. Less tangibly, there is no great tradition of Germany giving priority to its poorer and weaker eastern neighbors. Historically, when Germany looked east, it looked to Russia; this brings us to the third possible priority.

Moscow First

This is the classic eastern option of German foreign policy. The new-old great power in the center of Europe develops a new-old special relationship with what is still the most powerful state in eastern Europe. In doing so, over the heads of the peoples between, it argues that such a policy best serves the interests of Europe, indeed of the world. For what could be more important than a cooperative, peaceful or, at least, stable Russia?

For: Perhaps there is still gratitude for Moscow having agreed to German unification. Some may still see a grand symbiosis between Russia's abundant raw materials and primary energy sources and Germany's know-how (Germany as Ivan Stolz to Russia's Oblomov). There is also that part of German foreign policy tradition that puts order before freedom. Finally, there is fear.

Against: This is the great development that has not occurred over the last four years. In 1989-90 there was real German-Soviet euphoria. Germany's western and eastern neighbors looked anxiously for signs of one of Europe's oldest special relationships developing out of "Stavrapallo," as the Kohl-Gorbachev accord of mid-July 1990 was dubbed. Subsequently, Germany has given the lion's share of Western economic assistance to Russia (although much of the German contribution has been specifically related to unification or tied to trade promotion). Helmut Kohl has tried to establish with the Russian president, Boris Yeltsin, something of the personal rapport he had with Mikhail Gorbachev.

But, if anything, the Bonn government has privileged the relationship with east-central Europe over that with Moscow. And if anyone has had a policy of "Moscow First," it has been the Clinton administration. In one of those curious transatlantic role reversals that happen from time to time, the United States has played Germany to Yeltsin's Russia, while Germany has played America to east-central Europe.

If the Bill Clinton-Strobe Talbott gamble were to have paid off—that is, if Russia were set on course to become a cooperative capitalist democracy—then there would be a powerful case for Germany giving priority to its relations with Russia. But it has not, and it seems unlikely that it will in the foreseeable future. A strong but cooperative Russia would be a great partner for Germany. A weak but cooperative Russia could still be a partner. A strong but uncooperative Russia would be a sparring partner. But a Russia that is both weak and uncooperative?

World Power

Germany would give top priority to seeking both the rights and the duties of a world power, starting, of course, with a permanent seat on the U.N. Security Council. The Federal Republic would seize with both hands the United States' offer to be "partners in leadership." As once America was (reluctantly) prepared to "take up the White Man's burden" from Britain, to use Rudyard Kipling's disgracefully non-PC phrase, so now Germany would take up the GI's burden. This would mean enhancing its military power to match its economy, size and social magnetism. Thus equipped, Germany would be the captain of a great European trading bloc, dealing as an equal with the United States, the captain of the North American bloc, and with Japan and China, rival captains of the Asian bloc(s).

For: Such a prospect would appeal to many nations. The quiet widening of the bounds of German power has been a central purpose of the foreign policy of the Federal Republic for more than 40 years, and old habits die hard. The idea of Germany as a normal nation-state, taking its rightful place at the head table of world politics, is one of the two main visions of Germany currently being canvassed there.

The United States seems to have few qualms about German leadership in Europe; it has even pressed the role on it. This American encouragement is accompanied by the implied threat of a continued reduction of the American military commitment to Europe—an old familiar theme from the history of transatlantic relations, but more credible in the post-Cold War world.

This priority could find support among both the Atlanticist and the economic *mondialiste* tendencies in Germany. America, too, was historically drawn from being a continental trading state, protected by the military power of others, to doing its own protecting and power projecting.

Against: Germany is not like most nations. It has special burdens of history and self-doubt. Hitler and Auschwitz are less than a human lifetime away. For all the profound, historic changes in Germany, for all the trust in the liberal, democratic Federal Republic, many people around Germany and—quite as important—many Germans would be loath to see it even attempting to play such a role. Moreover, it is not big enough, not powerful enough, not rich enough. Germany does not even have that preponderance in Europe that America had in the world in 1945. If, however, the proposition were that of being junior partner to the United States, this policy would soon reactivate the complex but deep reactions known by the simplistic label of "anti-Americanism." The other three possible priorities seem closer to German concerns and better matched to Germany's means.

THE RIGHT CHOICE

WHAT, THEN, will Germany choose? It will, I think, choose not to choose. True to its foreign policy tradition, the Federal Republic will try to do a little of all the above. *Sowohl-als-auch*, or, in the immortal words of Yogi Berra, "If you see a fork in the road, take it!" This tendency will be strengthened by any likely outcome of the 1994 elections.

Even without Genscher, Germany will genscher. To some extent this is inevitable for a major power in Germany's complex geopolitical position. But with increased demands on limited resources, the danger is that by trying to do everything Germany will end up achieving nothing.

Moreover, to choose not to choose does not mean you make no choices. It means only that the choices will be made reactively, as a response to the combination of unexpected external developments (especially in eastern and southeastern Europe) and internal pressures from political, published and public opinion. Again, this phenomenon is not peculiar to Germany. In a way, it is further proof of the Americanization of the Federal Republic. That may be small consolation.

In a probably vain attempt to make this prophecy self-negating, I shall now take the liberty of saying what I think Germany should do.

I am deeply convinced that Germany should pursue the second option: giving top priority for the next 20 years to building a wider Europe, extending the EU and NATO eastward step by step.

Of course Germany could not do this alone. It would need to win the agreement and active support of the United States, France, Britain, Italy and, so far as possible, other EU partners, for this priority. American support should and probably would be the easiest to secure.

> The danger is that by trying to do everything Germany will end up achieving nothing.

Although on present form one must seriously doubt the capacity of British politics to produce any coherent European policy at all, such a redefinition of European purpose—starting with the advance planning for the EU's intergovernmental conference in 1996—would be a way out of Britain's present hiding to nowhere. Britain could and should take it.

Italy has traditionally been a passionate advocate of deepening rather than widening the existing European Union, but with a new foreign minister who was a founding member of the Thatcherite Bruges Group, with its own interests in central and eastern Europe, and with scant likelihood of itself being included in a Carolingian inner core of European monetary union, Italy too might now be ready to embrace this priority. The most difficult partner to win for such a course is also the most important one: France. Helped by the United States, Britain and Italy, Germany would simply have to argue the case to its closest European partner, and even now there are signs of a revision of France's defensive little-Europe strategy.

In Germany, the argument for this priority is generally made negatively, in terms of the threat of mass immigration, the dangers of instability in eastern Europe, even the need for a *cordon sanitaire*. It can and should be made positively.

The voluntary westernization of what became West Germany after 1945 was a peaceful revolution for the better. (A revolution was proclaimed in the East, but happened in the West.) With all its faults, the old Federal Republic was a model bourgeois democracy and the best German state in history. But the job was only half done: West

Germany's inner security and peace of mind came from its firm geopolitical and existential anchoring in the West; its insecurity, uncertainty and even schizophrenia came from the ghosts of the past and the fact of division.

Now it has a historic chance to finish the job. To recreate those virtues of the old Federal Republic across its larger territory, and find a lasting inner equilibrium, Germany not only needs to achieve the westernization of the former East Germany. It also needs to assist in the westernization on which the new democracies to its east have themselves embarked, and to bring them into the structures of Western and European integration to which the Federal Republic already belongs. If you really want to be a normal country like Britain, France or America, then you need Western neighbors to your east.

The strategic goal of German foreign policy in the 20 years after 1970 could be summarized in one sentence from the so-called letter on German unity: "to work toward a state of peace in Europe in which the German people regains its unity in free self-determination." The strategic goal of German foreign policy for the next 20 years should be to work toward a state of freedom in Europe in which Germany has Western allies and partners to its east.

This is not only a clear, positive goal. It is also a realistic one, proportionate to the country's size, resources and the limited readiness of its citizens to sustain larger external commitments. More would be less. ✪

Freedom and Its Discontents

Fritz Stern

THE TRAVAILS OF THE NEW GERMANY

IN 1983 THE PRESIDENT of the Federal Republic, Richard von Weizsäcker, published a collection of essays under the title *German History Has Not Stopped*. Even he could not have predicted the pace of progress since then. And as the process of unification has unfolded, one can see the drama of German history continue as well. The economic consequences of unity are becoming apparent; the moral and psychological consequences are harder to grasp and may prove longer lasting. It is these that this article addresses.

While the two states of postwar Germany existed, Germans could believe in the unity of their nation, of a people with a common language, a common past, even a common fate. Now unified within one state, the deep divisions among Germans are more visible. No doubt there is truth in Freud's words about "the narcissism of small differences" that divides neighborhoods and family members, and yet in 1989 there was an expectation that Germans would understand Germans. In the first flush of enthusiasm, people forgot the estrangements that had grown so strong over 40 years, as West Germans came to regard the French or the Tuscans or the Dutch as closer, and perhaps more attractive, to them than the East Germans. For their part, East Germans lived with a prescribed if gradually attenuated hostility to the Federal Republic of Germany (F.R.G.), and with a nonprescribed envy and resentment of its freedom and prosperity, witnessed

---

FRITZ STERN is a University Professor at Columbia University. His article is an abridged and revised version of the second of two Tanner Lectures that he gave at Yale in April 1993.

[108]

The fall of the Berlin Wall, 1989

nightly on their television screens.

Visitors to East Germany, including this author, sensed the estrangement. And in the Federal Republic, for all the ritualistic invocations of German solidarity, for all the many individuals who did genuinely care about their fellow Germans in the East, one sensed an enormous, unacknowledged indifference to them. Sudden commonality, sudden huge demands, did not instantly transform indifference to openhearted solicitude.

DIFFERENT KINDS OF FREEDOM

BOTH GERMANIES GAINED greater, if sharply different, kinds of freedom after unification—and with that freedom came new uncertainties and discontents. In the East it was the freedom from the knock at the door, freedom to travel, release from a regimented, intimidating, false existence, freedom to examine one's life. But almost immediately 17 million East Germans discovered that freedom also meant freedom to face an uncertain future, freedom to lose a job, to lose support nets, however inadequate they may have been.

For 40 years, most East Germans had accommodated to life in a world of public lies and private doubts. Totalitarian regimes mobilize people into passive participation in politics. After 12 years of Nazi rule and 40 years of communist rule in the German Democratic Republic (G.D.R.), they may have survived psychologically by practicing denial, by wishing not to see.

After 1989 avoiding reality became impossible, given the economic dislocations of transforming a dysfunctional, decaying command economy into a market economy—as if there was but one type of market economy. The closing of state-run enterprises led to mounting unemployment. Moreover, economic affairs were only part of what had been prescribed under the old command economy. So much of life had been lived in the public realm. So much of it had been ordered from above or came by inherited routine. Suddenly the East Germans, released from public control, had to learn to make their own choices, think their own thoughts, find their own truths. They were indeed privatized at a time when the associational life of a civil society was being but slowly introduced.

Market economies presuppose legal structures, a system of private and public law—a legal code that has to be taught, learned and gradually assimilated. But the art of evasion also flourishes in market economies—as the 1980s so vividly illustrate. Western enthusiasts for the free market in the former G.D.R. often ignored the social costs of the transformation. Worse, the abrupt introduction of new forms of economic life also created what sociologists and Marxists have long identified with modern capitalism: alienation, anomie, insecurity. For the East Germans, the move from the rigid world of communist rule to the demands of a mobile society was hard. The very notion of planning for a market economy had an ironic ring to it. A new dependency developed. Much of life in the new eastern *Länder* of the united Germany came to be organized by Westerners who were practiced in taking decisions, in making things work and assessing the risks of the market, and who had the skills and the funds to take charge. East Germans had been taught to live and work by plans that bore little relation to reality; they had learned to suffer and endure but not to take responsibility or to live by trial and error.

East Germans hoped that the end of communism would bring instant rehabilitation as well as instant improvement in their living standard. But soon they began to think they were being "colonized"—a word commonly used that was infuriating to Western ears. Defeated, humiliated, more object than subject, many East Germans expressed their disappointment in terms of self-pity and resentment. Was there no end to their being victimized? In the early years of occupation, the Russians had dismantled and taken what was left of German industrial plants in their zone. A current estimate is that the Russians extracted some 54 billion Deutsche marks in reparations—all this while the Western zones and later the Federal Republic received Marshall Plan aid. Of course the balance sheet is far more complicated: West Germany also benefited from the huge influx of refugees from the Soviet zone and of Germans expelled by Poles and Czechs, and on the other hand, Bonn did make restitution payments to Israel and gradually gave support to the G.D.R. But East Germans believed, with some justification, that they had paid disproportionately for Hitler's war.

Fritz Stern

SEPARATE AND JOINT PASTS

AFTER 1990 BOTH East and West Germans had to consider their separate and joint pasts. Former G.D.R. citizens had to address questions that have beset other countries at other times in the twentieth century: questions of collaboration and collusion, of culpability and trustworthiness. Which of them were so compromised that they could no longer be teachers or judges, civil servants or plant managers, professors or members of renowned academies? Who was to make these judgments, and on what basis?

West Germans, hardly at peace with their own past, seemed ready to make their judgments about Easterners. From the moment of unification I was concerned that the West Germans would be far more cheerfully, self-righteously assiduous in punishing suspected collaborators with the communist regime than their forbears had been in dealing with the servants of the Nazi regime. The very popularity of that regime had made de-Nazification difficult. Even now, West Germans with an undetected compromised past continue to flourish. Earlier this year a prominent West German physician was forced to resign from a major post in an international organization because it was revealed that he had participated in the Nazis' euthanasia program.

The Nazi past divides West Germans still, as shown by the controversy surrounding President Reagan's visit to Bitburg in 1985, by the so-called historians' debate, and by the decades it has taken to document the complicity of the German army in the atrocities on the Eastern front. To this day many Germans, in and out of uniform, choose to believe in the *Wehrmacht's* innocence. National Socialism never needed a wall; there was never a threat of a mass exodus. By comparison, millions of East Germans voted with their feet. Under the Nazis an indeterminate number of Germans had gone into "inner emigration," tried to remain insulated, to purchase peace at the price of silence. West Germans who were confounded by this past—and divided among themselves about it—were now called upon to judge fellow Germans who had lived for a further 40 years under a totalitarian regime initially held in place by foreign bayonets.

Most East Germans knew that their leaders, piously mouthing slogans of peace, had believed in violence and had no mercy. What they could not have known, because the tape was released only last February, was that in 1982 Erich Mielke, head of the Stasi, the state security police, had told his closest colleagues that to save the lives of millions one might have to kill a bandit: "All this drivel about not executing and no death sentences, all crap, comrades."

The tone does remind one of Nazi evil. In the post-Stalinist era East German leaders, like leaders throughout the Soviet bloc, sought to replace torture with other kinds of intimidation, including the abomination of psychiatric wards. Party leaders ordered alleged enemies of the regime to be tortured, incarcerated or shot; they organized espionage and initiated or facilitated international terrorism. But these same leaders after 1970, and especially in the 1980s, garnered official recognition by other states. Chancellor Helmut Kohl received them in Bonn; Franz Joseph Strauss visited them and arranged for the G.D.R. to receive a one billion Deutsche mark credit. West German Social Democrats collaborated with functionaries of the East German Communist Party to hammer out a joint paper defining areas of agreement and disagreement. Today the former East German leader, Erich Honecker, is free in Chile, and only a few frontier guards are in prison, while tens of thousands of teachers and other East German civil servants have been suspended or dismissed.

> Questions of collaboration and collusion beset East and West Germans alike.

As the communist regime crumbled, East Germans, left in their crowded, drab, decaying dwellings, saw pictures of how the *nomenklatura* had lived in insulated comfort and read about the perquisites that ranged from special medical care to Swiss bank accounts. Had they really not noticed that the much-touted egalitarianism of the first German socialist state had been traduced daily, visibly and invisibly? The apparatchiks had their own Volvos, their children had privileged access to education, and all of them could shop in the Intershops, where Western goods could be bought for Western currency. The revelations of the extent of these special benefits—petty by Western standards—enraged many East Germans. They felt betrayed. They remembered the leaders' endless invocations that, unlike the rapacious capitalist West, the G.D.R. was an egalitarian society where austerity and sacrifice provided a psychological guarantee of a better future. But they must have had at least an inkling that their leaders had not practiced the virtues of delayed gratification that they preached.

The resultant outburst sprang from what I think was an ambivalence about deprivation. They minded it, of course, but they may have felt that austerity was virtuous—in old Germanic terms, ennobling. To have stark proof that their leaders had mocked this notion was offensive. In this largely Lutheran country, was this a distant echo of Martin Luther's attacks on a Roman hierarchy that preached poverty but lived in corrupt luxury?

THE STASI LEGACY

THE EAST GERMANS were made to realize something far worse. Their insidious, malevolent regime had managed to entrap vast numbers of them in collusion and corruption. The state security police had organized an unprecedented web of surveillance. In its final days, the Stasi consisted of 97,000 full-time employees—with perhaps as many as 140,000 unofficial collaborators, most of whom had acknowledged their commitment in writing. Only the higher ranks of society, such as professors or members of elite academies, were allowed to register their agreement orally. In addition, membership in the Communist Party rose to two million people, who were particularly vulnerable to Stasi demands. All this machinery for 17 million Germans—while the Gestapo, helped by countless voluntary informers, at the end of the Nazi regime had only 32,000 members for 80 million Germans. The Stasi files—nearly 100 miles of them—offered poisonous proof of a poisoned society.

The Stasi were the eyes and ears of a regime deeply distrustful of its own people. Born of distrust, the Stasi became an agent of distrust. In a world without laws or enforceable rights, a person searches for the like-minded, for another person to talk to, if need be in some outside place where surveillance is more difficult. West German observers thought that East Germans had managed to have closer, more trusting relationships. Some East Germans probably did have a particular affinity for trust and friendship. They invested in them as rare human goods at a time of moral scarcity. Imagine then the shock, the retroactive dissolution of trust, when one discovered one's friend had been an informer; husbands had informed on their wives, wives on husbands, parents on children, friends on friends. Even now, as more information is divulged, the web of suspicion spreads ever wider.

During the 1970s, when the East German regime gradually replaced physical terror with calculated intimidation, the Stasi, like other secret police, learned to play with fiendish aptitude on people's vulnerabilities, operating an ever more elaborate system of carrots and sticks. The rewards for being an unofficial collaborator varied— advancement in a career, travel to the West; the sticks were more formidable, often involving the punishment of children for the alleged sins of their parents. The Stasi also resorted to more lethal methods, such as efforts to bring about "personal destabilization," including undermining marriages—a whole array of Iago-like villainies aimed at destroying trust among friends and potential critics.

Stasi revelations have threatened some of the most promising political careers in the new *Länder* of the united Germany. Two examples may suffice: Lothar de Mazière, the first vice chancellor of the unified Germany, resigned when it was said that he had had Stasi contacts; and insinuations continue to be made against the only socialist minister president in the new *Länder*, Manfred Stolpe of Brandenburg. Stolpe had worked in and with the Protestant churches and had helped them to help victims of the regime. He had regular contacts with the Stasi—how else to aid people entrapped by them? Knowledgeable defenders of Stolpe and others similarly accused insist that any responsible person who tried to help people who had fallen afoul of the regime had to deal with the Stasi. But critics claim that even talking to Stasi officials was to take the first steps on a slippery slope. Others, myself included, might argue that in a tyrannical system only absolute immobility can protect one from the dangers of that slope. Once upon a time the Stasi oppressed a people. Its legacy has been to demoralize them and perhaps to deprive them of the few good political leaders they might have had.

Opposition to the G.D.R. regime was feeble compared to that elsewhere in the Soviet bloc. After the one great outburst of June 17, 1953, when East German workers took to the streets to defy their ever more demanding and repressive regime and were crushed by Soviet tanks, there was apparent conformity. Not in East Germany the repeated uprisings or the great alliance of workers and intellectuals as in Poland's Solidarity Party, or in the Hungarian rebellion of 1956, or in the Czechoslovak Spring of 1968. It has often been said that Germans are somewhat untutored in civic courage. They have the word but not the all-essential practice. Albert Hirschman once wrote of moral resources, including civic spirit and trust: "These are resources whose supply may well increase rather than decrease through use . . . like the ability to speak a foreign language or to play the piano, these moral resources are likely to become depleted and to atrophy if not used."

The Ulbricht-Honecker regime, mixing German traditions with Soviet models, had time to promote a separate cultural life in the G.D.R. They wanted to create athletes of the spirit, writers and artists who could dazzle the outside world and satisfy at least some aspirations of their own people. As the East German molecular biologist and admirable citizen-thinker Jens Reich makes clear in a new book, the regime sought to implicate the entire intelligentsia—technicians as well as poets—and to a devastating degree it was successful. For many reasons the samizdat literature that flourished in Poland, Czechoslovakia and Russia did not exist in the G.D.R. In the early years of the regime, writers like Robert Havemann were imprisoned and gifted irritants like Wolf Biermann were expelled. This last decision prompted East German writers to protest for the first time. But by and large the limits of state tolerance for dissent were rarely, if ever, tested.

> The Stasi files—nearly 100 miles of them—offered poisonous proof of a poisoned society.

Gradually the demands for socialist realism were relaxed. Other kinds of art were allowed. The novelist Christa Wolf was able to depict life in the G.D.R. with some degree of candor. Writers jousted with censors, and parodists ventured the occasional mischief, as when the writer Heiner Müller said, "We are the most progressive state ever: 95 percent of the people are against it, such a thing has never happened before," or when he sang, "The Stasi is my Eckermann." Now come the revelations that these writers, too, were once part of the Stasi net. In the late 1950s and early 1960s Christa Wolf was an unofficial informant, unbeknownst even to her husband. Decades later she described at length how she too came under Stasi surveillance. As the most prominent of East German writers, she has been denounced and defended. She illustrates how easy it was under that regime to move from being accomplice and perpetrator to victim, and how difficult it is to judge the conduct of people enmeshed in a system with so many visible and invisible tentacles.

There is at present a great controversy about the conduct of East German authors and the intelligentsia. Some West German critics express outrage, and there is a danger that in time the work of these writers might be altogether forgotten. This would be a distortion and a loss. Some of them were guarded witnesses to life under dreadful conditions. Now, in the unified Germany, West Germans who were spared anything like these terrors have assumed a leading role in decision-making, in dismissals and recruitments throughout the eastern *Länder*. Their work is officially subsumed under the term *Abwicklung*. This sanitized bureaucratic term, once used by the Nazis, suggests legal procedures or business liquidations. It bespeaks distance and condescension; it is unattuned to tact or compassion.

The question of judgment is inherently difficult. In the case of many of the accusations against former East German citizens, one must ask: How reliable are the Stasi files, and how often were they slanted by inferiors trying to curry favor with their superiors? Finally, as Jens Reich has implicitly warned, the Stasi could easily become a scapegoat for the G.D.R. regime. The greater villains were the party and state functionaries; the Stasi were not autonomous villains, and some of their collaborators may have had mixed or honorable motives. Only the clearest picture of life in the G.D.R. can help to render humane judgments. There may be good reason to sympathize with those West Germans of an impeccable past who say of all these leaks and revelations: "Enough"—an "enough" that has been much heard in the countries of Eastern Europe.

LIVING WITH HISTORY

IN THE YEARS to come Germans of both East and West will continue to find it difficult to deal with the history of the 40 years of the G.D.R. and F.R.G., two entities that lasted almost as long as the Bismarckian Reich. Polemical, divisive arguments have already begun about who supported whom and when, who promoted unification and who opposed it. Right-wing Germans or newborn nationalists are already accusing the old Federal Republic's left of national neglect, of having slighted the goal of national unity, of having collaborated with the Communist Party or of having been "soft" on East German criminals or collaborators. In time, after the calumnies and the memories are extinguished or transformed, later generations may "bracket out" the G.D.R.'s history—as Germans call such a deletion—while finding that it remains hard to expunge the Nazi past. As President Weizsäcker has said, the G.D.R. neither started a war nor committed genocide. It may gradually fade from historical consciousness, be dismissed as a Soviet satellite, an alien excrescence of something called the Cold War. West Germans' earlier indifference to the G.D.R. will facilitate so convenient a lapse of memory. But the G.D.R. in all its ambiguity needs to be remembered and in some way integrated into the history of Germany and Europe in our century.

The beginnings of the G.D.R. are most likely to be forgotten, the time immediately after the war when in the Soviet zone of occupation a so-called socialist state was gradually established, expropriating the large estate owners and nationalizing what was left of German industry. In the baggage train of the conquering Red Army arrived Moscow-trained German communists—many of whom had been tortured in Nazi camps—determined to forge a union between socialists and communists and create what they called a great antifascist bloc, a bulwark against a revived German fascist-type nationalism. True socialists, remembering how at the end of the Weimar Republic communists had in fact aided the rise of Nazism, defied communist pleas and demands; men like Gustav Dahrendorf and Kurt Schumacher never had any doubts about the true nature of communism. A few socialists in the Soviet zone believed that the Communist Party was genuinely antifascist, that it would radically purge all former Nazis and would recruit its own cadre, mostly of young, untrained people from the unpropertied classes. The claim that the German Democratic Republic, formally established in 1949, would become the first socialist state in German history, that by its extrusion of Nazis and dismantling of capitalism it was cleansing German soil of Nazi poison, that out of devastation it was building up an egalitarian soci-ety—all had a certain appeal, particularly for writers and intellectu-als. Bertolt Brecht, long the lyricist of a proletarian culture, happily left his American exile, with its capitalist culture and McCarthyite hysteria, to win honors and his own theater in East Berlin. Lesser writers followed. Thomas Mann accepted an honor from the new state—though he decided to settle in Switzerland, spiritually equidis-tant from both Germanies. In the G.D.R., as elsewhere at the time, communists had the inestimable advantage of claiming to be the van-guard of a new culture; judge us by some distant future, they said, not by the bleak present. Intellectuals, once committed to the faith, found it hard to break with it, to confess to themselves their error.

In the last few months an old German word has reappeared over and over again in books and articles. Although there is no English or French analogue, *Lebenslüge* roughly means the lie that is life-giving, the lie that is essential to a particular life, the lie that a person or a people may know to be false but without which a person or state would perish. The G.D.R. was saddled with one *Lebenslüge* from the start: the fundamental insistence that the Soviet Union was at once liberator and fraternal master and model. The East Germans sensed the travesty of truth. They knew that the Red Army had raped and looted. They knew that the Soviets had despoiled their country, and they sensed as well that their rulers, at least in the beginning, were servile instruments of Soviet masters. One of the many East German witticisms—the one commodity in which they outperformed the West Germans—insisted that the Russians were indeed brothers with whom one had indissoluble fraternal bonds: friends one choos-es, brothers are unalterably inflicted. Gradually the antifascist prin-ciple, the G.D.R.'s sole threadbare claim to legitimacy, lost its cred-ibility as well: to call the Berlin Wall the great antifascist wall was too grim an absurdity.

The Soviets and the G.D.R.'s rulers needed each other. For the for-mer, East Germany was the frontier state, the most important defense post with the greatest arsenal of weapons. For the rulers of the G.D.R., the Soviet presence constituted the ultimate reserve army against their own people. The Federal Republic, its own legitimacy accepted by its people, had tied itself to the West, but these attachments enhanced security and prosperity and corresponded to the wishes of most of its people. In the 1980s the East German regime, encouraged by the Federal Republic's ever more enterprising Ostpolitik, sought to gain some greater room for maneuver, some independence from Moscow. Characteristically, Honecker's greatest moment of independence came at the end, when he banned Soviet publications carrying Gorbachev's liberalizing message. To the end, Honecker remained a German Leninist—German because there was a tinge of sentimentality to his inhumanity. He and his closest advisers, most of them ardent believers in the powers of repression, ignored younger members of the *nomenklatura* who understood the need for reform in East Germany. Their day came too late. The G.D.R. was founded on deception, on various *Lebenslügen*, and its end was hastened by the self-deception of its aged leaders.

The G.D.R. leaves an ambiguous legacy, as does the Federal Republic; the difference is that the institutions of the old F.R.G. have not ended but are in the process of having to adopt to different conditions. The old political culture of the Federal Republic is being tested and, in part, measured by Eastern ideals. In the historic rivalry between communism and social democracy, the former by its very collapse has scored a major triumph. Many people, especially on the political right, rejoice in confounding communism and socialism, interpreting the dismal failure of the one as irredeemably discrediting the other as well. The historic task of democratic socialism has been to correct the most grievous, ruthless qualities of what Jacques Delors once called "*capitalisme sauvage*." It is doubtful that this task will ever be totally completed.

The G.D.R. is dead, and some East Germans already have their nostalgic moments. Disappointed in the present, prompted by a selective memory, they ask: "Was everything wrong in the last 40 years?" And they tend to erase from memory the hopelessness of the old regime and remember that at some level of subsistence, however drab and uniform, even ordinary citizens could count on the essentials of life: housing, however wretched, food, however meager, medical care, however inferior and indifferent. They remember that in the old G.D.R. there was no crime, no drugs, no pornography. The communist rulers of the G.D.R. could have echoed President Nixon's boast: "We have taken crime off the streets." The government had assumed a monopoly on crime.

Citizens remember the much vaunted *Kinderkrippen*, a grandiose term for child-care centers to which working parents could send their children. The memory of the *Kinderkrippen* evokes the G.D.R.'s traditional concern for family life, for women's rights, including the non-traditional right of abortion, for social welfare—all this in contrast to the cold life in unified Germany, where the cash nexus rules all. These *Kinderkrippen* have become a kind of symbol for the better side of G.D.R. life. People forget that these benefits were palliatives for deeper pain. The *Kinderkrippen* were the decorous part of a controlled society that violated the home it pretended to protect.

MORE DIVIDED THAN BEFORE

ON SOME DEEP psychological level the unified Germany is more divided than before; the physical wall has been internalized. Where once had been the untroubled hope that at some future date the division of the country, unnaturally maintained, would be healed, there are now painful inequalities of power, wealth, experience and assertiveness. The living standard of East Germans is still much lower than that of West Germans; wages are lower and unemployment is at least three times higher. Economic inequalities heighten psychic discontent: East Germans are given to self-pity, West Germans to arrogance and exasperation. Some West Germans themselves complain of Western self-righteousness. Both sides deserve understanding. There are many Germans who demand solidarity not in words but in deeds, but their pleas are lost on pusillanimous politicians who, in confusion, think mostly of the next election.

In March 1993 the Bonn parliament finally approved a solidarity pact that has brought some predictability into the economic picture. It provides for new taxes to fund specified payments to the new *Länder*. Approximately seven percent of GNP will be transferred to the East over the next decade—roughly one trillion Deutsche marks. In July even the European Community agreed, reluctantly, to provide 27.5 billion Deutsche marks over the next six years to the new *Länder* out of its regional assistance funds. The strains are clear: Germany as a whole is in a deep recession, with continued negative growth; according to many observers, it is the most serious recession since the founding of the Federal Republic. Hence the great unease pervading both parts of Germany. Still, the solidarity pact affords real chances for the new *Länder*, as Kurt Biedenkopf, minister president of Saxony, made clear in a speech to the Saxon parliament in mid-March—a candid speech that exemplified the possibilities of democratic leadership.

The old Federal Republic has also gained greater freedom in 1989, but a very different kind of freedom from the East Germans'. Unification has fulfilled the old national dream and attenuated—even on some level removed—Germany's dependency on its Western allies. From the beginning of the Federal Republic, it needed Allied protection, most clearly in the ever vulnerable city of Berlin. For 40 years this dependency dictated the parameters of choice. Now questions about German national interest and purpose reemerge in full force. In the ongoing debate there are some who demand greater German assertiveness, who have grown tired of being held hostage to the memory of the Nazi past. That sentiment is so strong that Jürgen Habermas has warned against yet another *Lebenslüge* for Germany, the *Lebenslüge*, as he puts it, "of us being a normal nation." How understandable the wish of so many Germans to be liberated of the burden of the past, to "relativize" Nazi crimes, to seek a retrospective moral equality. How understandable, and probably how unattainable.

It is one of the tragic ironies of the 1989 revolutions that they coincided with deepening crises in the West. The newly liberated countries reached out for a market economy at a time of worldwide recession. They sought to embrace democracy when the democratic countries had plunged into scandals of corruption and a general paralysis of leadership. They looked to Europe just as the hopes of Europe 1992 faded in the post-Maastricht malaise and when the term "democratic deficit" seemed to have resonance beyond the internal arrangements of the European Community.

Germany's unanticipated unification, with its staggering demands, came at a time when the old Federal Republic was already experiencing mutually reinforcing pressures. The West German economy—in the past the guarantor of West German democracy—was slowing down. The capitalist world was not at its most dynamic, or at what

Joseph Schumpeter defined at its most destructively creative, when East Germans clamored for a free market and the many gurus of the market economy urged instant transformation. West Germans, including leading politicians, were not immune to the greed and corruption of the Reaganite 1980s. Faith in the political system was shaken. Put differently, the twin miracles of Bonn's beginnings, the economic miracle and the political miracle—that is, the emergence after the devastation of the Nazi years of unprecedented political leadership—had come to an end. Germany faces its gravest crisis since the end of World War II.

A new and ultra-right-wing party, the Republicans, has scored impressive victories. It is doubtful that the massive increase in asylum seekers between 1987 and 1992—an increase of some 800 percent—is solely or even primarily responsible for the dissatisfaction that this party exploits. People in all parts of Germany feel an imbalance between the economic and moral requirements of the newly unified state and their political response. There has hardly been a time in which the political classes were held in such low esteem—as is true in the rest of Europe. The present uncertainties prompted Marion Countess Dönhoff, Helmut Schmidt and a few like-minded citizens to issue a manifesto in November 1992 under the title "Because The Country Must Change." Or consider Jens Reich's fears of future unrest "when I observe our dance around the golden calf, called property, prosperity, consumerism ... which we hold sacrosanct. Even now I see the coming disgust and the helpless failure of the putative victors. Late socialism clung to the illusion of eternal growth and progress. We should not succumb to it under a different guise."

> On some deep psychological level the unified Germany is more divided than before.

The eruption of xenophobic violence, the killing of Turkish women and children, has horrified the world. Hundreds of skinheads are supported by thousands of nationalist, perhaps even neo-Nazi, sympathizers, while millions of Germans organize silent marches to protest this ugliness, a demonstrative solidarity never before seen in Germany. To some, the very silence of these marches, however impressive in themselves, is disturbing. Germans need speech, thought and moral authority, charged questions about asylum seekers and fiscal measures that would grapple with the needed transfer payments to the east. All these need public argument. Over and over again in the last few months Chancellor Kohl has been admonished to "tell the truth."

In all parts of Germany there is a palpable deficit of trust—trust in leaders, trust in almost all aspects of life. The English philosopher John Dunn has spoken of trust as the core element of democracy. And while trust is in short supply in all countries, its steady decline in Germany is alarming. Degrees of trust cannot be quantified, unlike the interest rates of the Bundesbank—yet the two are linked. The Deutsche mark remains the symbol and instrument of Germany's economic stability, and the unarticulated incantation could be "In the Deutsche mark we trust." In a decade or so that same Deutsche mark will—by the painful transfer of some thousand billion Deutsche marks—transform the new *Länder*, especially Saxony, into the most modern region of Europe; the moral-psychological recovery and unity will take much longer.

I say this with a certain sadness, sadness that the promise of 1989, or what I thought of as Germany's second chance in this century, has been trapped in pain and disappointment. Once again Germany's history did not have to be like this; there was nothing inevitable about it. More truth, better leadership and greater tolerance would have made a difference. Even now the pessimists see a political system without leadership—and see a repeat of Weimar. The optimists see the possibility of rejuvenation and reciprocal learning, of which there has been too little.

To seek freedom in defiance of the state is not part of the German political tradition, as it is of the English, Dutch, French and American traditions. And yet twice in the last half century Germans defied a tyrannical state: on July 20, 1944, a few Germans tried to overthrow Hitler—they failed, and the two Germanies have had a difficult time assimilating or celebrating their memory; and in the fall of 1989, hundreds of thousands of East Germans successfully defied their regime, admittedly at a time when neighboring countries had already thrown off the communist yoke; it was nonetheless a momentous achievement in German history. Their leaders have already sunk into oblivion, and the memory of those great days has faded. People refer to these events as *die Wende*, the turn, thus transforming what had been dramatic and heroic into something prosaic and bureaucratic. For all the disappointments that have followed, we should celebrate not merely the collapse of the Berlin Wall, but the men and women who by their demand for a better and freer life made that collapse one of the great moments in their history and ours.

The revolutions of 1989—however darkened in the meantime by the return of barbarism in many parts of the world—have given us an opportunity to live in trust and truth, to validate the hopes of Václav Havel. ☯

The Trouble with France

Dominique Moïsi

A ROTTEN MOOD

To AMERICANS, France is a beautiful country, home to that most elegant of cities, Paris, the seductive tones of the French language, and some of the world's finest wines, which makes it all the more difficult for them to understand how such a charming nation could be so irritating an ally. The French always seem to be opposing the United States on some issue or other, whether it is in the realm of international diplomacy, where between the lines of France's carefully worded diplomatic statements one can discern a distinct distaste for America's oft-proclaimed sole-superpower status, or on matters of culture, where France is always the first to denounce American "cultural imperialism." Lately, Franco-American friction has manifested itself most visibly in the Persian Gulf, where France's interests—in Iraq and Iran—seem to clash with America's security needs. Many Americans ascribe France's prickliness to the legacy of "Gaullism," the conservative, nationalist inheritance bequeathed by that country's greatest twentieth-century leader. But in France nobody even knows what Gaullism means anymore, apart from being able to say no to the United States.

In fact, the annoying behavior coming out of Paris is best explained by the fact that the country is, quite simply, in a bad mood, unsure of its place and status in a new world. The less confident France is, the more difficult it is to deal with. On the eve of the 21st century, France faces four major challenges, which are together the source of its melancholy. The first is globalization, which is often blamed for the erosion of France's culture and its depressingly high levels of unem-

---

DOMINIQUE MOÏSI is Deputy Director of the French Institute for International Relations and Editor in Chief of *Politique Étrangère*.

[94]

ployment. (Last year, one of Paris' biggest bestsellers was a tract titled *The Economic Horror*—a bitter philippic against globalization's ills.) The second is the unipolar nature of the international system, in which the United States leads and a once-proud France is grudgingly forced to follow. The third is the merger of Europe, which threatens to drown out France's voice. The fourth, and by far the toughest, challenge is France itself. The nation must overcome its economic, social, political, moral, and cultural shortcomings if it is to successfully face its other challenges. The rise of Jean-Marie LePen's extreme right National

Front is symptomatic of France's internal difficulties. To combat them, France must, in essence, transcend itself.

IT'S NOT EASY BEING MEDIUM

ALL MEN ARE equal, but some are more equal than others. In the age of globalization, size matters. If small is beautiful and big is powerful, then medium is problematic. The Internet, information technology, and other trappings of the global economy can reinforce the centrality of the United States or multiply the strength of a small city-state like Singapore, but they often penalize middle-size countries like France. France's special strengths are its culture and its heritage, and these are being worn away, replaced by a "universal culture" that looks strangely American. If France were a young state, less set in its ways, less burdened by the weight of old traditions or images from the past, it might be able to adapt. But France is an ancient country. It cannot forget its history, and in trying to reconcile it with elements of the modern world ends up merely superimposing it upon them, creating a hodgepodge that is true to neither. Tellingly, France's most popular computer game today is not a high-tech, outer space adventure, but a thriller called "Versailles," which takes place amid the grandeur of the court of Louis XIV.

Consider the difference between France and the United States. America is not only big and young; it is, above all, open. French society remains closed and rigid—incapable of attracting the best talent from other countries while unwittingly supplying its own to America. For example, Dr. Luc Montagnier, codiscoverer of the AIDS virus, now teaches and conducts research in the United States because he reached mandatory retirement age at the Institut Pasteur. Contrast the essential message of Hollywood—if you want to make a difference you can—with the classical archetype of the French movie: A loves B, who loves C, who loves D, all of whom end up in despair. America's flexibility can be seen in the success of its melting pot, which, in an age of globalization, is exported worldwide. Today, the sounds of the world are essentially African-American, everybody eats Italian-American pizza at least once a week, and children the world over delight in films by an Eastern European, Jewish American named Steven Spielberg. The American-accented brand of English is the closest thing we have to a universal language, while the French, obsessed with defending "Francophonie" and dreaming of a world united by their tongue, erect protective linguistic barriers, not understanding that this isolates them instead of preserving their culture. What France should seek to preserve—once it has conceded defeat in the language battle—is the context and originality of its message, not its medium.

France's struggle with globalization is complicated by its people's high quality of life. Most of the French feel they have little to gain and much to lose from globalization—the space and beautiful diversity of their countryside, the quality of their food and wine, and the respect for tradition. Why risk all these unique pleasures for the sake of an uncertain competition in a global world? The temptation for many Frenchmen is to retreat into the protective bubble of the good life.

TOPPLING THE GIANT

THE END OF the Cold War only reinforced French envy of America. They resent the global reach of America's power and Washington's presumption to speak in the name of the international community. Unlike the pragmatic British or the historically guilt-ridden Germans, the French feel that they, like the United States, carry a universal message. Remember that France, like the United States, is the font of ideas about "the rights of man," liberty, equality, and fraternity. French frustrations are exacerbated by the mixture of benign neglect, sheer indifference, and mild irritation with which Washington considers Paris' initiatives. In the absence of the unifying threat posed by the Soviet Union, Franco-American tensions can be eased only by shared interests. In the short run, France's jealousy of America will be muted by the political constraints imposed on it by a united Europe, the other members of which do not share France's feelings. The French know all too well that their secret dream—to build a Europe that will challenge the United States—is the nightmare of their continental partners. By openly expressing its differences with America, over the Middle East for example, Paris more often than not isolates itself from London and Bonn, not to mention the rest of the European Union. There are, however, subtle issues on which France can tilt Europe against America. If France is alone in supporting Iraq, for example, on Iran the rest of Europe is on its side and against the United States.

France's dream of challenging the United States is the rest of Europe's nightmare.

On security matters, Paris and Washington are at once allies and competitors. France's ambition to create a genuine European foreign and security policy, although formally welcomed by Washington, clashes with the United States' inclination to take the lead. France well knows that its long-term European ambitions will require it to rejoin NATO and give up on trying to attain some special status. France understands that more Europe tomorrow means more NATO today—a bitter pill, since expanding the alliance could reinforce the U.S. monopoly on security. But there is no alternative, since Europe lacks the political will to take on such a large commitment alone. In fact, the French have come to see any expansion of NATO without a corresponding widening of the European Union as an American attempt to preclude any specifically European initiatives in the security field.

In Paris, the peaceful end to the most recent crisis in the Persian Gulf was considered a triumph of French diplomacy over American belligerence. But it was a cosmetic victory, since Saddam Hussein's receptiveness to diplomacy was certainly the result of his fear of being bombed by America. The neat division of labor that France and the United States enjoyed in the Middle East in the 1970s—France in Baghdad, America in Tehran—did not exist this time around. U.S. and French policies over Iraq are antithetical—the French eschew military options, and the Americans show little faith in diplomacy. This essential difference will not disappear and could rebound at the first opportunity—most probably when Saddam takes his next adventure.

Exploiting its position as a permanent member of the U.N. Security Council, France can present itself as an alternative Western voice to the nations of the Third World. In the Middle East, for example, Benjamin Netanyahu's election and the resulting stall in the peace process has given a new legitimacy to Europe's and in particular France's role as an honest broker between Arabs and Israelis. Not content with merely bankrolling a peace process led by others, France intends to play a more active role, political as well as economic, complementing the United States but not replacing it. But the French cannot afford to balance America's pro-Israeli position simply by being pro-Arab. France must demonstrate that it is serious about peace. It has certain advantages: unlike the United States, it is not a prisoner of domestic politics. If Paris cannot make peace, it can at least facilitate it.

On the African continent, the French must admit that they need Washington's clout, just as Washington must admit that it needs France's experience and presence. Africa brings out the best and the worst in the French. France is per capita the largest donor of foreign aid in the world after Japan, and well ahead of most European countries. But French money has gone more to regimes and leaders than to the African people. Rivals in economic terms, Paris and Washington are necessary geopolitical partners in this area. The United States has been keen to reassure the French that America has no secret agenda, no ambition to become Africa's gendarme. In fact, the French are starting to realize that their views on the continent's future converge with those of the Americans. Both fear regional destabilization, as in the new Democratic Republic of the Congo, formerly Zaire.

LOST IN THE CROWD

ALTHOUGH "EUROPE" does not yet exist in security and diplomatic terms, it is very real in economic and commercial terms, an actor whose power and influence will be strengthened by the coming of the euro. This is the only hope for the Europeans to balance America—only in the monetary field does a new bipolarity seem within reach. There is an irony here: The only card with which France can challenge American hegemony is Europe, and to play it, Paris must abandon much of its sovereignty.

For the Germans, European unification has been, together with their participation in NATO, the way to sever their links with their Nazi past, to erase the grim legacy of that dark period. For the Italians, always in search of domestic stability and a way to overcome their low self-esteem, Europe provides legitimacy, allowing them to triumph over their doubts about themselves and the credibility of their nation-state. For France, however, Europe—in its various forms, from the confederal model favored by de Gaulle to the federal one preferred by François Mitterrand—has been at the very heart of the French nationalist project, a way to pursue France's past glory and power by multiplying its influence. For France to remain France, it must become Europe. Leaders of the left and the right, once in power, have strictly adhered to the European credo. France's allegiance to the cause of Europe is now focused on the achievement of a common currency. To create a common European identity, to strengthen the voice of Europe in the world, to forge a new economic power, there is only one answer: the euro.

Yet for all of France's devotion to the European ideal, one can sense its apprehensions. Beyond their fear of having created a technocratic monster, too intrusive for some, too impotent for others, the French worry about their country's place within this new and enlarged Europe. In 1992, the debate about the Maastricht referendum was really a debate about Germany. Did the treaty offer the best guarantee against the potential threat of a reunited and powerful Germany, or would it lead to German supremacy in Europe? Does France run the danger of being squeezed between an economically dynamic Britain and an ever more powerful Germany? The city of London has recovered its old financial power, bursting with energy and activity. Berlin, once torn, will soon become not just the capital of the new Germany, but the capital of the new Europe. But Paris, some French fear, is in danger of becoming a new Rome, a pleasant and beautiful metropolis but one that is mainly a museum of its own past.

For now it seems that France's best option is to continue to pay lip service to a united Europe and promote the euro, while taking

> nited Europe will
> ɔw France to
> ıltiply its influence.

advantage of the lack of a diplomatic and military "Europe" to pursue an independent French foreign policy. This is the kind of Janus-faced exercise for which France certainly has the cunning and skill but which could prove dangerous for the future of Europe—if France were to be imitated by the Germans, for example.

Hesitant about their influence within an enlarged Europe, with a strong Germany at its center, the French are also anxious about the applicability of France's model of state centralization to the requirements of a new Europe. There is a nagging fear in France that Britain's laissez-faire economic model, built by Margaret Thatcher and largely preserved by Tony Blair's New Labour, and Germany's form of decentralized government are more modern than France's old-fashioned statist recipe—a fear bolstered by the number of young French who are heading to Britain to find jobs in that dynamic economy. The state, once the pride of France, is now the main obstacle to adjustment and change.

L'ÉTAT, C'EST LA FRANCE

THE FRENCH behave toward their state the same way that adolescents behave toward their parents: with a mixture of rebellion and submission. They criticize its heavy-handedness and inefficiency, but they appreciate its reassuring presence and protection. The spring 1997 legislative elections, which brought the Socialists to power, perfectly demonstrated this contradictory attitude. Socialist leader Lionel Jospin's triumph showed that, on a moral and political level, the majority of the French want a less corrupt and more accountable government. At the same time, the electorate wants the state to protect the weakest, poorest elements of society and regulate the effects of the market. For example, Jospin's plan to cut the maximum working week from 39 to 35 hours, against the wishes of many employers, may not make sense economically but is in tune with the feelings of most Frenchmen, who want to be protected by the state from long working hours. It does not matter to them if the idea that governments can create jobs better than market forces is outdated. France is a conservative society—its majority clings to the status quo.

The centrality of the French state is compounded by the society's rigidity. France's work force, for example, is decidedly less mobile than Britain's. Too many people prefer to remain unemployed instead of moving to new towns or villages to fill jobs. This may contribute to family stability or the harmony of social life—which means that French families can always have Sunday lunch at grandma's—but certainly not to the dynamism of the economy.

Criticisms of the state extend to those who incarnate it at the highest levels. The prestigious but stiflingly conformist civil service training school, the National School of Administration, is the focus of most complaints about the administration and political class, since its graduates have long monopolized the corridors of power. The French often accuse their civil servants of knowing neither the importance of social dialogue nor the way to govern in a genuinely democratic environment in which all citizens expect to be treated as equals. These attacks are almost reminiscent of their ancestors' challenge to the nobility at the end of the ancien régime. If those who embody the state at the highest level cannot find an answer to unemployment and social injustice, the French ask, why should these mandarins enjoy virtual immunity from accountability?

Since the days of Alexis de Tocqueville, France has been described as a country forced into revolution by its inability to reform. Although today's France is not about to revolt, it is suffering from a lack of hope for the future, which in large part explains the success of rightist groups like the National Front. The French economy is actually doing far better than the unemployment figures suggest: French industry is increasingly competitive, the trade balance is positive, inflation is down, and the franc is strong. Nevertheless, the French are morose. Their country is slowly and painfully transforming itself from a welfare state into a modern one, learning to live within its means. France has not chosen the easiest path to its goals and certainly not the most direct one.

IN SEARCH OF IDENTITY

EUROPE'S ATTEMPT to transcend its fratricidal quarrels by integrating its resources, economies, currencies, and political institutions into a quasi-federal state will serve it well in the global era. Regionalization is the best way to meet the challenges of globalization, because it makes states bigger, and bigger is better. But globalization reinforces the likelihood of fragmentation. Today, the need to express one's difference in a global world leads to a desperate search for identity that can end in peaceful divorce between some nation-states and jingoistic tensions and bloody conflicts between others.

France is a perfect example of this identity dilemma. For decades the French have oscillated between celebrating their exceptionalism and proclaiming its end. Today

> France is a country forced into revolution by its inability to refor

France is torn more than ever between the desire to be a modern, normal country and the reflex to cling to the belief that France is not like other nations. The first choice presupposes openness, flexibility, and a secure sense of one's identity. The second opposes globalization, is wary of a more unified Europe, and embraces anti-Americanism. But the second choice is no choice at all; protectionism would lead to isolation and decay.

France is probably sicker politically than is generally thought. The fact that large numbers of the French have thrown their support behind LePen's National Front, which is highly represented in the country's regional assemblies, indicates that the people of France have reached the end of their tether. Gripped by despair over their country's high unemployment rate and declining importance in the world, they have begun to cast their lot with the exceptionalists, in a wistful but dangerous attempt to recapture France's past glory. The moderate right is falling by the wayside, incapable of producing a message that will resonate with the masses like LePen's and increasingly co-opted by it. The left and the Socialists, though in power, must contend with the fragility of their own coalitions. Corruption—and the threat that it will be exposed—hangs like the sword of Damocles over the heads of politicians on both sides. All of this combines to coarsen France's political life and plunge the country further into its depression.

Yet despite the weaknesses, there is hope for France. The exceptionalists may be making gains, but for the time being, they are in the minority. Indeed, the National Front has lost its only seat in Parliament. And the more successfully France's internal problems, particularly its unemployment, are tackled, the less political and social discontent men like LePen will have to exploit.

France has surmounted crises worse than this current crisis of confidence. Its long history will ultimately guarantee its stability. The land of Liberté, Egalité, Fraternité will not soon cede all of that for an imaginary kingdom of French supremacy, for its citizens know the despair that would bring. The French will come to realize that globalization, that most feared bogeyman on the streets of Paris, will not bring France's demise but rather force it to hone its skills and refurbish its message. A more unified Europe will not smother it but in fact give it new purpose, allowing it to determine its own destiny in the world far better than it could do alone. The depression will subside. In the end, France will endure.⊘